Winter of Entrapment

A New Look at the Donner Party

Joseph A. King
1-26-94

Winter of Entrapment

A New Look at the Donner Party

---

by

Joseph A. King

P. D. MEANY PUBLISHERS
Toronto

Canadian Cataloguing in Publication Data
King, Joseph A., 1925-
    Winter of Entrapment

Includes bibliographical references and index.
ISBN 0-88835-030-9 (bound) ISBN 0-88835-032-5 (pbk.)

1. Donner Party. 2. Overland journeys to the Pacific. 3. West (U.S.) - Description and travel - to 1848. 4. Breen family. I. Title

F868.N5K5 1992   978'.02   C92-093587-7

ISBN 0-88835-030-9 (bound)
ISBN 0-88835-032-5 (pbk.)

Reprinted January 1993

Cover by Jeffrey W. Brain

Printed and bound in Canada
for
P.D. Meany Company, Inc., Publishers
Box 118, Streetsville, Ontario, Canada L5M 2B7

TABLE OF CONTENTS

List of Illustrations

COVER. The Breens and others at Starved Camp, March 1847. Sketch by Jeffrey Brain.

page

FOREWORD

A central theme in American history is the westward movement of people, highlighted by the overland migration of families to California and Oregon beginning in 1841. This unique and colorful drama of pioneers with their ox-drawn covered wagons, spending six months on the trail, crossing plains and deserts, fording dozens of streams and rivers, fending off Indian raids, and scaling the Rockies and Sierras has provided a well-spring for national history, legend, literature, art, and movies. Of the tens of thousands who made the crossing, only a few names are widely-known today, and among these few, the Donner Party readily comes to mind. Undoubtedly, that is because of the tragedy resulting from their entrapment in the deep snow of the Sierra Nevada, and the publicity given subsequent events. Besides a great number of articles and fictional accounts about the Donner Party, there have been four major books tracing the history of the expedition; these were published in 1880, 1911, 1936, and 1950.

One might ask, "Why would someone write another history of the Donner Party tragedy?" Indeed, why should there be another book about any well-known event or personality in history, or why should anyone climb Mount Everest again? In the case of the Donner Party, there are obvious answers: different people looking at the same evidence can arrive at disparate conclusions; newly-discovered manuscripts and archaeological finds have surfaced since 1950; because of their ethnocentric prejudices, previous writers have minimized and denigrated the experiences of "foreign" members of the overland party. Based on his extensive teaching experience, qualifications in historical and genealogical research, and compassion for non-Anglo-Saxon immigrants, Professor King has successfully scaled the Mount Everest of the overland experience – the Donner Party story.

This book is a reinterpretation of the overland narrative, with special emphasis on the Irish-Catholic Breen family of nine persons who survived the ordeal intact. Professor King has scoured the primary and secondary literature to inform his readers about the Breens and others who made up the wagon train that headed west from Independence, Missouri, in mid-May of 1846. On July 19 at the Little Sandy River, twenty miles west of South Pass in the Rocky Mountains, they joined the Donner Party. The group continued westward to Fort Bridger and the Hastings Cut-Off. They numbered eighty-seven people, counting several who died in Utah and Nevada or went ahead on horseback to California, and a family of thirteen who caught up with them in Utah's Wasatch Mountains.

A major focus of the book is on the ordeal in the Sierra Nevada mountains after the party was trapped by snow. This is truly high drama, where the calamitous situation brought out the deepest human and spiritual characteristics of adult members of the party. The author makes effective use of Patrick Breen's unique diary and other eyewitness accounts. The dramatic rescue of the survivors is also reexamined in the light of historical evidence.

In addition to an entire chapter about the Breen family members after their arrival in California, there is much new material and fresh interpretation in this scholarly book. The author provides genealogical charts and copies of relevant manuscript letters, diaries, and reminiscences. He has also written a masterful critique of the vast published and unpublished literature on the subject. Five maps and two dozen illustrations enhance the book by letting us see the features of the principal people and lands discussed in the text. While shedding much new light on a familiar story, Professor King broadens the scope to ask philosophical questions and to make humanistic observations. In so doing, he has expanded our understanding of the Donner Party story and its place in the great drama of the American westward movement.

Robert Ryal Miller
Berkeley, California
July, 1991

Historian Miller is the author of a number of books, including MEXICO: A HISTORY *(1985) and* SHAMROCK AND SWORD: THE SAINT PATRICK'S BATTALION IN THE U.S.-MEXICAN WAR *(1989).*

PREFACE

My interest in the Donner Party began several years ago when I was working on a book about Irish emigration to rural Canada and America. In the process, I learned something about the Irish Breen family, who settled in San Juan Bautista, California. The nine Breens were the only Catholic family in the Donner Party, and they all survived.

My interest was aroused. I chose George R. Stewart's *Ordeal by Hunger: The Story of the Donner Party* as one of the readings for a college class in Freshman Reading and Composition, and continued research on the Breens.

What I had intended for two weeks of discussion and writing turned into about four weeks, in which the students addressed themselves to questions such as these: What is "heroism" by your definition? What persons in the Donner company do you consider the most heroic? What is "villainy," and were there any villains? Was Lewis Keseberg the demon that some Donner historians have made him out to be? How do you account for the survival of the Breens? Why did so many of the men die (especially those without families), and so few of the women? What is "morality"? Can cannibalism be morally justified? What roles do chance and choice play in human affairs? Were the emigrants in the Donner Party victims of bad luck or poor judgment? How do you account for an historian applying such sobriquets as "mongrel" to John Baptiste Trudeau, "half-breed" to rescuer Brit Greenwood, "cowardly" to some mountain Indians, "prodigal" to the Irish Breens? Can history be written without a "bias"? What is "racism"? Why is the Donner Party saga of continuing interest almost one hundred and fifty years after the events?

It was a stimulating teaching experience for four weeks, a fine end, I thought, to a thirty-five year teaching career. During those four weeks, I became more than ever convinced that a new examination of the documents pertaining to the Donner story was needed. Except for a few fictional works, no major book about the tragedy had been written since Stewart's *Ordeal* (1936, revised and enlarged in 1960) and Stookey's *Fatal Decision* (1950). And no book had been written about Patrick Breen, who kept the famous diary of the entrapment, and his family. Historians, I thought, may have given entirely too much credence to the testimony of one member of the party who had earned a reputation on the trail for telling tall tales involving himself.

My intention to write an article was expanded to a book. Hence hundreds of hours of additional research, and this book about the Donner Party with major focus on the Breen family.

In my research, I have been especially indebted to the following: Robert Ryal Miller of Berkeley for pointing out many lines of fruitful research; Father Nicholas Moore, Parish Priest of Borris, County Carlow, for searches of the oldest parish registers; Professor Kerby Miller of the University of Missouri at Columbia, always most generous in sharing his research, for first pointing out to me the five letters to the Breens (reprinted in this book); Barbara Warner of the Huntington Westerners in San Marino, California, for the Donner family genealogies; my sister, Dr. Margaret E. Fitzgerald of New York City, for her gifts of Irish books over the years, many of them quite rare, a fine resource which I have used countless times in writing this book.

Among the archivists and other researchers to whom I am grateful are Sister M. Teresita, C.S.J., Assistant Archivist for the Diocese of London, Ontario; Ben Watson and Jennifer Steen of the Gleeson Library, University of San Francisco; Dr. Jeffrey Burns of the San Francisco Archdiocesan Archives; Cathi Boronkay of the Diablo Valley Library staff; the staff of Bancroft Library, Berkeley; the staff of Sutro Library, San Francisco; the staff of the Genealogical Department of the Church of Jesus Christ of Latter-day Saints in Salt Lake City; Kay Schmidt-Robinson, Chief Ranger of the San Juan Bautista State Historic Park; Carla Hendershot of Hollister, California; the staff of the Donner Memorial State Park at Truckee, California; Michael Tucker, Curator of the Historic Sites Unit, Sutter's Fort; Stephen E. Michel, ranger at Donner Memorial

State Park at Truckee, California; Stanleigh Bry, Director of the Society of California Pioneers library in San Francisco; Peter Blodgett of The Huntington Library, San Marino, California; Nicholas N. Lapkass of the Mendocino County Library; Mr. and Mrs. Hugh L. Wallace of the Marin County Genealogical Society; Jack Steed of Sacramento; and Dr. Duayne J. Dillon of Martinez, California.

Major resources for both documents and family folklore have been the following descendants of Patrick Breen and Margaret Bulger: Philip Hudner of Kentfield, California; Joseph Cullumber of San Juan; Barbara Breen of Hollister; Isabelle Breen Raven of Walnut Creek; and Dr. Peter Raven of St. Louis, Missouri. Other descendants who have been very helpful are Marilyn Harrison of Stockton, California; Harvey Nyland and Dorothy Avila of San Juan Bautista; Anne Breen of Pacific Grove; Edwina Kump of San Francisco; Jay Barrington of Scott's Valley; and Ed Ordway of Angel's Camp. Chief resources for the family of Patrick's brother, Samuel Breen, have been Vivian Breen Manka of Fort Madison, Iowa; Jeanne M. MacLardy of Oceanside, California; and Sandy Dacon of San Diego.

I wish to thank the Bancroft Library for permission to print the entire Breen *Diary* (as transcribed by Frederick J. Teggart in 1910), the Weddell map of the "Historic Emigrant Road," and John Breen's "Pioneer Memoirs."

Finally, I am indebted to my publisher, Patrick Meany, who must surely be one of the finest editors, especially of books pertaining to things Irish, in this world; and to my wife of thirty-six years, Betty Wayne King, another superb editor, but additionally an expert at word processing. She has come to my aid scores and scores of times, patiently and soothingly, in response to loud cries of anguish as the disastrously obedient word processor insists on implementing to the letter my wrong commands.

Joseph A. King
Lafayette, California
January 2, 1992

Ireland

Donegal
Derry
Antrim
ULSTER
Tyrone
Down
Fermanagh
Armagh
Monaghan
Sligo
Leitrim
Cavan
Louth
Mayo
Roscommon
Longford
Meath
CONNAUGHT
Westmeath
Galway
LEINSTER
Dublin
Offaly
(King's)
Kildare
Leix
(Queen's)
Wicklow
Clare
Carlow
Limerick
Tipperary
Kilkenny
Wexford
MUNSTER
Waterford
Kerry
Cork

50 mi.

80 km.

PROVINCE BOUNDARIES

Mizen Head

Chapter 1

IRELAND TO THE NEW WORLD: CANADA AND IOWA

At four in the afternoon on March 12, 1847, seven men on a rescue mission from Sutter's Fort reached the head of the Yuba River in California's High Sierras. At an altitude of seven thousand feet, they found a pit twenty-four feet deep. It had been created by a campfire, kept burning for about seven days, descending as it melted the snow. At the bottom of the pit around the fire were huddled eleven miserable human beings, barely alive. At the surface were the mutilated bodies of three other human beings, their flesh stripped from their arms and legs, their hearts and livers and brains removed. A pot was boiling on the fire. It was one of the most pitiful sights in the history of the Old West.

The eleven survivors numbered two adults and nine children, ages one to fifteen. The adults were two immigrants from County Carlow, Ireland, Patrick Breen, fifty-one, and his spouse Margaret, whom he called Peggy, forty-one. They were members of the tragic Donner Party. Patrick Breen was the author of one of the most remarkable documents of the American West. Entrapped with his large family in the snows for over four months near what came to be known as Donner Lake, Patrick Breen kept a diary of the ordeal, now a prized possession of the Bancroft Library at Berkeley, California.

The story of the Breens, from Ireland to that horrible pit in the snow and their eventual escape, has never been told completely or accurately. It has been partially told, and somewhat prejudicially, I think, by some of the foremost chroniclers of the Donner Party. This book is an attempt to present an historically accurate account of events with a major focus on the family of Breens.

1

GENEALOGY

Patrick Breen was baptized on June 11, 1795, the son of Ned (Edward) Breen and Mary Wilson of Barnahasken Townland, near the tiny village of Killedmund in County Carlow, Ireland's smallest county.

Patrick's grandfather was also Patrick, who died in 1802 at age seventy-seven, the husband of Bridget Ryan, who died in 1799 at the age of seventy-three. Patrick's father, Ned, died in 1816 at age fifty. They are all buried under a substantial headstone in Kiltennel Cemetery. The inscriptions on the stone, which is topped by a cross and the symbols "IHS," are still readable almost two centuries after the stone was erected by Patrick's grandfather for his wife (see Notes to Chapter 1).

Margaret Bulger was baptized on March 1, 1806, a daughter of Simon Bulger and Margaret Bulger, no doubt distant cousins, of Rathgeran Townland, just a few miles away from Barnahasken. Eleven years younger than Patrick, she would one day become his wife. The Breens and the Bulgers attended the Catholic chapel at Ballymurphy, a fact that Margaret would remember with gratitude many years later when she was settled in California (see Chapter 16).

REASONS FOR EMIGRATION

We can only guess at the reasons for the migration of the Breens to Canada in the late 1820s, but some good guesses can be made. Ireland had experienced a period of prosperity during the Napoleonic Wars when European ports were closed to British trade, and exports of Irish grain drew premium prices on the British markets. With the reopening of European ports in 1815 after Napoleon's defeat at Waterloo, Irish grain prices dropped dramatically. Landlords in Ireland turned to more profitable grazing. As leases expired in the province of Leinster, which included County Carlow, wholesale evictions of tillage farmers took place, these evictions sometimes based on the religious and political convictions of the tenants. A well-off Catholic in County Carlow expressed bitterness over what he described as "the exclusive orange [Protestant] system of letting practiced in this County." A shopkeeper in County Wexford reported, "The people are so divided....[that] landlords are driving their unfortunate Tennants out, Especially Roman Catholic." The evictions, together with falling grain prices, were powerful incentives for both Catholics and Protestants to book passage to the New World, if they had the means.

Another spur to emigration was the system of "partible inheritance," especially practiced by Catholic families. When Ned Breen, father of Patrick Breen of the Donner Party, died in 1816, his land passed into the hands of his widow and his three oldest sons. By 1826, according to the *Tithe Applotment Books* (see Notes to Chapter 1), widow Mary Breen and sons Patrick, William, and Samuel were the occupiers of six lots totalling 161 Irish acres (256 English or statute acres) on lease from the head landlord, the Third Earl of Courtown. Patrick Breen's holding was 21 acres. Through partible inheritance, as distinct from primogeniture (oldest son inheriting all), the Breens had been reduced from "strong" to "middle" tenant status. For the next generation partible inheritance meant poverty for the Breens, and even landless status for some of them.

A further cause of political and religious unrest was the burdensome and hated tithe. In addition to the rents paid to the head landlord, the Breens, although Roman Catholic, had to pay a total of £4.14s.11d. in tithes annually to the established Protestant Church of Ireland. This was a considerable sum. A laborer could not expect to earn more than ten pounds per year, if he were fortunate enough to obtain work for nine or ten months of that year. The tithe was a festering sore that had contributed to the Rising of 1798, when the village of Killedmund was burned to the ground by insurrectionists.

OPPORTUNITY TO EMIGRATE

Timber ships from Canada served ports both small and large in Ireland. By 1828, the system of "timber in, passengers out" was widely employed by ship owners in the timber trade. As a consequence, fares had been substantially reduced from about five pounds to about one pound per adult, much less for children. But passage was still affordable only to strong tenants, skilled artisans, and tradesmen, mostly Protestant. The Breens were among the relatively few Catholics with the means

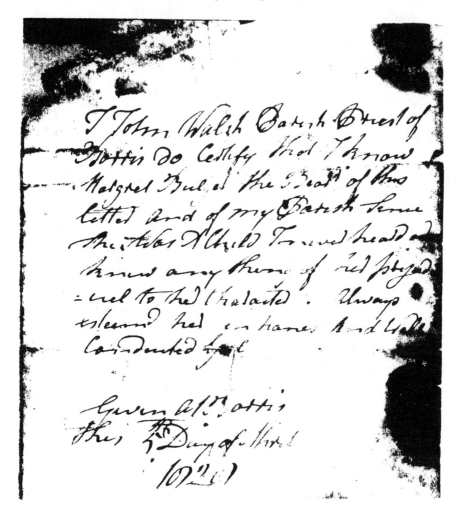

Letter of introduction for Margaret Bulger from John Walsh, Parish Priest of Borris, County Carlow: *"I John Walsh Parish Priest of Borris do certify that I know Margret Bulger the bearer of this letter and of my Parish since she was a child   I never heard or knew any thing of her prejudicial to her character   Always esteemed her an honest and well conducted girl   Given at Borris this 5th day of April 1826"*

to emigrate. By selling off their leaseholds, they could acquire the capital for the ship fares and for purchase of land in Canada.

TO CANADA

Patrick Breen, age thirty-three, sailed for Canada in 1828, perhaps from New Ross in County Wexford, a port that had long served the Canadian trade. It was a six-week journey on a sailing ship. He was joined in Canada by other members of the family. By the early 1830s, Patrick, four younger brothers, a sister, and their widowed mother were settled in Southwold Township near the village of St. Thomas in Ontario. About 1830 or 1831, Patrick married Margaret Bulger whom he had known in Ireland. Sons John and Edward were born in 1832 and 1833.

It was a pioneering community. The land needed clearing for farming. For the Breens and their smattering of Catholic neighbors in a sea of mostly Irish Protestants, a resident priest was of the utmost importance. The mission stations at Yarmouth, St. Thomas, and London were served only irregularly by priests of the Diocese of Kingston.

On September 7, 1830, ten residents of the St. Thomas area, one of whom was Patrick Breen, addressed a petition to Bishop Alexander Macdonnell of Kingston. The petitioners wrote that they represented sixty-seven Catholic families of two hundred souls. They said that "from here Catholicks are almost shut out in consequence of not having a Priest stationed as there are many of them on that acct., will not remain, and those who settled are dissatisfied, and will not encourage their friends to come here, which many of them would if there was a Priest...." It would be three more years, however, before the bishop was able to assign a resident priest to St. Thomas, and by that time Patrick and Margaret Breen had decided to cross the border to the United States.

ILLINOIS AND IOWA

Patrick and Margaret and their two infant children left Canada about 1834 ("when John was two") and headed for the American West. They resided briefly at Springfield, Illinois, where they may have become acquainted with brothers George and Jacob Donner, farmers, and James Frazier Reed, a carriage maker. These affluent residents of Springfield would later share with the Breens the miseries of the California trail. Two of them, and their wives, would perish during the winter of entrapment in the mountains.

In 1835 the Breens moved two hundred miles south of Springfield and across the Mississippi to Lee County, Territory of Iowa, near a point where the great river touches the states of Missouri, Illinois, and Iowa. A son James, born in 1835, died the following year.

For a time, Patrick was employed on a riverboat. On the 1840 census for Lee County, the Patrick Breen household was listed consecutively with James Ryan and Patrick Dolan, both of whom were living alone. Four male children under ten years of age were living in the Breen household. On December 13, 1841, Richard F. Barrett of Springfield, Illinois, deeded to Patrick Breen the south half (320 acres) of Section 10, Township 65, North of Range 5, for one hundred dollars to be paid in five equal installments at twelve percent interest. The land was about three miles northwest of Keokuk, rolling and wooded country, not very suitable for tillage. Today, it is partly within the city limits and has been sub-divided into a score of large, irregularly-shaped lots. The residences, among the trees, are accessible by a gravel road (Wirtz Lane), off North Main Street. There are no ruins or other marks of the presence of the Breens one hundred and fifty years ago.

In Keokuk, five more children were born to Patrick and Peggy: Patrick Jr. (1837), Simon (1839), a second James (1841), Peter (1843), and Isabella (1845). Patrick applied for citizenship about 1840. His final papers were accepted in the District Court at West Point, Lee County, October 15, 1844. His Irish-born neighbor, Patrick Dolan, testified that Patrick had been in the United States at least five years.

Keokuk was a rough river town. The Breens probably shared the negative opinion of missionary Fr. Lucien Galtier concerning it. Wishing to be relieved of his duties in Keokuk, Galtier wrote his superior, Bishop Loras, in 1844, "I really see no advantage of remaining in this post, which according to all standards, temporal and spiritual, is perhaps the very lowest in America."

Another letter to Loras, dated January 13, 1845, was more insistent:

I am giving you the report of my parish. I do not know what the number of inhabitants is in Keokuk. That of the Catholics is seventy-four (74), large and small. I have baptized six children, one of whom was later buried by a minister. I have blessed two marriages and rehabilitated a third. One person made his First Communion and fourteen persons received Communion. One Christian was converted to the Catholic religion, two boys are taking catechism. I have no Catholic school. The revenue of the church is nothing. I have received small offerings of victuals. I have been obliged to do all the furnishings of the church. The church is naked and without benches. It will soon be a widow and without a priest like other places of little importance. For the good of the parish a neighboring priest should visit it from time to time. I do not see any good that can be done. I do not visit any other place, although twice I have journeyed in Missouri taking care of the sick, and twice I have been at West Point and Fort Madison....if refusal for my *exeat* comes with your response, which I hope will be accelerated, I shall write to France the necessary comment to my disappointment.

The unhappy priest was assigned to the Milwaukee diocese sometime in 1845, before the Breens left Keokuk. (See Notes to Chapter 1.)

Patrick Breen (1795-1868), born in Barnahasken Townland, County Carlow, Ireland; died in San Juan Bautista, California.

Margaret Bulger Breen (1806-1874), born in Rathgeran Townland, County Carlow, Ireland; died in San Juan Bautista, California.

Chapter 2

CALIFORNIA BOUND

The year 1846 has been called by historians the "year of decision." In the spring of that year about two thousand immigrants in about five hundred wagons left Mississippi and Missouri River points for the journey to Oregon and California.

Precisely why Patrick and Margaret Breen decided to uproot their family in the spring of 1846 and head for California is, like the move from Canada, a matter of guesswork. Their oldest son, John, recalled that his parents and their neighbor Dolan had been talking about California for several years. Certainly by 1845 news had reached them of the Murphy/Stevens Party. In 1844, the large extended family of County Wexford-born Martin Murphy Sr., comprising about half the members of the fifty-member Murphy/Stevens Party, had succeeded in bringing wagons for the first time across the Sierras to Sutter's Fort. They made the two thousand mile journey from Council Bluffs, Iowa, across the plains, deserts, and mountains to California's Sacramento Valley without the loss of a life.

According to a grandson, Patrick had read Captain Fremont's account of his 1843-44 expedition. Fremont's band had crossed the Sierras on horseback and in winter. Patrick, the grandson reported, had also talked to Jim Bridger during a visit down river to St. Louis. In 1843, Bridger and a partner had established a trading post about one hundred miles east of the Great Salt Lake.

Patrick Breen, like just about all others on the overland trail in 1846, must have been acquainted with a best-selling book by Lansford Hastings, *The Emigrants' Guide to Oregon and California* (1845). Hastings was a lawyer from Ohio with grand plans for colonizing the Far West and profiting thereby. In 1845, on horseback, he crossed on a new route that took him south of Salt Lake. Prior crossings to California had been made in recent years but they were by a route through Fort Hall in Idaho which avoided the grassless, treeless and waterless Great Western Desert of Utah. Hastings, in what was essentially a salesman's pitch for California settlement, mentioned what he claimed was "the most direct route" to California, south of Salt Lake, although Hastings himself had never taken wagons over it.

Apart from all of this, the Breens may have decided that Keokuk was simply not a good place to raise their family.

KEOKUK, IOWA, TO INDEPENDENCE, MISSOURI

The sale of Patrick Breen's farm was not recorded on the grantor or grantee indexes for Lee County, Iowa, so we have no way of knowing what he received for it. Considerable cash was needed to purchase the equipment needed for the long journey. Work oxen per yoke of two cost $25 to $40. A well-built wagon with three yoke of oxen cost $250 to $300. A horse cost $30, a domesticated mule anywhere from $40 to $90, depending on the degree of obstinacy. Food and other provisions for four to six months had to be carried. Additionally, cash had to be on hand in coin for purchases at the few private trading posts ("forts") along the way, and for purchasing land in California. Breen's oldest son, John, who had turned fourteen in February, recalled that his father carried with him from Keokuk around $500, no more. The westward journey was by no means for poor people. Laborers toiling at one dollar a day could hardly afford it, unless they attached themselves to one of the families in the wagon train as a teamster or other employee.

On April 5, 1846, the nine Breens and their friend Patrick Dolan began the first leg of their two thousand mile journey. Before Father Galtier had departed for Wisconsin, he gave the family his blessing, and left Patrick a Bible or a prayer book (accounts vary as to which) that would serve the family well during their months of distress in the snows of the Sierras.

The Breens had three wagons drawn by a total of seven yoke of oxen, some cows and saddle horses, and the dog

Towser. Two of the wagons were loaded with provisions. A lighter wagon carried the children and some beds. Bachelor Dolan had one wagon. He was described by one of the Breen children who could remember him as "red-faced, light-haired, handsome, well-built, honest, very religious." Another described him as having "dark complexion, brown hair, blue eyes....medium height, strong build, quick of motion....a favorite with children [with whom] he would romp and play." He was "not as wealthy" as their father, but "well-equipped."

The journey to Independence was "tedious," as John Breen recalled it. The spring of 1846 was especially wet, he said, and the teams found it hard going in the mud. They crossed the Missouri River at a bend at Glasgow in mid-Missouri, and went on to Independence, where they arrived in early May.

INDEPENDENCE, MISSOURI, AND ACROSS THE PLAINS

Independence was a thriving frontier community. Here, and at St. Joseph fifty miles to the north, hundreds of wagons were gathering to make final preparations for the long journey. W.H. "Owl" Russell, a self-styled "colonel," was in Independence, gathering together a huge company of over one hundred wagons, but the Breens and Dolan did not join this group.

It was past the middle of May before the Breens and Dolan left Independence. Across the Missouri line they arrived at a camp where they met some hunters returning with furs. "They gave us some dried buffalo meat," wrote John Breen in his memoirs, "and told us that we had no idea of what we would suffer before we reached California." The camp was appropriately named Lone Elm. "At the time what made the matter still lonelier," wrote John, " [was that] we were only one family, not having yet....joined any other of the families crossing the plains that year."

Many of the five hundred or so wagons of the 1846 emigration were not tightly organized but were strung more or less loosely along the trail, grouping together at evening campsites. Groups split up and wagons merged into new groups as the days and weeks went by.

It was relatively easy going along the Kansas River in the northeast corner of Kansas and along the Little Blue in Nebraska, then overland to the Platte. Indians maintained ferryboats on some river crossings. Cooperative efforts in negotiating difficult mountain passes and streams, requiring strong male bodies and the doubling of ox teams, were not yet absolutely required. A letter written on the trail by Donner Party member James Frazier Reed (such letters were entrusted to travellers returning to eastern points) may suggest why the Breens travelled alone. Reed was "3 miles west of the Cansas [Kansas River]" when he wrote his brother-in-law, James Keyes of Springfield, Illinois, on May 20, 1846. He had camped, he said, in the vicinity of Colonel Russell and forty-nine of his wagons. Reed wanted to join the nine wagons of his small company (which included the brothers Jacob and George Donner and their large families) to the Russell train. Russell was choosy, having rejected several recent applications for admission to his caravan. But Russell must have been impressed by the affluent and imperious Reed. His application was accepted after the matter was put to a vote. Whether the Breens made application unsuccessfully to join the Russell group is unknown. But the possibility cannot be dismissed. The Breens were "foreigners" and Irish Catholics, and this was the age of Know-Nothingism. The prejudices reached to the frontier.

Large emigrant companies tended to break up in Nebraska after the fear of raids by the Sioux had passed. Another reason, John Breen recalled, was that very large companies sometimes had difficulties at a single campsite competing for water and pasturage for their animals. There was also the obvious problem of a company having to proceed from campsite to campsite at the pace of the slowest wagons.

And so the four wagons of Breen and Dolan proceeded across the plains alone, though they were doubtless joined in the evening by other travellers. The routine was to rise at dawn and start the campfires. After breakfast the oxen would be yoked, and the wagons rotated, the lead team yesterday following in the rear today, and eating the dust. The Breens, like other emigrants, quickly learned that the dust of an old trail eventually weakened the animals. There would be a one-hour break for lunch, and then westward at the oxens' pace of about two miles per hour, drivers beside them, sometimes walking, sometimes on horseback.

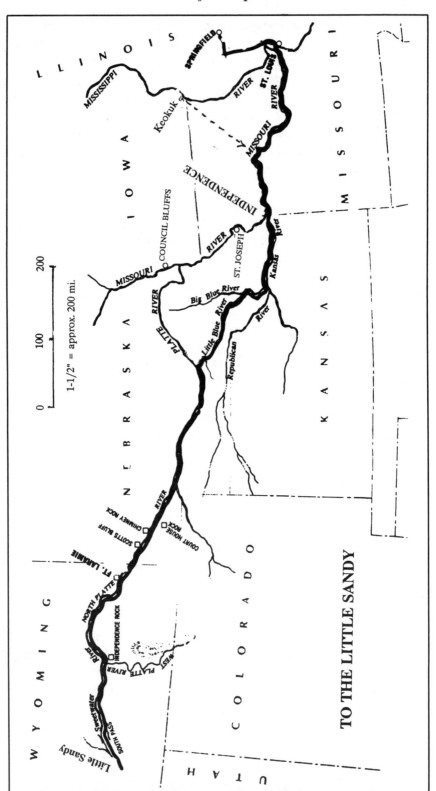

TO THE LITTLE SANDY

Covered wagon "palace car" drawn by four yoke of oxen.

Fort Laramie in 1849, drawing by Frederic Remington.

The journey from Independence to Fort Laramie, a private trading post in what is now eastern Wyoming, was over six hundred miles, requiring over forty days of travel. Much of it was along Nebraska's Platte River. Patrick Breen reached his fifty-first birthday about June 10. About June 16 the Breen and Dolan wagons approached the junction of the North and South Platte.

The crossing of the South Fork must have required all of the strength and ingenuity of Breen and Dolan, and Breen's two oldest sons, John and Edward. At the fork, the river was six hundred yards to one and a half miles wide, and two feet deep. From there to Fort Laramie was about one hundred and eighty miles. They were now in the "real West," arid country, trees only along the riverbank. The plains had turned into rolling prairie. Many buffalo were about. They passed remarkable natural formations such as Jailhouse, Courthouse and Chimney rocks. From many diaries kept by travellers on the overland trail in 1846, and from John Breen's memoirs, we know something of what daily life must have been for the Breens. Hunting parties went out in the evenings. If the hunt were successful, all families gathered at the campsite to feast on the buffalo meat. Occasionally an antelope would be brought in. In the morning, the usual fare was boiled hard corn and wheat, covered with cream, making a fine cereal. Or maybe a breakfast of buffalo steak, as Tamsen Donner reported in a letter to Springfield. But bread, rice and beans were the staple foods.

The older children helped with milking the cows and churning the butter. They cleaned the cooking utensils with sand. It was the duty of the children to keep the kettles bright and shining. Children would also gather buffalo "chips" (dried buffalo dung) for the fire. It was recommended by past travellers to make camp about four in the afternoon. The families ate their suppers by individual fires, afterwards gathering for talk around a common bonfire. Sometimes they would be joined by trappers and other traders returning east. Some trading was done with Indians. Families carried musical instruments and Patrick Breen could play the violin. Patrick Dolan liked to amuse the children with songs and tales of Ireland. Younger folks danced. One thirteen year old,

Virginia Reed, whose family would soon join the Breens, later said that she was "perfectly happy" during this part of the journey. In a letter to the *Springfield Journal*, Tamsen Donner, whose family wagons the Breens would also join, described the prairie between the Blue and Platte rivers as "beautiful beyond description."

The Breens reached Fort Laramie about July 1 and may have spent Independence Day there. Many Sioux were camped that summer at this small but important outpost of the American Fur Company. A few supplies might be purchased.

FORT LARAMIE TO THE LITTLE SANDY

Beyond Fort Laramie were one hundred and thirty miles and about ten days of travel through somewhat rough country to the North Fork of the Platte, and a difficult river crossing. Three days and fifty miles more brought the travellers to Independence Rock. The Breens, like others, may have inscribed their names on this famous formation. Eight days and about one hundred miles more, along the valley of the Sweetwater, brought the wagons to South Pass in the Rockies. This was the Continental Divide and here were the headwaters of the Sweetwater River. Beyond the pass the waters for the first time flowed west.

Small companies began to get a little skittish. There were tales of the fierce Sioux and raiding Crows from the north, and even war-parties of Blackfoot and Snake. At the 8,000-foot pass the Breens found that nights were much colder than before. Frost and ice were in their buckets when the Breens arose in the morning. Little did they imagine what was yet in store for them.

FATEFUL DECISION ON THE LITTLE SANDY

From the pass to the Little Sandy River was twenty miles, a long one-day march. It was now about July 19. The camp at the Little Sandy was the place of decision. Here emigrant parties bound for California had to decide whether to take a right-hand turn or a left-hand turn. If they chose the right-hand turn on the trail known as the Greenwood or Sublette Cut-Off, about twenty miles west of their camp, they would continue with the Oregon-bound parties to Fort Hall, a Hudson's Bay

Company trading post in what became Idaho. At Fort Hall, those bound for California would take a southwesterly course to the Humboldt River in Nevada. They would then follow that lazy river to its sink, east of Truckee Meadows (today's Reno), go up the canyon of the Truckee and over the pass, thence down to the sparse settlements in the Sacramento Valley of California. This was roughly the route followed by the Murphy Party of 1844. Some of the parties of 1845 had also followed this route.

But even at the Little Sandy the die need not be cast. It was still possible at Fort Bridger to take the old route to Fort Hall, east of the Great Salt Lake, avoiding the salt desert.

The left-hand turn at Fort Bridger meant negotiating the formidable Wasatch Mountains and a long, dry drive across the salt desert before reaching the Humboldt River, where the Hastings Cut-Off merged with the trail coming down from Fort Hall, just west of today's Elko.

At Fort Laramie, Hastings had left word urging emigrants to take his cut-off. He would be waiting for them, he promised, at Fort Bridger to lead them across his new route.

A contingent of the Russell company was there on the Little Sandy. Most of them made what turned out to be a very wise decision, to take the right-hand turn. James Frazier Reed, vigorous and adventurous, argued for the left-hand turn and convinced the elderly Donner brothers of that course. The Breens and their faithful friend Dolan, until then travelling more or less alone, agreed to join the party of Reed and the Donners, as did several other families. After all, there was still time to take the Fort Hall route at Fort Bridger.

Stewart in *Ordeal by Hunger* gives the camp at the Little Sandy as the place where what came to be known as the Donner Party was formed. Actually, however, the company as history has come to know it took its final shape later.

Chapter 3

JOINING THE DONNERS

George Donner, age sixty-two, was elected the nominal leader of the company. This choice was probably because the rich and haughty Reed, with his fine horses and "palace car" and several servants, had already earned the jealousy of some of the families. The leader had little power, however, beyond choosing where and when to camp. Reed, scouting ahead on horseback, often accompanied by his step-daughter Virginia on her prize horse, generally made that decision anyway.

The company left the Little Sandy about July 20. Even from the beginning problems developed because of clashes of personalities. Many years later, Leanna Donner App, twelve years of age on the trail, remembered that a destructive spirit of clannishness emerged because "the party was composed of different nationalities, Germans, Irish, Americans...." The clans worked together when they absolutely had to, Leanna re-called, but there was "a great deal of unnecessary trouble and confusion [and] jealousy....when they would meet at the camp-fire morning and evenings." Early on the trail Lewis Keseberg may have been shunned after an argument with Reed, and still later for allegedly desecrating an Indian grave by removing a buffalo robe, thereby risking the wrath of the Sioux. (The evidence for this comes only from the unreliable William Eddy and J. Quinn Thornton, of which more later.) The Keseberg wagons were always close to those of the Breens.

There can be little doubt that the Breens and the Germans had less help than the Donners and Reeds in getting their wag-ons across the plains, prairies, mountains, and river crossings. For adult male muscle, Breen and Dolan had only each other to lean on, although the Breens' two oldest boys, fourteen and thirteen, could be helpful. The aging Donner brothers had no fewer than five young adult males, employees and travellers, to do the heavy work. Reed had four adult male employees and a servant, Eliza, who did all the cooking. Margaret Breen, cooking for ten, including Dolan, and nursing her infant, may have had reason to envy Mrs. Reed. Widow Murphy had two adult daughters and their husbands.

FORT BRIDGER

They arrived at Fort Bridger in the last week of July. The fort was actually a small trading post established three years before by Jim Bridger and his partner, Luis Vasquez. It was in a pleasant valley on one of the tributaries of Black's Fork west of the Green River. Its original purpose was to serve emigrant trains taking the Fort Hall route to Oregon and California, but the cut-off near the Little Sandy was now being used by most of the emigrants, by-passing Fort Bridger. That was certainly not good for the business of Bridger and Vasquez, who became strong supporters of the Hastings Cut-Off route south of Salt Lake.

The Donner company was surprised to find that Hastings, who had promised to wait for them, had already departed with a train of over sixty wagons. He left word for them to follow in his wagon tracks. Bridger and Vasquez were, of course, also encouraging. However, unknown to anybody in the party, Edwin Bryant, author of *What I Saw in California,* had left a letter for Reed urging him not to follow Hastings but to follow the old trail from Fort Bridger to Fort Hall. The letter was not given to Reed, perhaps because the fort's owners did not want to discourage travel on Hastings' route.

Already it was getting late in the season. The wagons of the Donner Company were among the last to leave the Little Sandy. They still had almost one thousand miles to go to the California settlements. There was nothing between Fort Bridger and California except deserts and mountains, but at Fort Bridger it was possible to repair wagons (Bridger and Vasquez maintained a blacksmith shop), put tired animals to grazing in the lush grass, and buy some supplies. Prices were reasonable: $40 for a yoke of oxen, $40 for a mule, $25 for a horse, to replace tired animals. It was also still possible to make a sharp right-hand turn to Fort Hall. However, for most of those who had become part of the Donner Party on the Little Sandy, the die was cast. They were determined to go due west on the new cut-off, following several days behind the pied-piper, Lansford Hastings, and the wagons of the Harlan-Young group.

At Fort Bridger, John Baptiste Trudeau, age about eighteen, attached himself to the Donners as a teamster. Also joining the company was William McCutchen from Missouri, with his wife Amanda and one-year-old daughter.

At Fort Bridger, some of the families had second thoughts about the Hastings Cut-Off. They left the company in favor of the old route from Fort Bridger to Fort Hall. Those who continued with the Donner Party consisted of the following families and individuals. (In many cases the ages, shown in parentheses, are merely the guesswork of William C. Graves, a survivor, but I have used more reliable evidence when available.)

PATRICK BREEN (51) - three wagons. His wife Margaret (40) and their seven children: John (14), Edward (13), Patrick Jr. (11), Simon (9), Peter (7), James (5), and Isabella (a nursing baby of about six months). With them was PATRICK DOLAN (about 35), one wagon.

GEORGE DONNER (62) - farmer of Springfield, Illinois, three wagons. His third wife Tamsen (45) and their three children: Frances (6), Georgia (4), Eliza (3). Also George's daughters from a previous marriage: Elitha (14) and Leanna (12). George was born in North Carolina, with German roots several generations back. Nevertheless, he was known as "The Dutchman," perhaps because he still maintained a German affiliation as a member of the German Prairie Christian Church in Springfield.

JACOB DONNER (65) - farmer of Springfield, Illinois, three wagons. His wife Elizabeth (45) and their five children: George Jr. (9), Mary (7), Isaac (5), Samuel (4), Lewis (3). Also two of Elizabeth's children by an earlier marriage: SOLOMON HOOK (14) and WILLIAM HOOK (12).

Travelling with the Donner brothers were two employees, NOAH JAMES (20) and SAMUEL SHOEMAKER (25); CHARLES STANTON (35), an educated American, recently of Chicago; JOHN DENTON (28), a cutler and inlayer of gold from Sheffield, England. Additionally, ANTONIO_____ (about 23), a young sheepherder perhaps from New Mexico, who had attached himself to the Donner and Reed families somewhere along the trail; LUKE HALLORAN (25), a consumptive with considerable money, left behind by another party, who was taken in by the

Donners at the Little Sandy and who had not long to live; and JOHN BAPTISTE TRUDEAU (18), as previously mentioned, hired at Fort Bridger.

JAMES FRAZIER REED (46) - Irish-born (Protestant) contractor and furniture maker of Springfield, Illinois, three wagons. His wife Margaret (32), and their four children: Virginia Backenstoe Reed (13), daughter of Margaret by a previous marriage; Martha, called "Patty" (9), James Jr. (5), and Thomas (3). (Mrs. Reed's mother, Sarah Keyes, started out with the Reed/Donner group, but died and was buried in Kansas.) The Reeds, the wealthiest of the Donner Party, travelled in style. One of their wagons was two stories high, probably the largest "prairie schooner" ever to be seen on the trail. They were accompanied by two longtime servants from Springfield: ELIZA WILLIAMS (25), who did all the cooking, and her half-brother BAYLIS WILLIAMS (24). Also three teamsters: MILFORD ELLIOTT (28), WALTER HERRON (25), and JAMES SMITH (25).

WILLIAM H. EDDY (28) - a carriage-maker from Belleville, Illinois, one wagon. His wife Eleanor (25) and their two children: James (3) and Margaret (1).

LAVINIA MURPHY (50), neé Jackson - widow of Jeremiah Burns Murphy of North Carolina, who arrived in Missouri via Tennessee and Illinois (where Lavinia was converted to Mormonism), two wagons. Her seven children: Landrum (15), Mary (13), Lemuel (12), William (11), Simon (10), Sarah (23) and her husband WILLIAM M. FOSTER, and one child, George (4); and Harriet (21) and her husband WILLIAM M. PIKE (25), and their two children, Naomi (3) and Catherine (1). Considering the size of this extended family of thirteen, they were travelling light with only two wagons. The roots of this family were unmistakably Irish, but they were not thought of as "foreigners" by members of the Donner Party. (Mrs. Murphy's first name is spelled "Lavina" in the Donner literature, but "Lavinia" in Murphy family records.)

LEWIS KESEBERG (32) - an Ohio settler from Berleburg, Westphalia, Germany, two wagons. His wife Philippine (23), and their two children: Ada (3) and Lewis Jr. (1), born on the trail. Keseberg was described as a tall, blonde, handsome fellow who, early on, incurred the dislike of other families, perhaps because of his alleged harsh treatment of his wife, perhaps simply because he was a German and a well educated one at that. The son of a Lutheran minister, he spoke four languages and the less educated of the company considered him haughty.

[Jacob?] WOLFINGER (perhaps 26) - one wagon. His wife Doriss (19), sometimes "Doris" and "Dorothy" on the records, maiden name unknown.

Mrs. Wolfinger was German-born (according to California census records), as was, probably, her husband. See notes to this chapter.

Travelling with the Kesebergs or the Wolfingers (with which is not clear) and without wagons: KARL BURGER (about 30), a German speaker known as "Dutch Charley"; AUGUSTUS SPITZER (age unknown), a German speaker, probably from Indiana; JOSEPH REINHARDT (about 30), also a German speaker and perhaps a partner of Spitzer (Stewart in *Ordeal* assigns one wagon to Spitzer and Reinhardt, but there is no evidence for that); and MR. HARDCOOP (about 60), said to be a native of Antwerp, Belgium, who had a farm near Cincinnati, but see notes to this chapter.

WILLIAM McCUTCHEN (30) - from Jackson County, Missouri, who was, it seems, without a wagon. His wife Amanda (30) and infant daughter Harriet (1). The McCutchens apparently had had bad luck travelling with another party. They joined the Donners at Fort Bridger. Spelled "McCutchen" in all the literature, but he signed his name "McCutchan."

Thus the company venturing west from Fort Bridger on the Hastings Cut-Off consisted of seventy-four persons and about nineteen wagons. Some more were to join them. For economy's sake, they will be mentioned here:

FRANKLIN GRAVES (57) - from Sparland, Marshall County, Illinois, three wagons, who caught up with the Donner company in the wilds of the Wasatch Mountains and joined the company. His wife Elizabeth (47), maiden name Cooper, and their nine children: Mary (20), William (18), Eleanor (15), Lovina (13), Nancy (9), Jonathan (7), Franklin Ward Graves Jr. (5), Elizabeth (1); Sarah (22) and her husband, JAY FOSDICK (23). Travelling with them was teamster JOHN SNYDER (25), who was to meet with grief in Nevada, killed by James F. Reed. A total of thirteen in the Graves' group.

LUIS and SALVADOR - Indians from Sutter's Fort who, with Charles Stanton, crossed the mountains with six mules on an early relief mission to the Donners. Since they spent two and one-half months with the Donner Party, and were both murdered and cannibalized, they should certainly be considered among the members of the company.

HOW MANY PEOPLE IN THE "DONNER PARTY"?

"Eighty-seven" is usually cited in the literature as the number of people in the Donner Party, but it is a confusing figure. If we say, as Stewart does, that the Donner Party was organized on the Little Sandy, we have no way of knowing how many people and wagons considered themselves under the elected

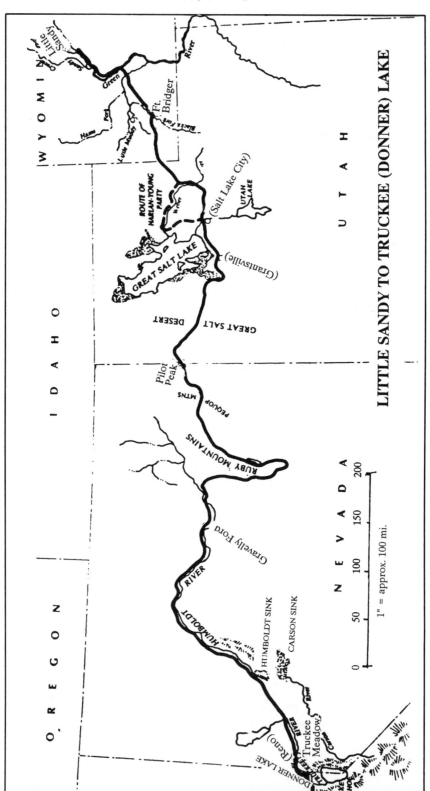

LITTLE SANDY TO TRUCKEE (DONNER) LAKE

captaincy of George Donner on the trail from the Little Sandy to Fort Bridger. At Fort Bridger the McCutchen family of three joined the Donners. So did John Baptiste Trudeau. On leaving the fort, the company consisted of seventy-four people in about nineteen wagons. Later, when the thirteen members of the Graves group (including teamster John Snyder) over-took the Donners in Utah's Wasatch Mountains, the company consisted of eighty-seven people in about twenty-three wagons. Before the company reached Truckee Lake, Halloran, Hard-coop, Snyder, Pike, and Wolfinger were dead; Reed, Herron, Stanton, and McCutchen had departed on horseback for California; and Stanton had returned with the two Sutter's Fort Indians, Luis and Salvador. The number to be entrapped in the high camps, including the Indians, was eighty-one.

THE IRISH IN THE DONNER PARTY

Unlike the Murphy/Stevens Party of 1844, more than half of whose fifty-one members were Irish and Catholic, the Donner Party has generally not been considered an "Irish" com-pany. Yet at least thirty of the eighty-seven (Breens, Reeds, Murphys, Dolan, and Halloran) or 34.5% had distinctly Irish roots. Additionally, McCutchen is a Scots-Gaelic name of frequent occurrence in Ulster. The only Catholics in the Donner Party were the Breens, Dolan, Trudeau, and most likely Antonio and the Sutter's Fort Indians, Luis and Salvador.

EDWARD BREEN BREAKS HIS LEG

The following story was told by Harry J. Breen, son of Edward:

....I must relate an incident that my father told happened to him when the party was not far west of Fort Bridger. He says that Patty Reed and he were galloping along on their saddle ponies, when his horse put one or both front feet into a badger or prairie dog burrow and took a hard fall. He was knocked out and when some of the others came to pick him up they found he had a compound break of his left leg between the knee and ankle. Someone was sent back to the Fort for aid in repairing the damage, and after what seemed to him a long time a rough looking man with long whiskers rode up on a mule. He examined the boy's leg and proceeded to unroll a small bun-dle he had wrapped in canvass and tied behind his saddle. Out of this came a short meat saw and a long bladed knife. The boy of course set up a loud cry when he sensed what was to be done and finally after long discussion convinced his parents that he should keep his leg. The old mountain man was given five dollars and sent back to the Fort muttering to himself for not being given a chance to display his skill as a surgeon. The mother fashioned splints from wood strips and my father said by the time they had reached the Humboldt River he was able to ride his horse again. Youth and a good constitution no doubt. He grew to be six feet one and a half inches tall and weighed in his prime 230 pounds, and one of the finest horsemen in California.

Virginia Reed, more than thirty years later, confirmed this event, but had a slightly different version. She wrote C.F. McGlashan, when he was preparing a history of the Donner Party in 1879, that her father, James F. Reed, had fashioned the splint for Edward's leg and had tended to it until the leg healed. When McGlashan informed her of Edward Breen's recollection of the event, Virginia replied: "Do not say anything [in the book] about the dressing of Ed Breen's leg unless the Breens mention it, it is nothing one way or the other." Virginia was ever anxious that her father be presented heroically in the McGlashan history. It seems likely that she rescinded some of her testimony when confronted with Edward Breen's own account.

THE WASATCH MOUNTAINS

The events of the next two months, until the company reached the high camps near Truckee Lake, can be dated only approximately, as the sources differ. There were many more calamities on the trail. If anticipated, any one of them would have driven the emigrants back to Independence, or at least to Fort Bridger and the trail to Fort Hall. One such ordeal was the crossing of the Wasatch Mountains of Utah.

On leaving Fort Bridger about July 31, they were approximately one hundred and twenty five trail miles from the Great Salt Lake. It was easy going for several days and the company made good time. They crossed several mountain ridges, traveled down Echo Canyon, and arrived at the present site of Henefer, Utah, during the first week of August. Here they found a letter, fixed to the top of a bush, which Hastings had left for them. The note advised them not to take the Weber Canyon route which Hastings had taken. It was too difficult, and they might not have the manpower to manage the many river crossings. Make camp, the note advised, until Hastings could show them a better route. Send a messenger on horseback ahead, he said, and he would return with him and point out the better route. We have Reed's account of this episode, understandably designed to show himself in the best of possible lights, as Reed himself was soon to choose, and lead the party over, a time-wasting alternate route.

The season was getting late. Reed, McCutchen, and Stanton volunteered to go ahead down the Weber Canyon on horseback to find Hastings. Reed overtook Hastings, who was encamped with his wagon train on the south shore of the Salt Lake. He left Stanton and McCutchen there with their worn-out horses. According to Reed, Hastings furnished him with a fresh horse and took him to a mountain peak where he pointed out to Reed a possible course south of the Weber Canyon route. Hastings then returned to the lake. Reed explored part of the new route, which Hastings himself knew nothing about, and blazed trees to mark the intended path. More than a week passed in the camp before Reed returned, without Stanton and McCutchen, who later would re-join the company, half-dead from exhaustion and about to eat their horses, having gotten lost in the mountains.

Back at the Donner encampment, Reed convinced the members of the party to try his route. It turned into a back-breaking and oxen-breaking disaster every yard of the way, ax swing by ax swing, cutting trails in heavily wooded canyons, crossing and re-crossing streams, events which were minimized when Reed gave his written testimony twenty-five years later but which contributed to the general dislike of Reed by some members of the party. They were several days in this thicket when the three wagons of "Uncle Billy" Graves caught up with them, the last of the wagons to leave Fort Bridger. They were a party of thirteen, including four adult males, welcome additions in the work of cutting the trail. The company now numbered eighty-seven people and about twenty-two wagons. The Donner Party was complete, taking its final form in the Wasatch Mountains.

Nevertheless, it took them about eighteen days (twenty-one and more days according to the accounts of some witnesses) to bring their wagons a distance of about thirty miles to the pass or saddle of the Wasatch Range. They had blazed a trail to the historic "Reed-Donner Pass," over which Brigham Young led his pioneer Mormon party the following year. Over this same trail came many more thousands of travellers in the next two decades before the coming of the railroad in 1869.

William C. Graves, son of "Uncle Billy" (Franklin Graves) and not always a credible witness, placed much of the blame for the debacle in the Wasatch on Reed who, he said, "told us if we went the Canon [*sic*] Road we would be apt to break our wagons and kill our oxen, but if we went the new way we could get to Salt Lake in a week or 10 days."

It was still hard going to the valley of the Great Salt Lake. Finally they passed the site of what is today the "This Is the Place" monument of the Mormons, where Brigham Young first saw the valley. They descended to cross the present site of Salt Lake City and during the last week of September (or a week earlier than that, according to the Miller-Reed Diary) encamped on the eastern bank of what later became known as the Jordan River at a point just west of today's Utah State Fairgrounds.

Chapter 4

THE LONG DRY DRIVE

It was getting late in the season and fears of survival began to permeate the company. They did not delay at the Jordan River camp but pushed on the next day without additional rest, camping near to the shore of the Salt Lake. They could see the wheel tracks and other marks of the Hastings company. An axle on one of Reed's wagons broke. His men had to ride fifteen miles on horseback to find the right timber with which to fashion a new axle.

One of the wagons brought in a dead man, the consumptive Luke Halloran. He was buried with Masonic ceremonies conducted by Reed, a Master Mason himself. Halloran's emaciated body was wrapped in a buffalo robe and blanket and buried by the southern shore of Great Salt Lake, at what would one day become the pier site of Sunset Beach, Utah. Halloran left his possessions, which included $1,500 in coin, to George Donner. The company rested one day.

On the trail again, they rounded the lake and, crossing the Tooele Valley, came to Twenty Wells (today's Grantsville). There they found natural springs with the purest of water. The following day they passed another spring with undrinkable salty water, but finally found a campsite in a fine meadow with good, potable water. They were in the Skull Valley on the site of what would one day be the Kimball-Knowlton Ranch. Hastings had been there and had left them a note on a post. It was so tattered that the advice could barely be read. He wrote that it would take them two days and nights of a hard and dry drive before they reached the next grass and water below Pilot Peak. The Salt Desert had to be passed.

As in the past, Hastings underestimated the difficulty. He led the Donner company to think that the dry drive was only about thirty-five or forty miles, which would stretch the oxen to their very limits, even if their tongues were bathed with wet towels from time to time.

They rested the animals for a day and a half, gathering and storing grass for them, filling up their water casks for people and animals for what they thought would be a forty-eight hour drive. The women cooked the food they would need. There would be no chance of making a fire on this desolate landscape of mud, salt, and sand.

After a long day's drive across Skull Valley, climbing a low ridge now known as Cedar Mountain, they could see the salt plain ahead. It was surely a sickening sight. As far as the eye could see, to the mountains far to the west, there was desert. Men cursed Hastings, as they had in the Wasatch Mountains. Now they even talked of killing him if and when they got to California. Feelings also ran high against Reed who, some felt, had led them astray in the Wasatch, and whose huge two-story wagon had slowed down the train for months. Many years later, an embittered William C. Graves wrote C.F. McGlashan, "Reed, being an aristocratic fellow, was above working so he had hired hands to drive his teams and he gave orders, although no one paid much attention to him, but his wife was a lady and the company humored him a good deal on that account."

At night they began their crossing of the salt dunes, wagon wheels sinking into the sand and mud. They pushed on, every-body walking who could walk to lighten the load on the teams. The wagons were soon spread out in a line of several miles. It was every family for itself. The heaviest wagons, driven by the Donners and Reed, were falling farther and farther behind. Their teamsters were of little use in driving the weakened oxen. The lightest wagons were the first to make it through the dunes to the hard desert surface of salt. The Breens and Dolan seem to have had little trouble in the crossing. They were gen-erally more prudent and perhaps luckier than the other fami-lies, as time was beginning to tell. It was not like the Breens to take the minimum of water.

On the morning of the third day, after three nights and two days of driving with only occasional rests, William Eddy's wagon, with Breen, Dolan, and Graves not far behind, reached the water below Pilot Peek. Reed was there too, having ridden ahead on horseback in search of the water. The dry drive, as measured by Charles Kelly and William Stookey, was actually seventy-five miles, twice the estimate of Hastings. The springs were about twenty miles north of today's Wendover, at what later became the ranch of J.W. Cummins, next to Charley McKellar's Ranch, on the Utah-Nevada border.

Still about twenty miles back on the salt plains were the Donners with their heavy wagons, and ten miles behind them were the even heavier wagons of Reed. Eddy wanted to go back to look for an ox and Reed returned with him. It was nightfall, and Reed was carrying a few buckets of water to revive his ox teams and bring in his family. Late that night he met his teamsters, still far back in the desert, driving his unyoked oxen to water. He continued on and would later learn that the teamsters, soon after he left them, lost control of the thirst-crazed animals. Eighteen of them stampeded, away from the direction of the water, and were never recovered. He was left with but one ox and one cow. Reed, the richest in possessions, had become the poorest.

At daylight, Reed finally reached his wife and children walking with their dogs. They waited all day, expecting their teamsters to return with horses and oxen. In the evening the six Reeds proceeded on foot, became exhausted and tried to sleep, cuddling up with five dogs for warmth during the cold desert night. They moved on at daylight and caught up with the Jacob Donner family. Jacob had gone ahead by himself, but soon returned with refreshed animals and took his own and Reed's family to the water.

Other families succeeded in driving their unyoked oxen to the water. Reed managed to retrieve only one of his wagons, the two-story one, known as the "palace car." William C. Graves wrote that "Father [Franklin Graves] loaned him one ox and Mr. Breen one and with his cow and ox made two yoke to one wagon." It was not a strong team, especially for Reed's huge wagon.

Despite all this, Reed had an eye out for future business enterprise. Three years later he wrote his relative, James W. Keyes, in Springfield: "....fifty miles west of Great Salt Lake, where I met my defeat, and while helping to catch [cache] a wagon, I found at least one half an ounce of very small gold."

The company camped for seven or eight days to rest and engage in fruitless searches for Reed's oxen. All adult males participated in the search. Valuable time was lost. Much personal property had to be abandoned. The company was reduced to about eighteen wagons. George Donner and Lewis Keseberg had each abandoned one wagon, it seems, in addition to the two that Reed had abandoned.

Stewart, a colorful stylist and story-teller, probably exaggerated somewhat the ordeal of the long drive across the Great Salt Desert. A few wagons were abandoned, but no person perished. It was mainly Reed's ordeal, for several reasons. He had over-burdened his oxen with the extraordinarily heavy load of personal possessions he had brought from Springfield. He had built himself the largest wagon that had ever been seen on the trail, and the like of it would not be seen again. Pulling this wagon over mountains and fording rivers had delayed the entire company along the difficult trail from Fort Bridger. Now in the desert Reed himself had ridden ahead cavalierly in search of water, leaving the heavy work to his teamsters, and they had been careless with the oxen.

Breen, Dolan, Graves, Wolfinger, the Murphy/Foster family, and Eddy seem to have crossed handily with little or no loss of livestock. The greatest problem was the one week or more delay below Pilot Peak while everybody was obliged to turn out for the unsuccessful search for Reed's lost teams. This delay was almost certainly a major contributing cause of the tragedy that the company was to experience.

It is small wonder that Reed, whose strong voice had prevailed concerning the choice of the Hastings Cut-Off, was blamed by some for the plight of the company. It is even less wonder that he would soon be banished for the killing of the popular John Snyder, the Graves' teamster, in a moment of anger.

Chapter 5

A DIGRESSION ON INDIANS, SURVIVAL AND CHARITY

Few Indians had been seen since the company left Fort Bridger, but they would soon be getting into the territory of the "Digger" Indians along the Humboldt and Truckee rivers. Historian Bernard DeVoto said the term Digger (a pejorative) applied to castoffs from various tribes, "degenerate bands," many of them "physically decadent" who had "lost their culture." His view is simplistic. The Indians of central and western Nevada, who were of Shoshone and Piute stock, were by no means without "culture," although they were, indeed, among the most primitive of North American Indians.

The culture of the Indians of the Nevada river basins was early Stone Age. They were frequently not organized above the family level. They had neither agriculture nor horses. They dieted on roots (hence "Digger"), rabbits, an occasional antelope, ducks, rats, insects, nuts of the piñon tree (when available) and, most importantly, the seeds of the vegetation along the river. The women gathered these seeds in late summer and stored them for the winter months. They made shallow baskets for winnowing seeds. They had decoys for ducks, made of rushes, feathers and paints. Naked in summer except perhaps for a covering of mud for protection from mosquitoes, they used rabbit skins for robes in the winter when they retreated to sheltered canyons or to caves. They had primitive bows and arrows, and shields. Families and groups of families occasionally made war on each other, but the warfare tended to be more ritualistic than bloody.

In summer months several families might join up for a foraging expedition. They harvested grass here and there, dug

33

bulbs, hunted rabbits and grasshoppers. For the latter, they would build a fire and let it burn down to the coals. Meanwhile, they encircled the fire, gradually tightening the circle and forcing grasshoppers into the coals to roast like peanuts.

Their lives were mean and harsh. Life expectancy for a male who survived infancy was about twenty-five years; for a female slightly longer. In 1859, an Indian of eastern Nevada was asked by an officer of the Army Corps of Engineers if he liked his country. The Indian said it was better than any other place he had seen because it had lots of rats.

Surely many of the Indians remembered the company of trappers under Joe Walker in 1834. Walker's men murdered many Indians, whom they considered sub-human, for mere sport as well as vengeance. The Indians remembered the more benign emigrant parties of 1841 to 1845. By 1846, however, they had become aware of the devastation to their precarious existence caused by the grazing of livestock along their river. The vegetation was being devoured even before it could bear seed. The Diggers quickly developed a taste for beef and mule-meat, easier to get late in the 1846 season than rats, antelopes, rabbits, and seeds. Accomplished thieves even before the arrival of the white man, they now applied their skills to raiding the wagon trains.

They ran off horses and cattle in the night or maimed them with primitive bows and arrows, coming back later as the animals dropped on the trail. They feasted for a few days until the carcasses began to spoil, then came back for more. Usually the lowly Diggers could be frightened off temporarily by sight or sound of guns, but they sometimes stood and fought.

The best method of protection from the raids of the Indians at night was to form the wagons in a circle with the livestock *inside* it. The campfires would then be lighted outside this circle, where the adults and the older children would also make their beds. Sentries would be posted. However, no memoirs of surviving Donner Party members mention this strategy, while many recall devastating Indian depredations near the Humboldt and Truckee river basins ("sinks"). These were not people experienced in the West. Unlike the successful Murphy Party of 1844, they did not have an experienced mountain man like Caleb Greenwood as their guide. Greenwood was able to negotiate with Indians such as "Chief" Truckee, who directed the Murphy Party to the lake and the pass over the Sierras.

Another problem was that the company sub-divided itself into groups, each pursuing its own course along the Humboldt and Truckee. It was every family or little group for itself. This gave the Indian raiders a distinct advantage.

The Breens and Dolan lost fewer of their animals than did other families. Margaret Breen recalled later that "all of the Breen wagons and animals" were brought to the camp of entrapment near Truckee Lake. As was becoming evident on the trail, Patrick and Margaret Breen seemed to possess a strong sense of survival. Their own children always came first; others had to wait in line.

To people who can travel Interstate 80 today in the comfort of their automobiles, some of the decisions that Patrick and Peggy and other members of the party had to make may seem harsh and uncharitable. They were decisions such as few of us have to make in our own lifetime as we go from cradle to grave over relatively placid waters. The Donner Party members had to find answers to the most difficult of moral questions. What to do when helping another with food or drink would seriously endanger the lives of one's own children? Should one lend a weakened horse for the almost certainly fruitless search for an elderly man last seen dying on the desert, when that horse, needed for the survival of one's own family, would probably die in the process? Should dead human flesh be shunned as food, if children would starve to death without it? The family heads of the Donner company were faced with such dreadful questions in the days and months ahead.

Patrick and Margaret Breen, while always putting their own children first, seem to have been the most generous in sharing what they had with other families. Even Stewart, no great admirer of the Breens, somewhat reluctantly granted that they were "a little more charitable" than the rest. Like others in the party, they adopted a strategy of trading rather than giving anything away outright. "You need an ox? All right, promise me two in return when – and if – we get to California. Meanwhile I will take some jewelry as security." Such became the strategy of those who had and those who had not, as the greater part of the emigrants' goods were cached futilely in the desert and as some found themselves without even one yoke of oxen. These were not poor people lacking in the treasures of the civilized world, but such treasures were of little use to them now. Some carried considerable quantities of coin in gold and silver. The Donner brothers may have had as much as $14,000, according to the research and estimate of C.F. McGlashan.

Martha "Patty" Reed Lewis explained how things worked in a letter to McGlashan in 1879.

> Your paper received, I am not at all satisfied with Hon. James Breen's statement of Mr. Dolan's generosity or kindness to Mrs. Reed and their children. Mr. Dolan demand[ed] security from my Mother for beef which she bought from him, agreeing to pay him two in California for one there, if by lb. or otherwise (like agreement she made with all other parties of whom she bought[t] meat or any thing else). Mother was obliged to part with articles of clothing or waring apperal and beding, and to get anything hauled by their teams, from the time we made our first cashee really....

Patty Reed also wrote that Dolan took her mother's watch and her father's Masonic medal, giving a promise to return them in California when payment was received for the meat. Dolan "had plenty" of that, said Patty. (The items were later returned at Johnson's Ranch, retrieved from Dolan's effects.)

Chapter 6

TO THE HUMBOLDT AND TRUCKEE

It was mid-September before the company abandoned the search for Reed's lost oxen and broke camp below Pilot Peak. They moved along the base of a mountain range, the peaks already snow-capped. Dispiriting to the emigrants was the news brought in by their horsemen that there was another dry drive just ahead of them, many miles to water. They followed Hastings' tracks, going due south along the foot of the Ruby Mountains. They found water, but it was three days before they turned westward again, around the Rubys. They then headed due northward for another three days, along the south fork of the Humboldt to where it joined the main branch of the river, about ten miles west of today's Elko. That was the end of the Hastings Cut-Off, the point where it met the trail coming down from Fort Hall.

Meanwhile, it was becoming evident that death by starvation was facing them. Consequently, Stanton and McCutchen agreed to go ahead on horseback, all the way to Sutter's Fort, to obtain food. Reed finally had to cache most of his considerable personal possessions in the desert. William Eddy yoked his oxen to Reed's wagon and William Pike took Eddy's wagon.

The last of the parties that had taken the Fort Hall route from the Little Sandy had already passed this point. Hastings too. The Donner Party members were not to hear from him again. Hastings did manage to get his entire company of over sixty wagons, what came to be known as the Harlan/Young Party, to the California settlements with few casualties.

The Donner Party was now much less than half way across the present state of Nevada. The Humboldt River – also known as Ogden's or St. Mary's River – followed a leisurely course to its sink in the desert over two hundred miles farther westward.

REED KILLS SNYDER

The company divided into two groups. The teams of the Donners seemed to be in good shape. They went on ahead. With them went Reed's teamsters, with the exception of Milt Elliott. The Murphy extended family, including the Pikes and Fosters, went ahead too. The group behind included Reed, Eddy, Breen, Graves, and Keseberg. The troubles continued. Indians stole a horse and a yoke of Uncle Billy Graves' oxen. Ahead, some of the oxen of the Donners were maimed by the arrows of Indians in a night raid. The party was now making twenty miles in a day's long march, but tempers were becoming short. This led to a tragedy, the facts of which would be debated for decades to come. About October 5, Reed's teamster, Milt Elliott, was driving his team up a difficult hill. The event was vividly described by John Breen in his manuscript "Pioneer Memoirs." John recalled that Reed's team was on a sand bank. Snyder was driving Graves' team behind Reed's enormous wagon and attempted to pass. Snyder called Reed a name and threatened to strike him. Reed jumped across the tongue of the wagon and stabbed Snyder in the chest. In the melee, Snyder managed to lash Reed across the head with his whip. Although Reed and his apologists later claimed that Snyder also struck Mrs. Reed, John vigorously denied that such had happened. "Mrs. Reed had nothing to do with the affair....Snyder would not strike her....he was too much of a man for that."

Snyder died in a few minutes in the arms of Patrick Breen. "Uncle Patrick, I am dead," were his last words as one witness reported. James Breen recalled that Snyder was "strong, handsome, entertaining....in the evenings....when other amusements failed [he would] remove the 'hind grate' of his wagon, lay it on the ground, and thereon perform the 'clog' dance....Irish jigs....and other steps....he was a most expert dancer." John Breen wrote that "Snyder's loss was mourned by the whole company; still Reed was not blamed by many."

Feelings were mixed as to justice in the matter, and reports of survivors conflict. Probably the most unreliable account was given by J. Quinn Thornton in his *Oregon and California in 1848* (1849). Thornton depended exclusively on the testimony of William H. Eddy, who gave a bizarre account of Keseberg proposing to hang Reed with the consent of all but Eddy and Elliott. According to this account, Reed and his two supporters had guns at the ready; finally, Eddy proposed that Reed be allowed to leave the camp and he left the next morning.

It is surprising that Stewart in *Ordeal* took Thornton's account seriously. "Reed's situation was desperate....Keseberg, cherishing the grudge [against Reed], propped up his wagon-tongue with an ox-yoke for the hanging....The Graves' clan was crying for vengeance." Stewart, in a later book *(The California Trail)*, bettered his own fiction by adding that Patrick Breen joined Keseberg and Graves in crying for vengeance. According to Thornton, as informed by Eddy, Reed went off into exile and almost certain death without horse or gun, but Eddy, always the hero in his own accounting, followed Reed with a gun and some ammunition. As Virginia Reed recounted the event forty-five years later, the horse was first denied her father, but she and Milt Elliott, carrying rifle, pistols, ammuniton, and some food, followed after him, left him with the horse and provisions, and walked back to the camp. As John Breen, and even Reed himself, told the story, Reed proposed voluntary exile from the party. He offered to go ahead on horseback to Fort Sutter, much as Stanton and McCutchen had done, and bring back provisions. Reed's proposal was accepted by Patrick Breen, with these words, as his son remembered them: "We all seem to be doomed, and I think we had better not have the man's blood on our hands."

William C. Graves, who wrote a vivid account of Snyder's death and the subsequent council, said: "It was not a brutal decision to banish Reed. He killed a man." In any case, there could have been no danger of Reed's being hanged at the insistence of Keseberg, Breen, and Graves, without at least consulting George Donner, the elected leader of the company. But the story was a good one for Thornton and irresistible for Stewart.

Reed's wife and four children remained with the company. Reed caught up with the Donners, where his teamster, Walter

Herron, joined him. They went on to reach the California settlements, and that story will be told in its place.

The elderly Belgian travelling with Keseberg, Mr. Hardcoop, fell far behind the second group.   Like all other adults
and most of the children, Hardcoop had been reduced to
walking. He asked Eddy to let him ride in his wagon. Eddy refused, saying "maybe later." Reed's family was having problems too. Their huge wagon had to be abandoned and substi-
tuted with one of the Graves wagons.

Patrick Breen also had to make a hard decision. On the
evening of October 8, old Hardcoop had not made it to the
camp. He was still not there in the morning. According to
Eddy, Patrick Breen and Franklin Graves twice refused to lend
him a saddle horse to go search for the Belgian. Even assum-
ing Eddy's uncorroborated statement was true, a horse was po-
tential food for the mouths of the nine children of Graves and
the seven of Breen. The animals might be lacking in flesh and
fat, but they could provide edible brains, heart, and liver, not to
mention a valuable hide.

The Indians continued to run off cattle. Another wagon
was abandoned. As the sink was approached, water became
less and less potable and grass was scantier. The Indians ran
off eighteen oxen and a milk cow, mostly belonging to the
Donner brothers and Wolfinger. The two groups joined and
camped together as they approached the sink. Breen's horse
got bogged down in the mud. Eddy refused to help Breen extract the beast, and it was left to die. Oxen continued to be
wounded by the weak bows of the Diggers. On the night of
October 12, the Indians maimed twenty head of cattle. The
animals were slaughtered for food on the spot, but there was
no time for drying and preserving what meat was left on their
wasted bodies.

Eddy abandoned his wagon. Wolfinger remained behind
to make a cache of his wagon, with the help of Spitzer and
Reinhardt. Mrs. Wolfinger proceeded ahead, walking like
everybody else who could walk. Mothers and fathers carried
their small children. Mrs. Reed, now without husband, and the
Donners were in the advance group. Mrs. Reed still had two
saddle horses capable of carrying her children. Patrick Breen
allowed the wagonless Eddy to throw his goods in one of the

Breen wagons. Eddy and family trudged along with their one remaining ox. The Breens trudged beside them. By the time the company reached the sink of the Humboldt over one hundred cattle had been lost in the Indian raids, according to one report, but that may be an exaggeration.

THE FORTY-MILE DESERT

Reaching the sink had no rewards. The grass had become sparse and the water saltier, hardly fit to drink. This was no place for dallying. Ahead lay forty miles of desert before they would reach the Truckee River basin. It meant a hard drive of twenty-four hours with little rest for people or livestock.

Only about fourteen wagons remained on October 13 when the company left the sink of the Humboldt. Far out in the desert they came to Geyser Springs. The boiling water was barely potable if allowed to cool. They wasted little time at the Springs. Unfortunately, William Eddy had failed to carry enough water, although his ox was capable of carrying it. When he ran out, he demanded water from the cask of the Breens. Eddy later recalled that Patrick Breen refused him, saying the water was needed for his own children. Eddy reported that he took the water anyway, threatening to shoot Breen if he interfered. Such was one of Eddy's many uncorroborated stories reflecting poorly on his companions.

The wagons reached the Truckee River, near today's town of Wadsworth, on October 25 or thereabouts. The famished livestock feasted on the lush grass. William Eddy later claimed that his family was starving and that both Graves and Breen refused meat to them. Later he shot some geese and shared them, he said, with others including the Breens. Eddy, according to the Breens in their later recollections, had already earned the sobriquet of "Lying Eddy" for his constant boasting around the campfires of past heroic exploits. This opinion of Eddy was also expressed by Martha Reed Lewis in a letter to Eliza Donner Houghton:

> Of what value is the information given by men without principle....Mr. W.H. Eddy could not give you valuable or reliable information. On the plains I heard at various times – members of the Company say 'Did Eddy tell you that?' It is unfortunate that he [could] not tell the truth. ["Sutter's Fort Document Collection: Reed Family," folder 355]

The emigrants could already see snow on the peaks to the west. The Indian raids continued at the Meadows. Somewhere along the trail, it is not clear just where, Spitzer and Reinhardt finally caught up with the company. Wolfinger was not with them. They said he had been killed by the Indians. In the Thornton/Eddy account of this, Reinhardt is made a murderer:

> I [Thornton] was informed by Mr. Eddy that George Donner, with whom Rianhard [*sic*] subsequently traveled, told him that Wolfinger had not died as stated – that this fact he learned from a confession made by Rianhard a short time previous to his death....

This was a demonstrable untruth. As we shall learn, Eddy left the high camp with the "Snowshoe Party" on December 16 and never again saw Reinhardt or George Donner alive. Those at the lake did not learn of Reinhardt's death until December 21, according to Breen's diary. When Eddy returned to the lake camps in mid-March with the third rescue party, he never visited the Alder Creek camp where George Donner was either dead or dying. Even George R. Stewart says that the rescuers had been at the lake "only two hours" before they headed for the valley. Yet Stewart accepted Eddy and Thornton's tale of Reinhardt's "confession." It made for a good story, and the devil with any evidence for it.

The strongest evidence that Wolfinger was the victim of foul play in the hands of Spitzer and Reinhardt came from William C. Graves who, so he claimed more than thirty years later, went with two others in search of Wolfinger. They found his wagon and his two yoke of oxen, grazing nearby on the banks of the Humboldt, but no Mr. Wolfinger nor any Indian tracks thereabouts. "We hitched the oxen to the wagon and drove them on till we overtook the company and delivered them up to Mrs. Woulfinger [*sic*]. She hired another German by the name of Chas. Berger to drive it, after that, and there was nothing more said about it."

There was good news. Somewhere along the Truckee, Stanton and two Indians from Sutter's Fort arrived with seven pack mules full of provisions. But tragedy also struck on the Truckee. William Pike of the Lavinia Murphy extended family was accidentally killed. As he handed a pistol to his brother-in-law William Foster and turned to take care of the campfire, the weapon fired and Pike was hit in the back. He died in minutes. In another incident, one night Eddy killed an Indian archer caught in the act of maiming the cattle.

Breen and Dolan, fearful of the snows and anxious to get going, took the lead in the drive up the Truckee. By the time they had reached today's Verdi, west of Truckee Meadows (today's Reno), they had forded the river for the forty-ninth time. At Verdi, they decided to depart from the Truckee Canyon. They made their way in a northwesterly direction to a mountain pass and then down a steep pitch into Dog Valley, after which the unmapped trail turned generally south for about twenty miles to the Alder Creek Valley, a few miles south of which was the site of the present town of Truckee.

The wagons were stretched out for miles. Keseberg and Eddy joined Breen and Dolan in the lead group. In the second group were the Reed, Graves, and Murphy wagons, and Stanton with his mules. The Donners in the rear fell farther behind when an axle broke. A new one was fashioned, but in the process George Donner's chisel slipped, making a terrible gash in his hand. He was never to recover from that, although it did not seem fatal at the time.

On October 31, Breen and the advance group approached Truckee Lake, now known as Donner Lake and referred to hereafter by that name in this book. They made camp on the ground in an inch of snow. They were at the six thousand foot level, twelve hundred feet below the pass. In the morning they passed a deserted cabin that had been built by the Murphy Party two years before. They worked around the north shore of the lake before driving their teams toward the pass, about three miles from the western end of the lake. But as the snow got deeper they had to return to the lake.

Chapter 7

ENTRAPMENT IN THE SNOWS

As well as they could, the Breens settled into the cabin at the eastern end of the lake where young Moses Schallenberger of the Murphy Party had spent the whole winter in 1844. The roof of pine boughs did little to impede the rain, but that problem was soon remedied by a covering of hides. James Breen said that the cabin was about sixteen by twenty (another estimate was twelve by fourteen), built of rough logs, with a fireplace and chimney at one end and sleeping space at the other. Later, when Mrs. Reed and her four children were taken into the cabin, a sheet separated the two families.

In the first week of November another try for the pass was made, this time with Stanton and the Indians to guide them. Keseberg had badly damaged his foot with an ax and had to be hoisted up and tied to a horse. They failed to make the pass that night and made camp below the summit in over five feet of snow. By the following morning an additional foot of snow had fallen. Again, the party had to turn back to the lake. The date was November 4, 1846. They were six miles from the pass, about seventy miles from the nearest settlement, and more than one hundred miles from Sutter's Fort.

THE LAKE CAMPS

The emigrants chose three campsites. All but the Breens had to construct their own cabins.

(1) BREEN AND KESEBERG CABIN

Breen/Dolan cabin:

Patrick Breen, 51	Simon Breen, 9
Margaret Breen, 40	Peter Breen, 7
John Breen, 14	James Breen, 5
Edward Breen, 13	Isabella Breen, 1
Patrick Breen, 11	Patrick Dolan, 30-34

Keseberg extension to Breen cabin:

Lewis Keseberg, 33   Ada Keseberg, 3
Philippine Keseberg, 23   Lewis Keseberg Jr., 1
Augustus Spitzer, also possibly with Keseberg

(2) MURPHY AND EDDY CAMP (double cabin 200 yards from Breen)

Lavinia Murphy, 50   George Foster, 4
Landrum Murphy, 15   Harriet Murphy Pike, 21
Mary Murphy, 13   Naomi Pike, 3
Lemuel Murphy, 12   Catherine Pike, 1
William Murphy, 11   William Eddy, 28
Simon Murphy, 10   Eleanor Eddy, 25
Sarah Murphy Foster, 23   James Eddy, 3
William M. Foster, 28   Margaret Eddy, 1

(3) GRAVES AND REED CAMP (two or three cabins on Donner Creek, more than half a mile from the Breen cabin, one for the Graves family, another for the Reeds, and perhaps a third for others, including Stanton and the fort Indians)

Franklin Graves Sr., 57   Amanda McCutchen, 24
Elizabeth Graves,47   Harriet McCutchen, 1
Mary Graves, 20   Margaret Reed, 32
William Graves, 18   Virginia Backenstoe Reed, 13
Eleanor Graves, 15   Martha "Patty" Reed, 8
Lovina Graves, 13   James Reed, 5
Nancy Graves, 9   Thomas Reed, 3
Jonathan Graves, 7   Milford Elliott, 28
Franklin Graves Jr., 5   Baylis Williams, 24
Elizabeth Graves, 1   Eliza Williams, 25
Sarah Graves Fosdick, 23   Charles Stanton, 35
Jay Fosdick, 23   Luis
                                     Salvador

THE ALDER CREEK CAMP

The Donner brothers, caught in the heavy snows a few days before, never reached the lake camps and were obliged to camp six miles away in the extreme upper end of the Alder Creek Valley, about three miles north of today's town of Truckee. Tents on each side of the creek were constructed of poles propped diagonally against a tree. Canvas, quilts, and buffalo robes were draped over the poles. The fire inside meant that the melting snow was constantly dripping in. A Donner survivor recalled that her clothes and bed covers were wet for weeks at a time. A rude structure resembling a wigwam was put together for teamsters and other males travelling without family. There were three camp sites, several hundred yards apart.

(1) GEORGE DONNER TENT

George Donner, 62	Eliza Donner, 3
Tamsen Donner, 45	Elitha Donner, 14
Frances Donner, 6	Leanna Donner, 12
Georgia Donner, 4	Doriss/Dorothy Wolfinger, 19

(2) JACOB DONNER TENT

Jacob Donner, 65	Samuel Donner, 4
Elizabeth Donner, 45	Lewis Donner, 3
George Donner, 9	Solomon Hook, 14
Mary Donner, 7	William Hook, 12
Isaac Donner, 5	

(3) EMPLOYEES, SINGLE MALES (wigwam-like structure)

Noah James, 20	James Smith, 25
Samuel Shoemaker, 25	James Denton, 28*
Joseph Reinhardt, about 30	Charley Burger, 30*
John Baptiste Trudeau, 18	Antonio, probably at Alder Creek

Denton and Burger later moved to the lake camp.

So, at the beginning of the entrapment, there were fifty-six persons at the lake camps and twenty-five at Alder Creek, for a total of eighty-one. Only forty-six of them would live to see the California settlements.

In November, a few other attempts were made to scale the pass, with and without ox teams. None was successful. Without pasturage, the livestock, mules, and horses died quickly in the snow. The most prudent of the emigrants, such as Breen and Dolan, seem to have been quicker than other families to accept the fact that they were snowbound for the winter. They slaughtered their animals quickly, dried as much of the meat as they could, and stored what was left in the snow, probably marking the spot with stakes. Patrick Breen wrote nothing in his diary about having any problems finding his livestock or meat under new snows, unlike the situation at the Donner camp, where unsuccessful probes were conducted for buried animals.

Top: Site of Murphy cabin with bronze plaque listing names of Donner Party members (entrance of cabin faced the rock, where there was a fireplace). *Bottom*: author, Donner Lake in background, from old Highway 40 west of the lake and near the pass. Photos by Betty Wayne King, 1991.

DOWN IN THE VALLEY

As mentioned earlier, four men had gone ahead of the party in Utah and Nevada, Stanton and McCutchen first, then Reed and Herron. They all reached Sutter's Fort safely. It will be recalled that Stanton, with two fort Indians, had returned over the mountains to the company, meeting them near Truckee Meadows, with a mule train of provisions. In October, Reed and McCutchen also equipped themselves at Sutter's Fort for a return journey, with no knowledge of just where the company was. They got as far as Bear Valley where they were defeated by the soft snow, and they had to return to Sutter's Fort. Captain Sutter advised them that relief was impossible until the snow hardened.

But there were other problems in getting relief efforts under way. One of them was the Mexican War, which had broken out in April 1846. The war and the Bear Flag Revolt in California (June-July 1846) were the major subjects of interest, not emigrants in trouble. American military authorities in California were busily recruiting all the Americans they could find, and there were not many of them. In 1845, the American population of California was only about five hundred. In 1846, the number perhaps doubled with the arrival of the wagon trains, but these people were hardly in a position to engage in expensive rescue efforts requiring considerable provisions, horses, etc.

Reed was not a man content to weep over what he could not do. He therefore busied himself during the months of December and January in things he could accomplish. He successfully petitioned the alcaldes (mayors) in San Francisco and San Jose for parcels of land. He joined John C. Fremont's California Battalion, was placed in charge of Mission San Jose, and participated in the so-called Battle of Santa Clara. Most importantly for the entrapped Donner Party, he made contacts with people who would be needed for raising money and men when rescue efforts could commence.

Chapter 8

THE HISTORIC DIARY OF PATRICK BREEN

The story of that long winter entrapment is a tragic tale told, amazingly, by Patrick Breen himself. Huddled in the rude shanty with his large family for over four months as the snows fell to depths of twenty feet and more, and suffering from kidney stones, Breen somehow managed to take pencil in hand almost every day to record the historic events. It was a unique achievement, considering the circumstances. "Factually, the diary nearly always proves to be correct, when it can be checked," wrote George R. Stewart.

The diary of this remarkable Irishman from County Carlow was kept in a little book which Patrick made from eight small sheets of letter paper. He trimmed and folded the sheets to make a book of thirty-two pages, each 3-3/4 by 6 inches. He filled twenty-nine of these pages by the efforts of fingers that were probably often numbed from cold, from November 20, 1846 (first entry) to March 1, 1847 (last entry).

THE DIARY OF PATRICK BREEN

[NOVEMBER 1846]
Friday Nov. 20th 1846 came to this place on the 31st of last month that it snowed we went on to the pass the snow so deep we were unable to find the road, when within 3 miles of the summit then turned back to this shanty on the Lake, Stanton came one day after we arrived here we again took our teams & waggons & made another unsuccessful attempt to cross in company with Stanton we returned to the shanty it continueing to snow all the time we were here we now have killed most part of our cattle having to stay here untill next spring & live on poor beef without bread or salt [2] it snowed during the space of eight days with little intermission, after our arrival here,

First page (full scale) from the *Diary of Patrick Breen*, Nov. 20, 1846.
Courtesy of Bancroft Library, University of California, Berkeley,
California.

the remainder of time up to this day was clear & pleasant frezeing at night the snow nearly gone from the valleys.

Sat. 21st   Fine morning   wind N:W   22 of our company are about starting across the mountain this mor[n]ing including Stanton & his indians, some clouds flying   thawed to day   wnd E.

Sunday 22nd   froze hard last night   this a fine clear morning,   wind E.S.E.   no account from those on the mountains.

Monday   23rd   Same weather wind W   the expedition across the mountains returned after an unsuccesful attempt. [3]

Tuesday 24th   Fine in the morning   towards eve[n]ing cloudy & windy wind W   looks like snow   freezeing hard.

Wendsday 25th   Wind about W N W   Cloudy   looks like the eve of a snow storm   our mountainers intend trying to cross the mountain tomorrow if fair   froze hard last night.

Thurssday the 26th   Began to snow yesterday in the evening   now rains or sleet   the mountainiers dont start to day   the wind about W.   wet & muddy.

Friday 27   Continues to snow, the ground not covered, wind W   dull prospect for crossing the mountains.

Saturday 28th   Snowing fast now about 10 o clock   snow 8 or 10 inches deep soft wet snow, weather not cold   wind W.

Sunday 29th   still snowing now about 3 feet deep, wind W   killed my last oxen today   will skin them tomorrow   gave another yoke to Fosters hard to get wood. [4]

Monday 30th   Snowing fast   wind W   about 4 or 5 feet deep, no drifts looks as likely to continue as when it commenced   no liveing thing without wings can get about.

[DECEMBER 1846]

December 1st Tuesday   Still snowing   wind W   snow about 5½ feet or 6 deep   difficult to get wood   no going from the house   completely housed up   looks as likely for snow as when it commenced, our cattle all killed but three or four [of] them, the horses & Stantons mules gone & cattle suppose lost in the Snow   no hopes of finding them alive.

Wedns. 2nd   Continues to snow   wind W   sun shineing hazily thro the clouds   dont snow quite as fast as it has done   snow must be over six feet deep   bad fire this morning. [5]

Thursd. 3rd   Snowed a little last night   bright and cloudy at intervals all night, to day cloudy   snows none   wind S.W.   warm but not enough so to thaw snow lying deep allround   Expec[t]ing it to thaw a little to day   the forgoing written in the morning   it immediately turned in to snow & continued to snow all day & likely to do so all night.

Friday 4th   Cloudy that is flying clouds   neither snow or rain this day it is a relief to have one fine day,   wind E by N   no sign of thaw   freezeing pretty hard   snow deep.

Saturday 5th   Fine clear day   beautiful sunshine   thawing a little   looks delightful after the long snow storm.

Sund. 6th   The morning fine & clear   now some cloudy wind S-E   not [melting] much in the sunshine,   Stanton & Graves manufactureing snow shoes for another mountain scrabble   no account of mules. [6]

Mond. 7th   Beautiful clear day   wind E by S   looks as if we might [have] some fair weather   no thaw.

Tues 8th   Fine weather   Clear & pleasant   froze hard last night   wind S.E.   deep snow   the people not stiring round much   hard work to [get] wood suffficient to keep us warm & cook our beef.

Wedns. 9th   Commenced snowing about 11 Oclock   wind N:W   snows fast   took in Spitzer yesterday so weak that he cannot rise without help caused by starveation   all in good health some having scant supply of beef Stanton trying to make a raise of some for his Indians & self   not likely to get much. [7]

Thurs. 10th   Snowed fast all night with heavy squalls of wind   Continues still to snow the sun peeping through the clouds once in about three hours   very difficult to get wood to day   now about 2 Oclock   looks likely to continue snowing   don't know the debth of the snow   may be 7 feet.

Friday 11th   Snowing a little   wind W   sun vissible at time   not freezeing.

Satd 12th   Continues to snow   wind W   weather mild   freezeind little.

Sunday 13th   Snows faster than any previous day   wind N:W   Stanton & Graves with several others makeing preperations to cross the mountains on snow shoes, snow 8 feet deep on the level   dull.

Monday 14   Fine morning   sunshine   cleared off last night about 12 o clock   wind E:S:E   dont thaw much but fair for a continueance of fair weather. [8]

Tuesday 15th   Still continues fine   wind W:S:W.

Wed'd 16th   Fair & pleasant   froeze hard last night & [so?] the Company started on snow shoes to cross the mountains   wind S.E   looks pleasant.

Thursd. 17th   Pleasant sunshine today   wind about S.E.   Bill Murp[hy] returned from the mountain party last evening   Bealis [Williams] died night before last   Milt. [Elliott] & Noah [James] went to Donnos 8 days since not returned yet, thinks they got lost in the snow. J Denton here to day.

Frid'd 18   Beautiful day   sky clear   it would be delightful were it not for the snow lying so deep   thaws but little on the south side of shanty   saw no strangers today from any of the shantys. [9]

Satd. 19   Snowd. last night   commenced about 11 o clock. squalls of wind with snow at intervals   this morning thawing   wind. N by W   a little singular for a thaw   may continue, it continues to snow   sun shining cleared off towards evening.

Sund. 20   Night clear   froze a little   now clear & pleasant   wind N W thawing a little   Mrs. Reid here, no account of Milt. yet   Dutch Charley

[Burger] started for Donnghs turned back not able to proceed tough times, but not discouraged our hopes are in God. <u>Amen</u>.

Mond. 21 Milt got back last night from Donos camp [at Alder Creek] sad news. Jake Donno Sam Shoemaker Rinehart, & Smith are dead the rest of them in a low situation snowed all night with a strong S-W wind to day cloudy wind continues but not snowing thawing sun shineing dimly in hopes it will clear of. [10]

Tuesd. 22nd Snowd. all last night Continued to snow all day with some few intermissions had a severe fit of the gravel [kidney stones] yesterday I am well to day, Praise be to the God of Heaven.

Wend. 23rd Snowd. a little last night clear to day & thawing a little. Milt took some of his meat to day all well at their camp began this day to read the Thirty days prayer, may Almighty God grant the request of an unworthy sinner that I am. <u>Amen</u>

Thursd. 24th Rained all night & still continues to rain poor prospect for any kind of comfort spiritual or temporal, wind S: help us to spend the Christmass as we ought considering circumstances. [11]

Friday 25th Began to snow yesterday about 12 o clock snowd. all night & snows yet rapidly wind about E by N Great dificulty in getting wood John & Edwd.has to get [it] I am not able offerd. our prayers to God this Cherimass morning the prospect is apalling but hope in God <u>Amen</u>

Satd. 26th Cleared off in the night to day clear & pleasant Snowd. about 20 inches or two feet deep yesterday, the old snow was nearly run soft before it began to snow now it is all soft the top dry & the under wet wind S.E.

Sun 27 Continues clear froze hard last night Snow very deep say 9 feet thawing a little in the sun scarce of wood to day chopt a tree dow[n] it sinks in the snow & is hard to be got. [12]

Monday 28th Snowd. last night cleared off this morning snowed a little now clear & pleasant.

Tuesday 29th Fine clear day froze hard last night, Charley sick. Keysburg has Wolfing[er]s Rifle gun.

Wedsd. 30th Fine clear morning froze hard last night Charley [Burger] died last night about 10 o clock had with him in money $1.50 two good loking silver watches one razor 3 boxes caps Keysburg tok them into his possession Spitzer took his coat & waistcoat Keysburg all his other little effects gold pin one shirt and tools for shaveing. [13]

Thursday 31st Last of the year, may we with Gods help spend the comeing year better than the past which we purpose to do if Almighty God will deliver us from our present dredful situation which is our prayer if the will of God sees it fiting for us Amen morning fair now cloudy wind E by S for three days past freezeing hard every night looks like another snow storm Snow Storms are dredful to us snow very deep crust on the [under? snow?] [14]

[JANUARY 1847]

Jany. 1st 1847 we pray the God of mercy to deliver us from our present calamity if it be his Holy will Amen. Commened. [commenced] snowing last night does not snow fast wind S.E sun peeps out at times provisions geting scant dug up a hide from under the snow yesterday for Milt. did not take it yet.

Sat. 2nd Fair & thawey snow got soft wind wind S-E looks thawey froze pretty hard last night.

Sund. 3rd Continues fair in day time freezeing at night wind about E Mrs. Reid talks of crossing the mountains with her children provisions scarce. [15]

Mond. 4th Fine morning looks like spring thawing now about 12 o clock wind S:E Mrs. Reid Milt. Virginia & Eliza started about ½ hour ago with prospect of crossing the mountain may God of Mercy help them left ther children here Tom's with us Pat with Keysburg & Jas with Gravese's folks, it was difficult for Mrs. Reid to get away from the children.

Tuesd. 5th Beautiful day thawing some in the sun Wind S-E snow not settleing much we are in hopes of the rainy time ending.

Weds. 6th Fine day clear not a cloud froze very hard last night wind S:E Eliza came back from the mountain yesterday evening not able to proceed, to day went to Graves, the others kept ahead.

Thursd. 7th Continues fine freezeing hard at night very cold this morning wind S.S.E. dont think we will have much more snow snow not thawing much not much dimeinished in debph. [16]

Friday 8th Fine morning wind E froze hard last night very cold this morning Mrs. Reid & company came back this mor[n]ing could not find their way on the other side of the mountain they have nothing but hides to live on Martha is to stay here Milt. & Eliza going to Donos Mrs. Reid & the 2 boys going to their own shanty & Virginia prospects dull may God relieve us all from this difficulty if it is his Holy will <u>Amen</u>.

Satd 9th Continues fine freezeing hard at night this a beatiful morning wind about S.S.E. Mrs. Reid here Virginia toes frozen a little snow settleing none to be perceived.

Sund. 10 Began to snow last night still continues wind W N W. [17]

Mond. 11th Still continues to snow fast, looks gloomy Mrs. Reid at Keysburgs Virg. [Virginia Reed] with us wood scarce difficult to get any more wind W.

Tuesd. 12th Snows fast yet new snow about 3 feet deep wind S:W no sign of clearing off.

Wens. 13th Snowing fast wind N.W snow higher than the shanty must be 13 feet deep dont know how to get wood this morning it is dredful to look at.

Thursd. 14th new moon Cleard. off yesterday evening snowd. a little during first part of night Calm but a little air from the North very pleasant to day sun shineing brilliantly renovates our spirits prais be to God, <u>Amen</u>.

Frid. 15th   Fine clear day   wind N W   Mrs. Murphy blind Lanth[ron] Murphy] not able to get wood   has but one axe betwixt him & Keysburg, he moved to Murphys yesterday   looks like another storm   expecting some account from Suiters [Sutter's Fort] soon. [15]

Satd. 16th   Wind blew hard all night from the W.   abated a little   did not freeze much   this is clear & pleasant   wind a little S of W   no telling what the weather will do.

Sund. 17th   Fine morning   sun shineing clear   wind S.S.E.   Eliza came here this morning, sent her back again to Graves   Lanthrom crazy last night so Bill [Graves] says, Keyburg sent Bill to get hides off his shanty & carry thim home this morning, provisions scarce   hides are the only article we depend on, we have a little meat yet, may God send us help.

Mond. 18th   Fine day clear & pleasant   wind W, thawing in the sun   Mrs. Murphy here to day   very hard to get wood.

Tuesd. 19th   Clear & pleasant   thawing a little in the sun   Wind S.W Peggy & Edward sick last night by eating some meat that Dolan threw his tobacco on, pretty well to day (praise God for his blessings,)   Lanthrom very low   in danger if relief dont soon come   hides are all the go   not much of any other in camp. [19]

Wed. 20th   Fine morning   wind N   froze hard last night. Expecting some person across the mountain this week.

Thursd. 21   Fine morning   wind W   did not freeze quite so hard last night as it has done,   John Battice [John Baptiste] and Denton came this morning with Eliza [Graves]   she wont eat hides   Mrs Reid sent her back to live or die on them. Milt. got his toes froze   the donoghs are all well.

Frid. 22nd   Began to snow a little after sunrise   likely to snow a good dale   wind W came up very suddenly, now 10 oclock.

Satd. 23rd   Blew hard & snowd. all night   the most severe storm we experienced this winter   wind W   sun now 12 oclock peeps out.

Sund. 24th   Some cloudy this morning   ceased snowing yesterday about 2 o clock. Wind about S.E   all in good health thanks be to God for his mercies endureth for ever.   heard nothing from Murphys camp since the storm expe[c]t to hear they sufferd some. [20]

Mo[n]d 25th   Began to snow yesterday evening & still continues   wind W.

Tuesd 26   Cleared up yesterday   to day fine & pleasant, wind S.   in hopes we are done with snow storms.   those that went to Suitors [Sutter's Fort] not yet returned   provisions geting very scant   people geting weak liveing on short allowance of hides.

Weds. 27th   began to snow yesterday & still continues to sleet   thawing a little   wind W   Mrs. Keyber [Kesesberg] here this morning   Lewis Suitor [*Breen means Lewis Keseberg, age one*] she says died three days ago   Keysburg sick & Lanthrom lying in bed the whole of his time   dont have fire enough to cook their hides. Bill & Sim. Murphy sick.

Thursd. 28th   Full moon   cleared off last night & froze some to day
fine & warm   wind S.E   looks some like spring weather   birds chirping
qu[i]te lively   full moon today.

Frid 29th   Fine morning   began to thaw in the sun early.   wind S.W
froze hard last night   there will be a crust soon   God send Amen. [21]

Satd. 30th   Fine pleasant morning   wind W   beginning to thaw in the
sun   John & Edwd. went to Graves this morning   the Graves seized on Mrs
Reids goods untill they would be paid   also took the hides that she & family
had to live on,   she got two peices of hides from there & the ballance they
have taken   you may know from these proceedings what our fare is in camp
there is nothing to be got by hunting yet perhaps there soon will.   God send it
Amen.

Sund. 31st   The sun dont shine out brilliant this morning   froze prtty
hard last night   wind N.W.   Lantron Murphy died last night about 1 o clock,
Mrs. Reid & John [Breen] went to Graves this morning to look after her
goods.

[FEBRUARY 1847]

Mond. February the 1st   Froze very hard last night   cold to day &
Cloudy   wind N W.   sun shines dimly   the snow has not settled much   John
is unwell to day   with the help of God & [deleted] he will be well by night
Amen.

Tuesday 2nd   Began to snow this morning & continued to snow untill
night   now clear   wind during the storm S. W.

Wend. 3rd   Cloudy   looks like more snow   not cold, froze a little last
night   wind S. S W   it was clear all last night   sun shines out at times.

Thurd. 4th   Snowd. hard all night & still continues with a strong S:W.
wind   untill now [not?] abated   looks as if it would snow all day   snowed
about 2 feet deep, now.

Frid. 5th   Snowd. hard all [yesterday] until 12 o'clock at night   wind still
continud to blow hard from the S.W: to day pretty clear a few clouds only
Peggy very uneasy for fear we shall all perrish with hunger   we have but a
little meat left & only part of 3 hides   has to support Mrs. Reid   she has
nothing left but one hide & it is on Graves shanty   Milt [Elliott] is livi[n]g
there and likely will keep that hide   Eddys child died last night. [23]

Satd 6th   It snowed faster last night & to day than it has done this winter & still continues without an intermission   wind S.W   Murphys folks or
Keysburgs say they cant get hides   I wish we had enough of them   Mrs Eddy
very weak.

Sund. 7th   Ceased to snow last [night] after one of the most severe
storms we experienced this winter   the snow fell about 4 feet deep   I had to
shovel the snow off our shanty this morning   it thawd so fast & thawd. during
the whole storm.   to day it is quite pleasant   wind S.W.   Milt here to day
says Mrs. Reid has to get a hide from Mrs. Murphy & McCutchins child died
2nd of this month.

it snowd faster last
night & to day than it
has done this winter & still
continues without an intermission
wind S W Murphys folks or
Keysburgs say they cant eat
hides I wish we had enough
of them Mrs Eddy very weak

Sund 7th Ceasd to snow last after
one of the most severe storms we
experienced this winter the snow fell
about 4 feet deep I had to shovel the
snow off our shanty this morning
it thaw so fast & thaw during the
whole storm to day it is quite
pleasant wind S W Milt here to day
says Mrs Reid has to get a hide
from Mrs Murphy & Mrs Eddys
child died 2nd of this month

Mond 8th fine clear morning
wind S W froze hard
last Spitzer died last night
about 3 oclock to we will
bury him in the snow
Mrs Eddy died on the night of the 7th

Page from the *Diary of Patrick Breen*, entries for February 6, 7, 8, 1847.
Courtesy of Bancroft Library, University of California, Berkeley, California.

Mond 8th   Fine clear morning   wind S.W.   froze hard last [night]
Spitzer died last night about 3 o clock to[today? so?] we will bury him in the
snow   Mrs. Eddy died on the night of the 7th. [24]

Tuesd. 9th   Mrs. Murphy here this morning   Pikes child all but dead
Milt at Murphys not able to get out of bed   Keyburg never gets up says he is
not able. John went down to day to bury Mrs Eddy & child   heard nothing
from Graves for 2 or 3 days   Mrs Murphy just now going to Graves   fine
mor[n]ing   wind S.E.   froze hard last night   begins to thaw in the sun.

Wednsd. 10th   Beautiful morning   Wind W: froze hard last night.
to day thawing in the Sun   Milt Elliot died las[t] night at Murphys shanty
about 9 o'clock P:M: Mrs. Reid went there this morning to see after his effects. J Denton trying to borrow meat from Graves   had none to give   they
have nothing but hides   all are entirely out of meat but a little we have   our
hides are nearly all eat up but with Gods help spring will soon smile upon us.

Thursd 11th   Fine morning   wind W.   froze hard last night   some
clouds lying in the E: looks like thaw   John Denton here last night very
delicate. John & Mrs Reid went to Graves this morning.

Frid. 12th   A warm thawey morning   wind S.E.   we hope with the assistance of Almighty God to be able to live to see the bare surface of the
earth once more. O God of Mercy grant it if it be thy holy will <u>Amen</u>.

Sat. 13th   Fine morning   clouded up yesterday evening   snowd a little
& continued cloudy all night.   cleared off about daylight.   wind about S:W
Mrs. Reid has headacke   the rest in health.

Sund 14th   Fine morning but cold before the sun got up,   now thawing
in the sun   wind S E   Ellen Graves here this morning   John Denton not well
froze hard last night   John & Edwd. E [*sic*]burried Milt. this morning in the
snow.

Mond. 15   Mor[n]ing cloudy untill 9 Oclock   then cleared off   wa[r]m
& sunshine   wind W.   Mrs. Graves refusd. to give Mrs. Reid any hides   put
Suitors pack hides on her shanty would not let her have them   says if I say it
will thaw it then will not, she is a case. [26]

Tuesd. 16th   Comme[n]ced to rain yesterday Evening   turned to snow
during the night & continued untill after day-light this morning   it is now
sunshine & light showers of hail at times   wind N.W by W.   we all feel very
weakly to day   snow not geting much less in quantity.

Wedsd 17th   Froze hard last night with heavy clouds runing from the
N.W. & light showers of hail at times   to day same kind of weather   wind
N.W.   very cold & cloudy   no sign of much thaw.

Thrsd 18th   Froze hard last night   to day clear & warm in the sun   cold
in the shanty or in the shade   wind S.E.   all in good health   Thanks be to
Almighty God <u>Amen</u>.

Frid. 19th   Froze hard last night   7 men arrived from Colifornia yesterday evening with som provisions but left the greater part on the way   to
day clear & warm for this region   some of the men are gone to day to
Donnos Camp   will start back on Monday. [27]

Saturd. 20th   Pleasant weather

Sund 21st   Thawey warm day

Mond 22nd   the Californians started this morning 24 in number some in a very weak state   fine morning   wind S.W. for the 3 last days   Mrs Keyburg started & left Keysburg here unable to go   I burried Pikes child this mor[n]ing in the snow   it died 2 days ago,   Paddy Reid & Thos. came back with Messr Graves & Mutry [Aquila Glover and R. Moutry, members of the first relief expedition].

Tuesd. 23   Froze hard last night   to day fine & thawey   has the appearance of spring all but the deep snow   wind S:S.E.   shot Towser [the Breen's dog] to day & dressed his flesh   Mrs Graves came here this morning to borrow meat dog or ox   they think I have meat to spare but I know to the contrary   they have plenty hides   I live principally on the same.

Wend. 24th   froze hard last night   to day cloudy   looks like a storm wind blows hard from the W.   Commenced thawing   there has not any more returned from those who started to cross the mts. [among those taken out by the first relief were Edward Breen, 13, and Simon Breen, 9].

Thursd. 25th   Froze hard last night   fine & sunshiny to day   wind W. Mrs Murphy says the wolves are about to dig up the dead bodies at her shanty, the nights are too cold to watch them, we hear them howl.

Frid 26th   Froze hard last night   today clear & warm   Wind S: E: blowing briskly   Marthas [Martha, known as Patty, Reed] jaw swelled with the toothache; hungry times in camp, plenty hides but the folks will not eat them   we eat them with a tolerable good apetite.   Thanks be to Almighty God.   Amen   Mrs Murphy said here yesterday that [she] thought she would commence on Milt. [Elliott] and eat him.   I dont [think] that she has done so yet, it is distressing   The Donnos told the California folks that they [would] commence to eat the dead people 4 days ago, if they did not succeed that day or next in finding their cattle then under ten or twelve feet of snow & did not know the spot or near it, I suppose they have done so ere this time. [29]

Satd 27th   Beautiful morning sun shineing brillantly, wind about S.W. the snow has fell in debth about 5 feet but no thaw but the sun in day time it freezeing hard every night   heard some geese fly over last night   saw none.

Sund. 28th   Froze hard last night   to day fair & sunshine   wind S.E. 1 solitary Indian passed by yesterday   come from the lake   had a heavy pack on his back   gave me 5 or 6 roots resembleing onions in shape   taste some like a sweet potatoe, all full of little tough fibres.

[MARCH 1847]

Mond. March the 1st To[day] fine and pleasant   froze hard last night there has 10 men arrived this morning from Bear Valley with provisions   we are to start in two or three days & cash [cache] our goods here   there is amongst them some old [mountaineers?] they say the snow will be here untill June.

Breen made one hundred and one diary entries, with three and one half months spanning the first entry and the last, which was on his wife's forty-first birthday. His words reveal people desperately struggling for life. They tell of the tensions that developed between families such as the Breens, who seem to have had more food than others, and the Graveses and Murphys, who seem to have had less. The entries generally reflect well on people in time of a great crisis. Breen is critical of people only once or twice, of Mrs. Graves, for example, who constantly besought the Breens for some meat while refusing to eat her own animal hides. She is a "case," wrote Breen. He is also very specific about the property of Dutch Charley Burger acquired by Spitzer and Keseberg immediately after Charley's death, as if a record were needed for future accounting.

Breen's words also reveal the moral dilemma in which he and his wife were placed, although Breen does not philosophize about it. That terrible question! What to do when giving to others would mean starvation and death for one's own children? The Breens seem to have struck something of a balance. They sometimes refused but they often gave.

A summary of events reported early in the diary reveals that by November 20, three weeks into the ordeal, Breen knew the company would be entrapped until spring. By November 29, he had killed his last ox after giving or trading two of his own to William Foster of the Lavinia Murphy family. According to Eddy/Thornton, Breen took from Foster a gold watch and some other property as security.

On December 1, the six mules that Stanton had brought up from the fort were lost, apparently buried by the recent very heavy snows. In time, they seem to have been found (though perhaps not all) because later Breen mentions that Stanton's hides covered one of the cabins. By December 8, the Breens were having trouble getting enough wood for the fire. (We later learn that this job fell heavily on the two oldest Breen boys, John and Edward.) By December 9, Stanton, who had unselfishly come with the two Indians with provisions for the company, was short of beef or mule meat (as to which, Breen's diary does not make clear) and was attempting to "raise" some animals buried in the snow. On December 16, the Breens' friend, Patrick Dolan, left with the Snowshoe Party. The Breens would never see Dolan again. We learn from sources other than the diary that one of Dolan's reasons for leaving was that it meant one less mouth to feed. He left his supply of dried meat to the Breens, with a request that they take care of the Reeds to the extent that they were able.

The importance of animal hides is evident in the diary entries. The hairs had to be removed by scorching; then the hides were boiled for many hours, even days, producing a gluey mass that some stomachs could not tolerate, but the Breens ate the hides with a "tolerable appetite."

Most of the adults, including the women, smoked tobacco. It was not only relaxing but also suppressed hunger pangs. We know from family sources that Margaret Breen was a pipe smoker, as were so many Irish and other women of the day. No doubt the pipe she used was the kind found in recent years by archeologist Don Hardesty of the University of Nevada in digs at the site of the Murphy cabin. This was a long-stemmed, white, kaolin (a kind of clay) "Dublin" pipe, the most popular 19th century model. It is an exciting thing when the work of scholars in different disciplines crosses, producing a small nugget of knowledge, generating a picture of women of the Donner Party engaging in the only luxury they had during the months of their ordeal: smoking their pipes in the mountain shanties.

Sex seems not to have been among the luxuries, or burdens, of life on the trail or at the camps of entrapment. At least, according to the records of adult survivors among the women, married or single, no babies were born as a result of conception along the trail or in the mountain camps.

Hardesty's excavations at the Murphy cabin site also un-earthed a religious medal with a loose wire loop, of the style used by Catholics between 1825 and 1875. On one side is a representation of Jesus encircled by the inscription, "SWEET HEART OF JESUS HAVE MERCY ON US." On the other side is a representation of the Virgin Mary, with the inscription, "BLESSED VIRGIN MARY PRAY FOR US." The Murphys were not Catholic, but may have had Catholic family connections.

Chapter 9

ATTEMPTS TO ESCAPE

On November 21 as many as twenty emigrants, including Stanton and the two Fort Indians, attempted to reach the pass on foot, but they returned two days later. On December 16, another try was made by a party of seventeen, fourteen of them on snowshoes. During the first day Charley Burger and Bill Murphy had to turn back. That left a party of fifteen, ten males and five females. They were to become known in the literature as the Snowshoe Party or the Forlorn Hope. Only seven survived. It took those seven snowshoers thirty-three days to travel the seventy miles to reach the first small outpost of civilization, amid much suffering and horror. The dead had been eaten, although it was said that no one would touch one of his own family members. The popular Irishman Patrick Dolan seems to have been the first among those cannibalized.

Those who died during this terrible ordeal were the two Indians and Dolan; Charles T. Stanton; Franklin "Uncle Billy" Graves Sr.; his son-in-law, Jay Fosdick; the young herder Antonio; and twelve-year old Lemuel Murphy. All but Stanton were cannibalized. At one point, the possibility was discussed of who should be killed so that the others might live. William Eddy claimed that a crazed William Foster had to be restrained by him when Foster considered killing one of the women. However, Mary Graves and her sister Sarah Fosdick recalled that Eddy himself worried them. They feared that Eddy wanted to get Mary away from the others and kill her for food, as they reported to their brother Billy, who passed the story along in a letter to C.F. McGlashan (see Notes to Chapter 9).

At one point, Eddy managed to shoot a deer. Meanwhile, Salvador and Luis had fled the party, fearing for their own lives. They were overtaken a few days later. Eddy claimed that the Indians had gone without food for three days, were almost dead, unable to move, and could not have had more than a couple of hours to live. They were shot in the head, said Eddy, by William Foster. Their starved bodies, with little meat or fat on them, were quickly consumed. In his "Personal Reminiscences" Captain Sutter, who talked with survivors, gave a brief and substantially different report of the death of the two "good Indians" who were under his protection. Luis and Salvador, he said, were "caught while scratching away [in] the snow for acorns and devoured."

Somewhere near Emigrant Gap the party had lost the trail to Bear Valley. They had gone southward, then travelled a rugged course westward for many miles between the Bear River and the North Fork of the American River. Finally, making their way out of the snows and into the foothills, they were befriended at two villages by Digger Indians who shared with them their poor fare of raw acorns, later some acorn bread and pine nuts. At the price of a little tobacco, the weakened and crippled Eddy was assisted by Indians to the cabin of Mr. and Mrs. M.D. Ritchie on the Johnson Ranch.

On January 18, the day after Eddy arrived, two parties of men from Johnson's set out to bring in the other six survivors, who were about eighteen miles eastward. John Howell, John Rhoads, Theodore Sicard, and Reasin Tucker with an Indian guide, travelling by foot with provisions, were the first to reach the survivors. The next morning Ritchie, William Johnson, Joe Verrot (Vero, Varro), and Sebastian Keyser arrived with horses to bring them in. They were barely alive, their bodies smeared with blood and their clothes in tatters.

All five of the women but only two of the males reached Johnson's Ranch. They were Eddy, Foster and his wife Sarah Murphy, Mary Graves, Sarah Graves Fosdick, Amanda Mc-Cutchen, and Harriet Murphy Pike. They were so hunger-crazed when they reached the ranch that they had to be restrained from eating too much food too quickly and killing themselves. Eddy later told his friend Peter Burnett that he "abused Mrs. Ritchie in harsh terms," but that she bore with him patiently.

Why did all the women survive? This is an intriguing question and no one has a satisfactory answer to it. Biological and even psychological differences between male and female may be partially accountable, but this is a complicated and controversial subject beyond the scope of this book. In any case, the answer is not that the women worked less hard than the men. They too gathered firewood, and they took turns carrying the only gun when it became too heavy for Eddy and Foster.

John Rhoads, who certainly qualifies as one of the great heroes of the Donner saga, volunteered to bring the news to Sutter's Fort, forty miles away. He crossed the Bear River on a couple of logs lashed together with rawhides. Travelling on foot because horses could not make it, he slogged his way down the valley through a quagmire caused by heavy winter rains, the water being one to three feet deep in long stretches. He arrived at Sutter's Fort about January 22 with the first news that the Donner Party was entrapped near the lake just east of the mountain pass.

JOHNSON'S RANCH

Johnson's Ranch at the edge of the Sacramento Valley was situated on the Bear River about three miles east of today's Wheatland and forty miles north of Sutter's Fort. For the history of the ranch, which played such an important part in the rescue efforts, I am indebted to Jack and Richard Steed's *The Donner Party Rescue Site: Johnson's Ranch on Bear River* (1988).

William Johnson's birth year is unknown. He was said to be a sailor from Boston who had been mate on the *Alciope*, coming to California in 1840. In 1842, when he and Jacob Leese (son-in-law of General Mariano Vallejo) bought a lighter for operation on the Sacramento River, Johnson's application for an operator's license noted that he was an Irishman and a naturalized Mexican citizen. At Sutter's Fort he met Sebastian Keyser, a German who had made John Sutter's acquaintance at a trapper rendezvous in 1838 in Wyoming and later worked for Sutter. The land which was to become Johnson's Ranch was part of the estate of Pablo Gutierrez when it was auctioned off at Sutter's Fort in 1844. Johnson was the highest bidder and in 1845 he and Sebastian Keyser received title to the property as partners for $150.

Heinrich Lienhard, an emigrant of 1846, wrote that he saw a new adobe at Johnson's being built by naked Indians and that there were only four men in the entire settlement – Johnson, Keyser, Theodore Sicard, and Joe Verrot. The testimony of Daniel Rhoads reveals that Johnson and Keyser did quite well for themselves. Rhoads' first experiences in the valley were at Johnson's Ranch, where he found prices exorbitantly high. Wheat bran was sold at three dollars a hundred pounds, wheat at two dollars a fanega (2.58 bushels), flour and meat at eight dollars a hundred pounds, peas at two dollars a bushel, "a good fat cow" ten dollars. Also sold were white and yellow domestic cloth, calico and "apron check," tea (two dollars a pound), coffee, sugar, plates, tea cups and saucers, knives and forks (from four to eight dollars each), and shoes (from two to five dollars a pair).

Rhoads wrote that one of the problems in organizing relief efforts to the Donners, after the survivors of the Snowshoe Party arrived at Johnson's Ranch in January 1847, was the shortage of manpower. The war with Mexico was still going on. A good many of the able-bodied men in the valley were busy with the American forces securing California for American rule. "They wasen't more than 14 men in the Sacrament Valley," wrote Rhoads, "[and it] was 2 weeks before aney person would consent to go." They wanted wages of five dollars a day, he said, a figure considered astronomical. Rhoads and his brother John, Mormons and men of conscience, finally concluded they "would go or die trying, for not to make aney attempt to save them....would be a disgrace to us and California."

BACK AT THE MOUNTAIN CAMPS

On December 17, the day after the Snowshoe Party left, the Reeds' servant Baylis Williams died, as noted in Patrick Breen's diary. He was the first of many single adult males to perish early in the entrapment.

On December 20, Mrs. Reed visited the Breen cabin. She and her four children were to spend more and more time there. Soon, all of the Reeds would be taken in by the Breens.

On December 21, Patrick learned that the situation was very serious at the camp of the Donners at Alder Creek. Jake Donner had died; so had Shoemaker, Smith, and Reinhardt.

On December 23, Breen gave some meat, apparently as a result of a trade, to Milt Elliott, employee of the Reeds. That evening, kneeling with his family by the light of the fire (the ritual of the evening prayer was vividly recalled by Virginia Reed, who later shared the Breen cabin), Breen recited the Thirty Days' Prayer for the first time. The prayer began with these words:

> Ever glorious and blessed Mary, Queen of Virgins, Mother of Mercy, hope and comfort of dejected and desolate souls, through that sword of sorrow which pierced thy tender heart whilst thine only Son, Jesus, our Lord, suffered death and ignominy on the cross; through that filial tenderness and pure love He had for thee, grieving in thy grief, whilst from His cross He recommended thee to the care and protection of His beloved disciple, St. John, take pity, I beseech thee, on my poverty and necessities....

It was a very long prayer, including some moments for reflection on a "lawful request," and must have taken Patrick, by firelight, at least fifteen minutes to recite, ending with

> ....I beseech thee, for the souls of my parents, brethren, relatives and benefactors, both living and dead, life everlasting, from the only Giver of every good and perfect gift, the Lord God Almighty: to Whom be all power, now and forever. *Amen.*

On Christmas Day, the enfeebled Patrick was no longer able to help his sons John and Edward in wood-gathering. On the same day, Mrs. Reed prepared a Christmas dinner for her four children, having hoarded some food for this special occasion. Patty Reed later recalled that the meat came from the ox Dolan had sold them. The Reeds also had beans, apples, rice, tripe. The hungry Reed children looked on delightedly at the stew, boiling over the fire. "It was simply grand," recalled Patty.

On December 30, Keseberg's employee, Charley Burger, died.

On the first day of the year 1847, two months into the entrapment, Patrick Breen, no doubt with the help of his sons, managed to dig up a hide in the snow for Milt Elliott and the Reeds.

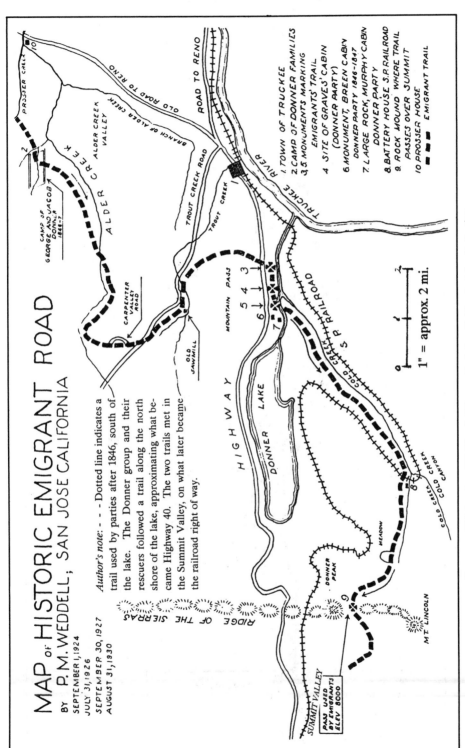

MAP of HISTORIC EMIGRANT ROAD
BY P. M. WEDDELL, SAN JOSE CALIFORNIA

SEPTEMBER 1, 1924
JULY 31, 1926
SEPTEMBER 30, 1927
AUGUST 31, 1930

Author's note: - - - Dotted line indicates a trail used by parties after 1846, south of the lake. The Donner group and their rescuers followed a trail along the north shore of the lake, approximating what became Highway 40. The two trails met in the Summit Valley, on what later became the railroad right of way.

1. TOWN OF TRUCKEE
2. CAMP OF DONNER FAMILIES
3,5 MONUMENTS MARKING EMIGRANTS' TRAIL
4. SITE OF GRAVES' CABIN (DONNER PARTY)
6. MONUMENT, BREEN CABIN DONNER PARTY 1846-1847
7. LARGE ROCK, MURPHY CABIN DONNER PARTY
8. BATTERY HOUSE S.P. RAILROAD
9. ROCK MOUND WHERE TRAIL PASSES OVER SUMMIT
10 PROSSER HOUSE
■ ■ ■ EMIGRANT TRAIL

1" = approx. 2 mi.

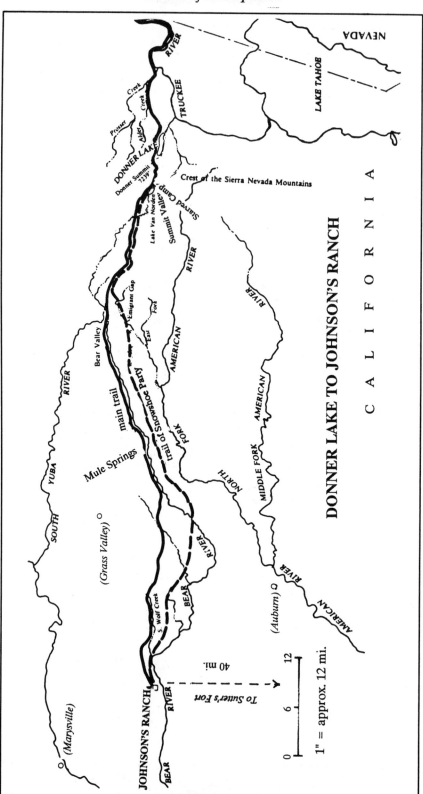

DONNER LAKE TO JOHNSON'S RANCH

On January 4, the Breens took in little Tommy Reed when their mother, her daughter Virginia, Milt, and the servant Eliza Williams made what would become a futile attempt to cross the mountains. Patty Reed was left with the Kesebergs, James Reed with the Graveses.

On January 5, Eliza returned from the failed attempt. She spent the night with the Breens, then went to the Graves' cabin.

On January 8, Mrs. Reed and the rest of her company returned, having failed to find the trail on the other side of the pass. Nine-year-old Patty (Martha) Reed was taken into the Breen cabin permanently. Mrs. Reed and her three other children stayed at their own cabin. On the next day, however, she was back at the Breens with daughter Virginia whose toes were frozen. The Breens took in Virginia permanently. Mrs. Reed moved into the adjoining Keseberg shack, apparently with Tommy and James, but soon after that she and her four children were all living in one end of the Breen cabin. Patty Reed recalled that the Reed's servant, Eliza Williams, also wanted to go to the Breens' cabin but Mr. Breen would not consent to that; therefore she had to stay at Mrs. Graves' shack, although "we had eaten our covering up [and] had no shelter for ourselves."

Food of any kind was growing scarce. Although unreported in Breen's diary, the Reeds, early on, dined in the Breen cabin on their remaining dog, Cash.

On January 15, Keseberg and family took up residence in the Murphy shack. They had a single ox to share.

On January 17, Eliza Graves came begging to the Breens and was "sent back."

On January 19, Margaret Breen and her son Edward became sick after eating some meat that had been fouled by Dolan's tobacco. There was little meat in camp, only the animal hides.

On January 21, Eliza Graves, arriving at the cabin with Trudeau and Denton, made another appeal for meat, claiming she could not eat hides. Mrs. Reed sent her back to her cabin.

On January 27, the infant Lewis Keseberg died, and there was much sickness at the Murphys. On the morning of January 30, John and Edward Breen went to the Graves' cabin, apparently to retrieve some of Mrs. Reed's possessions, but found that Mrs. Graves had seized Mrs. Reed's goods "until they would be paid." Mrs. Graves also took the hides that Mrs. Reed had to live on.

On the last day of January, Landrum Murphy died. The fifteen-year-old had been doing men's work for three months.

John Breen, Landrum's age, had also been doing men's work. On February 1, going into the fourth month of entrapment, Patrick Breen reported that his son John was unwell.

On February 2, Mrs. McCutchen's infant daughter died.

On February 5, Patrick reported that his wife was uneasy for fear that "we shall all parrish with hunger." The Eddy's infant daughter had died the night before. The mother was to die the next day. Little James Eddy, apparently now cared for by the Murphy group, had not long to live.

Many years later, John Breen wrote to McGlashan:

> I saw Mrs. Eddy the day before she died she lived in the Murphy cabin, I was there to help Mrs. Murphy bury her son Landrum. I made a grave in the snow and she and I laid him in it and covered [him] with the snow again – I then got them some wood as they had very little fire and no one in the house was strong enough....they were so light from starvation.

In another letter to McGlashan, John wrote:

> I put on plenty of wood, and as I was going Mrs. Eddy took my hand and said, 'God will surely [pay?] you, but I can not last another day.' The poor woman died that night, I think. I will never forget the expression of her countenance as she spoke to me on that occasion.

On February 7, one of the most severe storms ceased after a snowfall of several days. Patrick reported shoveling the snow from the roof that morning. Later, Patty Reed recalled just how Patrick did the job of digging out. Inside the shanty, he would first pace off the distance from the fireplace to the door. Then he would climb up the chimney (how wide it must have been!), shovel the roof snow, pace the distance from the chimney, and clear the snow below, unblocking the door.

SPITZER'S DEATH

Sometime before February 7, Augustus Spitzer approached the door of the Breen cabin. He was close to death.

James Breen, who had turned six years of age on January 21, later recalled the event:

One morning he [Spitzer] came into our cabin and was so weak and cold that he fell to the floor or ground. He was assisted to his feet, laid on a blanket, and some nourishment offered to his lips, but the appetite was gone. He uttered a few words and quietly closed his eyes to take his long sleep.

Patty Reed, who was nine, recalled the same event slightly differently. She said that Spitzer was taken in and laid with his head to the fireplace and feet toward the door. The Breens comforted him as best they could, she said. But just before he died on the night of February 7, he begged Mrs. Breen for a piece of meat. Mrs. Breen, with ten children and three adults to keep alive in her shanty, had to make another one of those terrible decisions. Patty, who always expressed much gratitude to Margaret Breen for her own survival, did not recall her responding to Spitzer's request. He was buried by the Breens in the snow.

MORE DEATHS AND TENSIONS

By February 9, Milt Elliott at the Murphys was not able to get out of bed and he died the next day. Keseberg was also not able to get up. The foot which he had severely damaged with an ax was giving him much trouble.

On February 10, John Denton tried to borrow meat from Mrs. Graves but she had "none to give," having nothing but hides, observed Patrick Breen in the *Diary*. The next day John Breen and Mrs. Reed went to the Graves' cabin, probably to get things belonging to Mrs. Reed.

On February 14, John Breen and his brother Edward buried Milt Elliott as best they could.

On February 15, Mrs. Graves again refused to give Mrs. Reed the hides that Mrs. Reed thought belonged to her. The severe tension between Mrs. Graves and both the Reeds and Breens, had become painfully evident.

On February 17, Patrick reported that all the Breens were "very weakly."

Chapter 10

THE RELIEF PARTIES

KERN ORGANIZES FIRST RELIEF EFFORT

At Sutter's Fort (or Fort Sacramento), Lieutenant Edward V. Kern of the California Battalion organized by Fremont and technically a part of the United States Army, was in command of the Sacramento District under Navy Captain Joseph B. Hull in Yerba Buena (San Francisco). Hull was in charge of the whole Northern District of California. When John Rhoads arrived about January 22 with news of the seven survivors of the Snowshoe Party, Kern wasted no time in organizing a relief effort for all those still entrapped. At a meeting at the fort, attended by the few men who were around, Kern called for volunteers, promising three dollars a day, considered very high wages, but he could not guarantee it until he received authority from Hull in Yerba Buena. Although the record is not clear which men Kern mustered at the fort, Aquila Glover, Riley Septimus ("Sept") Moultry, and Joe Sels (aka Foster) seem to have been among them. Provisions and horses were provided by Sutter and by John Sinclair, who was alcalde and justice of the peace for the Sacramento District.

The party arrived at Johnson's Ranch about January 31, accompanied by Sinclair. Kern arrived a few days later (see Notes to Chapter 10). With the help of Sinclair who, with Sutter, personally guaranteed the wages, several more men were recruited. These included Adolph Bruheim (known as "Greasy Jim"), Edward Coffeemire, and Daniel Rhoads, who were placed on Kern's payroll as of January 31. The next few days were busy ones at Johnson's as cattle and hogs were slaughtered, meat dried and prepared for packing, and flour bagged. These items were "cheerfully furnished" by Johnson, according to the Ritchie–Tucker Diary (to be sure, however, the goods came with a price).

According to Kern's papers, John Rhoads, Reasin P. Tucker, and William D. Ritchie were added to the payroll on February 5, and Jotham (aka Jonathan, James) Curtis at a date unspecified.

They were joined by George Tucker (son of Reasin), Joe Varrot, William Coon (considered a "half-wit"), and William Eddy after less than three weeks of recuperation from his ordeal. A party of at least fourteen men left Johnson's for the mountains on February 6.

The strategy was to set up provision points along the route. At Mule Springs about thirty miles away the snow was three feet deep. Eddy and Joe Varrot were assigned to bring the weakened animals back to Johnson's, for replacement with fresh stock. Young George Tucker and Billy Coon were to stay to guard provisions. The remaining ten men continued along the ridge between Steephollow Creek and the Bear River, into snow over five feet deep.

Years later Daniel Rhoads of this relief party gave a detailed account of how snowshoes were fashioned:

....snowshoes made up by cutting pine boughs, stripping the bark, heating them over the fire, and bending them in shape of an ox-bow with a lattice of raw hides for soles - about 2 ft. long, 1 foot wide. Attached to feet by means of rawhide strips with which we were provided - [we made a] fire platform of pine saplings, 6 inches diameter, 12 feet long. We then kindled a fire above it - if fire built directly on snow, in the morning it would have been 10 to 12 feet below the snow surface. This is what we did everynight, going up and coming back. Burned old dead logs to mark trail.

On February 15, Ritchie, Curtis, and Bruheim could not muster the strength to go any further, although Tucker promised each man five dollars a day. Seven men were able to continue – Glover, Moultry, Sels, brothers John and Daniel Rhoads, Tucker, and Coffeemire – and they camped in Summit Valley near the head of the Yuba River on February 17. The next morning they set out to climb the pass, five hundred feet above them and one mile away. Meanwhile....

YERBA BUENA GETS THE NEWS

On February 5, the day the first relief party left Johnson's Ranch, Sutter's schooner arrived at Yerba Buena bearing a long letter from Kern to his superior, Navy Captain Hull, telling of the seven survivors, describing the plight of those still in the mountains, and appealing for government funds for relief efforts. Even before this news arrived, James Frazier Reed had been promoting relief efforts, although he had no knowledge of exactly where the Donner Party, which included his wife and four children, had made camp for the winter. In January, some San Jose citizens at Reed's request petitioned Governor Hull in Yerba Buena for aid in a rescue mission to the Donners, wherever they were. Reed went to Yerba Buena himself to appeal to Alcalde John Bartlett and Hull. Consequently, on February 3, a public meeting was held in a saloon where various citizens and government officials subscribed $700 for relief efforts. More money was raised from sailors in United States vessels in the harbor. On the application of Alcalde Bartlett, Captain Mervine, commanding the United States frigate *Savannah*, furnished twenty days full rations for ten men, or two hundred rations. Hull and his committee appointed Passed Midshipman Selim E. Woodworth to take charge of the relief effort.

As Woodworth was about to leave Yerba Buena, Sutter's launch *Sacramento* arrived with Kern's letter of appeal. This news stimulated the efforts of Hull's committee. Governor Hull appropriated $400 of government money for the work and sent orders to Lieutenant Kern and Sutter at the fort to do all in their power to help. Reed and the old mountain man Caleb Greenwood set off for Sonoma and Napa counties with authority to hire recruits and purchase provisions. William McCutchen, whose wife and child were in the mountains, was in those parts too, and and he became involved in the recruiting. On January 27, McCutchen had written Reed from Younts Ranch in the Napa Valley, urging Reed to come to Younts and accompany him to Sutter's Fort. "No time to delay," wrote McCutchen, "we will start the first of February." Navy Lieutenant William L. Maury and Don Mariano Vallejo in Sonoma subscribed $500 and some horses and mules.

And so, finally, two relief organizations were at work, one headed by Woodworth, the other by Kern at the fort. Both were under the command of Governor Hull, and their efforts were to be coordinated. Both would set up provisions stations east of Johnson's Ranch.

THE ARRIVAL OF THE FIRST RELIEF

On February 18, the heroic seven men of the relief party organized by Kern with the help of Sinclair and Sutter scaled the pass and arrived at the lake camp. It had taken them fourteen days. Patrick Breen mentions their arrival matter-of-factly in the diary entry for Friday, February 19: "froze hard last night   7 men arrived from California yesterday evening with som provisions but left the greater part on the way   to day clear & warm for this region   some of the men are gone to day to Donnos Camp   will start back on Monday."

On February 22, they started back with twenty-three people from both the lake and creek camps. Two of them were Edward and Simon Breen, the children that Patrick and Margaret Breen thought were strong enough to make it. Another five were Margaret Reed and her four children, relieving the Breens of five mouths to feed. Near the pass, it became evident to the rescuers that Patty and her brother Tommy Reed were not strong enough for the journey. They were taken back to the Breens who were very upset by having this burden again placed on their shoulders. Nevertheless they reluctantly took the two Reed children back in, while at the same time expressing fear for the childrens' lives. The Reeds had already lived with the Breens for eight weeks and more, eating boiled hides, boiled bones from the Breens' beef, and occasional pieces of beef that the Breens were only willing to spare when the Reed children's lives appeared to be threatened. On February 26, Patty turned nine years of age.

THE GRATITUDE OF THE REED GIRLS

Years later, Patty Reed had an interesting story to tell. Mrs. Breen kept some little bags of meat, dried by Dolan before he left, in a hideaway over the cabin door. Mrs. Reed was aware of the cache and one day when rain was leaking through to it, she chided Mrs. Breen: "What could it be that is getting damaged up there?" Mrs. Reed would sometimes go to bed at night with a knife hidden under her blanket, with the idea of sneaking up to Mrs. Breen's cache. "But she could never do it," said Patty. "I cannot steal," she told her daughter. It is a touching story of two mothers fighting for the lives of their own children. Whatever the appearances of Mrs. Breen's hoarding, the fact is that neither Mrs. Reed nor her children would have survived were it not for the sustenance, both physical and spiritual, that the Breens gave them. The Reed girls would never forget that. Virginia Reed later wrote a beautiful testimony to the kindness of the Breens:

> We now had nothing to eat but raw hides and they were on the roof of the cabin to keep out the snow; when prepared for cooking and boiled they were simply a pot of glue. When the hides were taken off our cabin and we were left without shelter Mr. Breen gave us a home with his family, and Mrs. Breen prolonged my life by slipping me little bits of meat now and then when she discovered that I could not eat the hide....
>
> I am a Catholic, although my parents were not. I often went to the Catholic church before leaving home, but it was at Donner Lake that I made the vow to be a Catholic. The Breens were the only Catholic family in the Donner party and prayers were said aloud regularly in that cabin night and morning. Our only light was from little pine sticks split up like kindling wood and kept constantly on the hearth. I was very fond of kneeling by the side of Mr. Breen and holding these little torches so that he might see to read. One night we had all gone to bed – I was with my mother and the little ones, all huddled together to keep from freezing – but I could not sleep. It was a fearful night and I felt that the hour was not far distant when we would go to sleep – never to wake again in this world. All at once I found myself on my knees with my hands clasped, looking up through the darkness, making a vow that if God would send us relief and let me see my father again, I would be a Catholic. That prayer was answered....

Virginia's sister, Patty, confirmed this account in a letter in 1879 to McGlashan:

> Mr. Breen (God gless him) took us in and kept us from dieing, with *cold* when we had no place to lay our heads we had the shelter of his roof, and the warmth of Mr. Breen's fire, his good sons did get the wood, thanks! thanks! for all and Mrs. Breen *did*, kinely [*sic*], give to my mother a sip of her tea as they sat, oft-times by the fire trying to plan to escape from their *prison*....to do honor to that faithful Christian, Mr. Breen, he did worship his prayer book. I can see now the splits that were prepared by his boys, and placed to the *left* of that generous old fireplace, to be lit and held as a candle for the good old man to read the prayers, and all of us that were out of bed (on that day) would kneel to hear and feel, oh feel, yes! God have mercy, God have mercy!

Eighteen of the twenty-one emigrants led out by the first relief reached Sutter's Fort alive. William Hook, John Denton, and Ada Keseberg perished. Encamped at a spot in the Bear Valley where a cache of food had been left by the relief party, the twelve-year-old Hook had climbed up a tree in the night, feasted on the food, and the next morning was found dying from eating too much food too quickly.

Much credit for the survival of the others should go to Selim P. Woodworth, who has been generally maligned in the literature. He had wasted no time in setting up a provisions depot at Mule Springs, thirty miles east of Johnson's Ranch, and he was waiting for the rescue party when they arrived. George Tucker, fifteen years of age and the son of Reasin, was there too, helping to guard the provisions. In 1879, he wrote McGlashan about what his father told him of the experiences on the trail. Reasin Tucker's buckskins had ripped at the lower part of the leg and "the little children were so hungry they would cut strips of that wet buckskin from his pants [and] crisp it in the fire and eat it."

Reasin Tucker himself, writing to McGlashan from Goleta, California, in 1879, added some gruesome details. He recalled that he urged Mrs. Keseberg. who was holding her dead baby, to walk ahead with the company while the baby was buried in the snow "best we could." Tucker added that the baby's "sperrit went to heaven, her body to the wolves."

BETWEEN THE FIRST AND SECOND RELIEF

John Baptiste Trudeau, who wanted to leave with the first relief but was obliged to stay, later gave his recollections to Eliza Donner Houghton, who was a child of three at the time of the entrapment:

> To each of us who had to stay in camp, one of the First Relief Party measured a teacupful of flour, two small biscuits, and thin pieces of jerked beef, each piece as long as his first finger, and as many pieces as he could encircle with that first finger and thumb brought together, end to end. This was all that could be spared, and was to last until the next party could reach us.
>
> The outlook was dreary and often hopeless. I don't know what I would have done sometimes without the comforting talks and prayers of those two women, your mother and Aunt Elizabeth. Then evenings after you children went to sleep, Mrs. George Donner would read to me from the book she

wrote in every day. If that book had been saved, every one would know the truth of what went on in camp, and not spread these false tales.

I dug in the snow for the dead cattle, but found none, and we had to go back to our saltless old bullock hide, days before the Second Relief got to us, on the first of March.

Trudeau's story omitted the fact that the eating of human flesh began shortly after the first relief departed.

Counting the seven survivors of the Snowshoe Party, twenty-two of the eighty-one who arrived at the high camps around October 1 had so far made it alive to the Sacramento Valley. Still at the high camps were over thirty survivors. One of them was Lewis Keseberg. His badly damaged foot prevented him from joining his wife and infant daughter with the first relief. He had no way of knowing that his youngest child had perished. Nor could he know that in the mythology of the Donner Party to be created over the next few decades he would be labeled as a demon all over the world. His infamous reputation, undeserved, would follow him to his grave many years later.

On the day the first relief party left, Patrick Breen reported that he had buried the infant Catherine Pike. The next day, February 23, the Breens ate their dog, Towser. On the same day Mrs. Graves was back again to borrow "meat or ox." Patrick commented on the notion that he had meat to spare: "I know to the Contrary." He also noted that the Graveses had "plenty hides" and that his own family lived "principally on same."

On February 25, the diary notes the fears of Mrs. Murphy that the wolves were about to dig up the dead. "We hear them howl," wrote Patrick. The next day he commented again on the folks who would not eat hides, of which there were plenty. "We eat them with a tolerable good appetite," he wrote.

THE TERRIBLE THOUGHT IS SPOKEN

It was on February 26, the diary notes, that Mrs. Murphy talked about eating the dead Milt Elliott, buried two weeks before by the two Breen boys. She and no doubt others were thinking taboo thoughts. If Milt can be food for the wolves, why not the same to sustain my children? At the Alder Creek camp the same thought was a-borning. The refined and educated Tamsen Donner, the shining heroine-to-be of poems, novels, and histories of the Donner Party, fighting for the lives of her dying husband and children, had told the rescue party that she would instruct Trudeau to dig up the dead for eating, if he or the rescuers did not succeed in finding their cattle buried in the snow. Trudeau had been making unsuccessful probes for the animals.

On February 28, Patrick Breen was blest with a small but touching act of kindness by a lone Digger Indian who trudged, perhaps out of curiosity, by the camp. The diary mentions that the Indian left five or six onion-shaped roots on the snow. Patrick reported that they were fibrous, something like a sweet potato. John Breen remembered the incident, and recalled that the Indian stood a distance off on snow-shoes and made a sign, probably out of fear, not to approach him, before he left his gift on the surface of the snow. There were no reports that any other Indians were seen that near the mountain camps, at least not until the arrival of the fourth relief in April.

THE SECOND RELIEF AND BREEN'S LAST DIARY ENTRY

On March 1, ten men of the second relief arrived. They were James Reed, Hiram Miller, Brit Greenwood (son of the old mountain man, Caleb, by an Indian mother), William McCutchen (who, with Charles Stanton, had left the party in Nevada, travelling on horseback to Sutter's Fort). Charles Stone, John Turner, Matthew Dofar, Charles Cady, Nicholas Clark, and Joseph Jondro (Gendreau). The March 1 entry in Breen's diary noted that the relief party had arrived on a "fine and pleasant day" and would leave in two or three days. It was the last diary entry.

Certainly the diary reveals an unusual man. Patrick Breen was sensitive to suffering, but devoid of self-pity. He looked outward at the world – the people around him and the sun in the sky – with a clear eye and with hope, rather than probing his own psyche and dwelling on his own physical ills (only once did he mention his kidney stones, the "gravel"). He had a simple and strong faith in God, which sustained him and, no doubt, his own family and others; he never despaired. He and his oldest sons performed what in the Catholic Church are called "the corporal works of mercy," but his accounts were given without a suggestion of self-righteousness. He dug up hides for the sickly Milt Elliott. He took into his cabin the dying Spitzer and later Mrs. Reed and her four children. He and his sons saw to it that the dead were buried, including Spitzer, Milt Elliott, the infant Lewis Keseberg, the infant Catherine Pike, and Mrs. Eddy and her infant child. He allowed Franklin Graves, who had a large family, to have at least two of his oxen, which he could ill afford. He had the foresight to reserve the meat while living on the horrible hides, the reverse of what other families did. Experiencing terrible physical suffering, he nevertheless appreciated the sun in the sky on a clear morning after the worst of storms, and could thank God for his blessings. "With God's help spring will soon smile upon us," he wrote on February 10. Little could he know that his worst suffering was yet to come, at Starved Camp at the head of the Yuba.

CANNIBALISM

The second relief found the mutilated body of Milt Elliott in the Murphy cabin, probably the first instance of cannibalism at the lake camp. At Alder Creek, according to J. Quinn Thornton, the two rescuers who arrived there first discovered Trudeau "carrying across the snow the leg of a man cut off at the thigh." More, the surviving Donners had already consumed the bodies of Jacob Donner and the teamster Shoemaker. Jacob's wife Elizabeth was almost dead. Four Donner children, reported Thornton, "were sitting upon a log, with their faces stained with blood, devouring the half-roasted liver and heart of the father."

One would think that such specificity about the body parts would suggest to a scholar that Thornton was in the realm of fiction. But not to George R. Stewart, who slavishly accepted Thornton's hyperbole in all its specifics, including rescuers who had a fine eye for flesh not well done: "The two [rescuers] gazed upon the children sitting upon the log, their chins and breasts smeared bloodily as they innocently tore and ate the half-roasted heart and liver." The two rescuers who arrived there first were Cady and Clark. Stewart introduces his scenario with the words, "As Cady and Clark told their story...." This is simply not true, which Stewart's own notes make evident: "The facts are plainly and circumstantially stated in Thornton." Yet Thornton does not state his sources. And Stewart did not have access to any written testimony of Cady and Clark in the matter, for the simple reason that no such documents have been located.

Reed also visited the Alder Creek camp. His report in a letter to the *Illinois Journal*, published December 9, 1847, mentions the cannibalism but names no names, and his more detailed testimony, published in the *Pacific Rural Press* (March 25 and April 1, 1871) ignores the cannibalism.

Elizabeth Donner's oldest boy, Solomon Hook, fourteen, had become difficult to control. For that reason Trudeau had moved into the George Donner tent. Reed found Tamsen Donner in what he described as good health and tending to her bedridden husband, George. They were with three of their daughters, the oldest six years of age.

Reed decided to take only Mary and Isaac Donner and Sol Hook, all from the Elizabeth Donner tent and all capable of walking. Left behind were nine survivors: Tamsen and George Donner and their children, Frances, Georgia and Eliza; Elizabeth Donner and her children, Samuel and Lewis; and John Baptiste Trudeau. Trudeau, who was not allowed to leave with the first relief, was again asked to remain behind to take care of the Donner children, with whom he was popular. Reed assigned Cady and Clark to remain behind at Alder Creek. Why two of the rescuers, along with John Baptiste Trudeau, were left behind to take care of the remaining Donners is a mystery, but Cady's motives may not have been entirely altruistic, as we shall see.

JOHN BREEN

At the lake camp Reed's men set about choosing the survivors who they thought could make the journey to the valley. Patrick and Margaret Breen must have been overjoyed to learn from Reed that two of their children had already arrived safely in the valley with the first relief. Now they and their remaining five children were to get out too. But they must have been worried about their oldest, John, who had passed his fifteenth birthday on February 21. John was a sturdy and strong young lad, but his body was beginning to weaken severely. For almost four months, or at least since the ill-fated Patrick Dolan left with the Snowshoe Party in mid-December, the heaviest work had fallen on John's shoulders and, to a lesser extent, on Edward's. John had the main responsibility, so his mother later told Mrs. Eliza W. Farnham, for gathering the wood and helping to bury the dead from other cabins.

Despite John's heavy work, his share of the food was no more than was meted out carefully by his parents to each member of the family, with the exception of the infant Isabella. John also made many trips to the isolated Donner camp six miles away to lend what assistance he could. By the time he was taken out by the second relief, he was quite weak.

The second relief left the lake camp at noon on March 3. The party consisted of seven men of the relief and seventeen survivors: seven Breens, two Reed children, Mrs. Graves and her four children, and the three children from the Donner camp–Sol Hook, Isaac Donner, and Mary Donner.

Left behind at the lake camp were five persons: Lavinia Murphy and her son Simon, both of whom lacked the strength for the journey; Lavinia's grandchild, George Foster; James Eddy ; and Lewis Keseberg. Rescuer Stone also stayed behind but quickly hastened over to the Donner tents at Alder Creek. On Stone's arrival, Cady was there but Clark was off in the woods hunting a bear. In Clark's absence, Stone and Cady made a deal with Tamsen Donner to take her three children to Sutter's Fort. Instead they took the little ones only as far as the lake camp, leaving them within the cabin of the half-crazed Mrs. Murphy. They took cover during a three-day storm, probably in the empty Breen cabin, and about March 8 they headed for the pass carrying ample packs, including silks and silver spoons of the Donners, but no Donner children.

Meanwhile, on the first day out, the rescue party of twenty-four got only half-way along the northern shore of the lake and had to camp among the trees. All seemed to be in good spirits, buoyed by Patrick Breen's gay violin playing beside the camp-fire and by his nightly prayers. On the second night they made it only to the foot of the pass, where again Patrick Breen's fiddle playing kept up the spirits, while his older sons and the res-cuers gathered wood for the fire. But food was getting low, rations remained for only half a day, storm clouds were gathering over the pass, and it was about fifteen miles to the nearest cache left by the rescue party. They were already behind schedule and on half-rations, a few ounces a day.

Rescuers Turner, Dofar, and Jondro were sent ahead to find food at the cache and bring it back. That left four rescuers, Reed, Miller, McCutchen, and Greenwood. Those sent ahead found that the cache, in fact, had been robbed by animals. They got caught in a storm and were barely alive when they met a party consisting of Woodworth, Eddy, Foster and others, who were on their way up the Yuba from Bear Valley with provisions.

STARVED CAMP

On the third day out of the lake camp, March 5, the party of four rescuers headed by Reed, and seventeen survivors, crossed the pass at noon and by evening arrived at a spot in the Summit Valley close to the head of the Yuba River and just south of today's villages of Norden and Soda Springs. They had progressed only about ten or eleven miles from the lake camp, and were still five miles from what they hoped would be a cache.

A great storm came on that night. The length of the storm is difficult to determine from the records. Thornton said it lasted for two days and three nights, ending on March 8. Mc-Glashan also mentions a storm of "three days." Stewart concurs. Reed's "diary" of his rescue mission contains a long narrative section obviously composed some time after the events described. He refers to the place as "now [called] Starved Camp," and discusses other things that he "learned afterwards," such as the whereabouts of his advance men and of Woodworth, information that could come only from hindsight. Reed's memory was no doubt prompted by McCutchen, as it was again prompted in 1871 when they prepared simultaneous accounts for the *Pacific Rural Press*, both presenting themselves entirely heroically while describing the Breens in a highly unfavorable light. Reed's diary version of events is garbled as to chronology and duration, but he actually describes only two nights of the storm, in undated entries and in considerable detail, although he was blinded and unconscious much of the time.

Reed wrote that on the first night of the great storm, which would have to be March 5, John Breen almost fell into the firepit; that only three of his men (they could only have been McCutchen, Miller, and Greenwood) were able to get wood; that he himself had become snowblind, his sight not returning until the next day; and that there was much praying and crying among the men and women. On the second night, March 6, there was continued praying and crying, and the fire would have gone out "had it not been for Mr. McCutchen's exertions." (Hiram Miller is mentioned as also functioning as wood-gatherer, in a later scenario.) On the morning of March 7, the snow was "now nearly ceased." It seems likely then that on March 7, or on March 8 at the latest, the relief party made ready to continue the journey.

During the ordeal at Starved Camp, according to Thornton's account, the relief party members were too slow in gathering kindling wood for Margaret Breen's comfort. She allegedly hurled words of abuse at Miller and McCutchen, as they worked at piling up sticks for the fire. Holding her infant against her bosom, said Thornton, she was heard above the storm: "Were they not getting three dollars a day? Was it just to 'murther' people?"

Thornton wrote that big McCutchen, the strongest of the rescuers, let go some oaths of his own at Mrs. Breen before he finally managed to start a new fire. The Thornton scenario (accepted as fact and repeated by Stewart, including a long direct quotation in stage Irish) can plausibly be treated as fiction, however. Reed in his diary gave a very detailed account of that terrible night without mentioning Margaret Breen's faulting of the rescuers. McCutchen, in his 1871 article for the *Pacific Rural Press,* in which he described the first night of the storm, mentioned that *he* berated some (whom he does not name) who despaired and could not or would not help to build a fire. He does not, however, mention himself being bad-mouthed by Margaret Breen. Stewart names Mrs. Breen, and also directs moral judgments at Patrick Breen and rescuer Greenwood, accusing them of "funking."

Little Isaac Donner, age five, was found dead on the second morning (the third, according to some accounts), having passed away during the night, lying between his sister Mary, age seven, and Patty Reed, age nine.

Sometime during March 7 or March 8 the relief party prepared to continue the journey. Hiram Miller would carry three-year-old Tommy Reed. Patty Reed could not be carried by her weakened father, and agreed to walk. Solomon Hook also felt strong enough to walk. Left behind were fourteen bodies, thirteen alive and one dead: the seven Breens; Mrs. Graves and four of her children, ages nine, seven, five and one; Mary Donner, age seven; and the dead body of little Isaac Donner lying there on the snow.

Despite Reed's urgings, Breen knew that he and his family were just too weak to make the attempt without food. Reed himself had been so weakened that he could not carry either of his own children. Patrick and Margaret Breen would rely on the third rescue party, thought to be on its way. It was better to take their chances on that, rather than accept almost certain death for many, if not all, of the family on the trail. James Breen was failing rapidly. Mrs. Breen, now the strongest of them all, might have carried out her one-year-old, but she was not willing to abandon her husband and her four other children. Besides, how could she leave Mrs. Graves and her four small children, and little Mary Donner, to certain death?

Of the seventeen people who started out with them from the lake camp, rescuers Reed, McCutchen, Miller, and Greenwood succeeded in bringing out only three children, two of them Reed's own. This was a performance that might have to be explained later. After all, the first rescue party had brought out alive eighteen of twenty-one persons they started with. Realizing that he might have to answer for what could seem to be a poor and even selfish performance, Reed, according to a version of events that is not mentioned in his diary but which emerged in 1871, asked Greenwood, Miller and McCutchen to witness Patrick Breen's refusal to accompany him.

Actually, there was one additional "person." Unknown to her rescuers, little Patty Reed had secreted beneath her clothes a small doll. This famous doll is today on display at the museum at Sutter's Fort in Sacramento.

The rescuers left the Breens a three days' supply of fuel, but no food. Margaret Breen, however, had secretly stashed away some seeds, a little tea and coffee, and a one-pound ball of sugar. They had had very little food for five days and were to spend four more nights in that pit in the snow before the third relief arrived.

Mrs. Graves and her five-year-old son died on the first night after the rescue party left. It must be to the credit of Margaret Breen, possessed with an iron will for survival, that anybody remained alive. She had her own infant to comfort at her breast, as well as the Graves' infant. And there were other small children, barely beyond infancy, who needed the soft touch of a mother.

A few years later, Margaret told her story to Eliza W. Farnham, who published it in a long appendix to her book. *California, In-Doors and Out* (1856). Margaret, her husband, and all the children "lay feet to the fire." She had only moccasins on her feet and "a blanket drawn over her shoulders and head." Under the blanket she wore a shawl and under the shawl she "nursed her poor baby on her knees [although] her milk had been gone many days."

As the fire melted the snow and the platform of pine saplings on which it was built descended to a considerable depth, less and less warmth could be got from it. Finally the bare earth was exposed. With great difficulty John Breen used a long log or "tree top" which had partly fallen in and climbed down. Steps were made in the snow and all descended to a circle around the fire at the pit's bottom on the earth floor.

When it seemed that James Breen was dying, Patrick said, "Let him die, he will be better off than any of us." Margaret then applied snow water and a bit of the sugar lump she had carried about her waistcoat to James' tongue. His jaws were so tight that she had a difficult time opening his mouth. Margaret also took over the job of gathering wood, and she led the family in reciting the Litany.

Margaret Breen shared with infant Elizabeth Graves the last bits of loaf sugar and drops of tea. She and her husband now turned their eyes in another direction for food.

Little Mary Donner, who had accustomed herself to eating human flesh at the camp at Alder Creek, suggested innocently that they should eat the dead bodies. Margaret Breen, according to her own account, rebelled against the thought. Patrick, however, finally convinced himself that it was wrong to deny his family a chance of survival. The dead would provide the only means of survival for the living. And so the Breens themselves would finally break the age-old taboo. Patrick with knife in hand climbed the snow stairs to the surface to cut up the two dead children, who were eaten first. Margaret Breen turned her eyes away. When the children were consumed, Mrs. Graves was eaten. There could have been very little meat on the starved bodies.

Perhaps in the interests of not embarrassing Margaret Breen, Farnham suggested that Margaret herself did not engage in the cannibalism. But that is not credible. Besides, no moral theologians today would quarrel with Patrick's judgment, or with Margaret's eating of the only food available for giving her the strength to save herself and the children who entirely depended on her.

At some time during the ordeal in the pit, Cady and Stone must have passed Starved Camp, continuing on until they caught up with Reed and the second relief.

THE THIRD RELIEF AND A DEFENSE OF WOODWORTH

A precise chronology of the third relief is impossible to establish from the conflicting evidence of Eddy/Thornton, Reed, McGlashan, Stewart and others. Eddy and Reed, as to be expected, were inclined to show themselves in the most heroic of lights. Thornton and Stewart, as also to be expected, were willing to oblige them. Stewart attempted to reconcile the data in a suspenseful narrative (Chapters 25 and 27 of *Ordeal*) in which he pictures Woodworth as a weakling and villain.

Some facts in favor of Woodworth, however, do emerge from the record. On March 7 or 8, when the storm ceased, William Eddy and William Foster set off on horseback from Johnson's Ranch and arrived at Mule Springs that evening. Woodworth and a few of his men had already moved up to the Bear Valley, about ten trail miles away, to establish an advance camp. Woodworth was there at the Bear Valley camp when Eddy and Foster, travelling from Mule Springs on foot, arrived, probably on the evening of March 9. Meanwhile, Reed's rescue party had started down from Starved Camp. Somewhere along the Yuba River before reaching Bear Valley Reed's advance men – Dofar, Jondro, and Turner, half-dead themselves after the storm – met the party of Woodworth, who had advanced from the Bear Valley camp to the Yuba with provisions. Very shortly thereafter, Reed arrived with rescuers Greenwood, Miller, McCutchen, and three children, two of whom were Reed's own, everybody weakened and starving. Although they were only a long day's march away from Starved Camp, nobody seems to have been able or willing at that point to go to the rescue of the eleven persons who had been left behind there. In fact, Reed prevailed on the Woodworth party, including Eddy and Foster, to go back to the Bear Valley camp, a day's march further away from Starved Camp, to replenish their provisions and to discuss the matter of a relief party. At Bear Valley the next day, Woodworth organized the third relief, a party of seven. They left for the high camps on March 11 or 12.

The seven men were Hiram Miller and Charles Stone of the second relief, who volunteered to turn around and go back; John Stark, William Thompson, and Howard Oakley, whom Woodworth had brought up from Mule Springs; and Eddy and Foster.

A few other facts emerge, especially concerning Woodworth, who had been doing his job and doing it very well for over a month. When the first relief arrived at Mule Springs about February 27, Woodworth was there with food and horses. Within about a week, Woodworth had set up an advance base at Bear Valley and then had moved up to the Yuba with provisions to meet Reed's returning second relief, when they came down from Starved Camp after the storm. It is true that Woodworth did not venture to the high camps himself, but the notion advanced by James F. Reed that Woodworth let everybody down is untenable. Woodworth's movements up the mountains were delayed by the great storm just as much as Reed's movements down them. From February 5 to about March 9, when his party with Eddy and Foster met Reed's,

Woodworth was busy recruiting volunteers, establishing the bases at Mule Springs and Bear Valley and securing the provisions and animals with dependable guards, replenishing these bases, and maintaining liaison with Johnson's Ranch and with Lieutenant Kern, at his camp between Johnson's and Mule Springs. The fact is that all men available, willing, and able to undertake the journey over the pass and back again were occupied doing so during the five weeks when Woodworth was accused of doing nothing. Woodworth served these men and the emigrants well; Stewart, especially harsh toward Woodworth, failed to draw obvious conclusions from his own chronologies and other data. If anybody is to be faulted it should be Edward V. Kern, who gave little if any help to Woodworth and whose role seems to have been solely to place the men of the first relief and a few others on his payroll while he dawdled at his camp below the snow line with eight Indian servants and acted parsimoniously in doling out provisions to returning rescuers and the survivors (the testimony of Ritchie, who went part way with the first relief, and Tucker, who went all the way, is rather convincing in this matter).

JOHN DENTON

None of the third relief really expected to find anybody alive at Starved Camp when they broke camp in Bear Valley on the morning of March 11 or 12. On the way they found, sitting against a tree, the body of John Denton, who had been left behind by the first relief. His body and possessions had apparently been ignored by the second relief. The rescuers found in Denton's pocket a pencil and paper on which Denton had composed a poem, perhaps in his last hours before freezing to death. The first eight lines of his poem ran:

> *O! after many roving years,*
> *How sweet it is to come*
> *Back to the dwelling-place of youth,*
> *Our first and dearest home;*
> *To turn away our wearied eyes*
> *From proud ambition's towers,*
> *And wander in those summer fields,*
> *The scenes of boyhood's hours.*

ARRIVAL AT STARVED CAMP

On their second day out, late in the afternoon of March 12 or 13, they found the seven Breens, three Graves children, including the one-year-old infant, and Mary Donner. They had spent at least seven nights in their terrible prison-pit in the snow, during which time Patrick Breen Jr. reached his tenth birthday, and were to spend one more night before leaving.

Thornton, as usual relying only on Eddy as his informant, gave the following description of what Eddy saw:

....at 4 o'clock, they arrived at the camp of those whom Mr. Reed had been compelled to leave. The fire at the Starved Camp had melted the snow down to the ground, and the hole thus made was about twelve or fifteen feet in diameter, and twenty-four feet deep. As the snow had continued to melt, they made steps by which they ascended and descended.

The picture of distress which was here presented, was shocking indeed. And yet Patrick Brinn [sic] and his wife seemed not in any degree to realize the extent of their peril, or that they were in peril at all. They were found lying down sunning themselves, and evincing no concern for the future. They had consumed the two children of Jacob Donner. Mrs. Graves' body was lying there with almost all the flesh cut away from her arms and limbs. Her breasts were cut off, and her heart and liver taken out, and were all being boiled in a pot then on the fire. Her little child, about thirteen months old, sat at her side, with one arm upon the body of its mangled mother, and sobbing bitterly, Ma! ma! ma! It was a helpless and innocent lamb among the wolves of the wilderness. Mr. Eddy took up its wasted form in his arms, and touched even to tears with the sight he witnessed, he kissed its wan and pale cheeks again and again; and wept even more bitterly in the anguish of his spirit as he thought of his own dear ones, and the departed companion of his perils and sorrows. The child looked up imploringly into his face, and with a silent but expressive eloquence, besought him to be its protector. In a few minutes it nestled in his bosom, and seemed to feel assured that it once more had a friend. As soon as possible, he made some thin soup for the infant, which revived it, and, with the exception of an occasional short convulsive sob or sigh, it again appeared quiet and happy.

That scenario is repeated almost word for word by Stewart, with somewhat less emphasis on the sentimental. It has been repeated many times by lesser historians and novelists. But the details of the Thornton/Eddy scenario are factually incongruous, as well as unfair to the Breens. First of all, it is evident that Thornton never interviewed any of the Breens, as he consistently spelled their surname "Brinn" in his book, first published in 1849. Second, it is not likely that the rays of a late afternoon sun on March 12 could reach to the bottom of the pit as described. Third, the mutilated bodies of the dead were actually on or near the surface of the snow, above the pit. The picture of the infant Graves baby fondling the body of its mutilated mother clearly has the mark of pulp fiction. Finally, the picture ignores the fact that the Breens, allegedly sunning themselves and ignoring the infants and older children about them, had managed to nurture nine children in that pit for many days – with food, prayer, and the comforts of human touch. Yet the account makes it seem that Eddy was the first "protector" and comforter the Graves baby had experienced in those many days.

Stewart rejected almost all of the longest account of events at Starved Camp, that given by Margaret Breen to Mrs. Farnham. "This is so sentimentalized and so obviously a defense of Mrs. Breen....that it is not to be trusted." Yet Stewart accepted the version of Eddy/Thornton, so highly sentimentalized and patently false in many respects. Characteristically, Stewart had little patience with any evidence pointing to the heroism of the Breens and other ethnics in the Donner Party, such as John Baptiste Trudeau.

Eddy spent little time at Starved Camp before moving on to the high camps with rescuers Foster, Thompson, and Miller. Stark, Oakley, and Stone were left at Starved Camp to bring in the eleven survivors. But Stone remained true to form. He and Oakley argued that to try to take out eleven people would be courting disaster; four children would be enough, and the devil with the Breens. Did not the Breens have their chance with the second relief, and did not they reject the opportunity? Stewart sympathized with this point of view: "No one [of the rescue party]....had much sympathy for [Patrick] Breen, who by refusing to travel with Reed when he was still strong enough seemed to have forfeited his right to further consideration."

So, Stone took off with only the infant Graves, age one and close to death. Of like mind, Oakley took only little Mary Donner. They would give no help at all to the seven Breens and the two remaining Graves children, Nancy and Jonathan. Oakley and Stone headed down the trail to collect their $3 per diem and $50 bonus for carrying out a child not their own.

Easy bonus money. Starved Camp was closer to the prize than the lake camps. John Stark was left with nine people to lead to the valley. James Breen, who was five or six years old at Starved Camp, recalled Stark fondly. Many details he remembered clearly; regarding others, his mind was refreshed by accounts he heard from his parents and older brothers. He reminisced that when a vote was taken by the relief party members as to whether to abandon the Breens, only Stark voted against the proposal. "I will not abandon these people," he said. Stark was aware that, if the Breens had to wait for the other rescuers to return from the high camps, they would perish. James Breen, writing with an understandable gratitude toward the heroic Stark, said:

> Stark was finally left alone. To his great bodily strength, and unexcelled courage, myself and others owe their lives. There was probably no other man in California at that time, who had the intelligence, determination, and what was absolutely necessary in that emergency, the immense physical powers of John Stark. He weighed two hundred and forty pounds and was as strong as two ordinary men. On his broad shoulders he carried the provisions, most of the blankets, and most of the time some of the weaker children. In regard to this, he would laughingly say that he could carry them all if there was room on his back, because they were so light from starvation.

James Breen further told of how Stark cheered and encouraged the sufferers. He carried one or two of the little ones ahead, then returned for others. "I distinctly remember," he said, "that myself and Jonathan Graves were both carried by Stark, on his back the greater part of the journey." Mrs. Breen carried baby Isabella.

All of the people Stark led to the safety of the settlements reached Sutter's Fort. A doctor was sought to amputate one of little James' legs. He was hardly more than a skeleton and his feet were frozen and badly burned. Fortunately, a doctor could not be found; James survived, and lived to 1899 with both legs intact.

James Breen, who was to become a Superior Court judge in San Benito County, was quick to forgive those who would have left the Breens behind:

No one can attach blame to those who voted to leave part of the emigrants. It was a desperate case. Their idea was to save as many as possible, and they honestly believed that by attempting to save all, all would be lost. But this consideration – and the further one that Stark was an entire stranger to every one in the camps, not bound to them by any tie of blood or kindred, nor having any hopes of reward, except the grand consciousness of doing a noble act – makes his conduct shine more lustrously in the eyes of every person who admires nature's true and only nobility.

THIRD RELIEF REACHES THE HIGH CAMPS

Back at the Alder Creek camp, during or very soon after the terrible storm of early March, Elizabeth Donner and her two children, Samuel and Lewis, died. Left at Alder Creek were Clark, Trudeau, Tamsen Donner and George Donner. Clark hiked over to the lake camp one day and was surprised to find there the three Donner children that Cady and Stone were supposed to have taken to the valley. He hurried back to Alder Creek to inform Tamsen Donner. He and Trudeau told her of their decision to leave for the valley while they still had the strength. Tamsen hurried over to the lake camp to visit her children. She was there when Eddy, Foster, Thompson, and Miller arrived. Trudeau and Clark were also there, or arrived soon after.

At the lake, William Eddy learned that his little boy, James, age three, had died and been cannibalized. William Foster learned that his son George, age four, had met the same fate. George probably died in Mrs. Murphy's cabin. Georgia Donner, who was only four at the time, recalled many years later seeing the body of a child "hung up on the wall" in "Keseberg's cabin." (The memories of small children who survived were often refreshed and stimulated by lurid accounts about Keseberg, of whom they could have had little actual memory.) Eddy suspected that Keseberg had murdered his son.

Alive at the lake cabins were Mrs. Murphy and her son, Simon; Lewis Keseberg; and the three Donner girls.

Tamsen Donner said that she still could not leave her husband. So, she entrusted her three children to Eddy and the others of the relief party, and made her way back to her husband at Alder Creek.

John Stark, a native of Indiana and member of the third relief party, led Patrick and Margaret Breen, five of their children, and two Graves children from Starved Camp to the Sacramento Valley. Stark later served as sheriff of Napa County and represented that county in the state legislature.

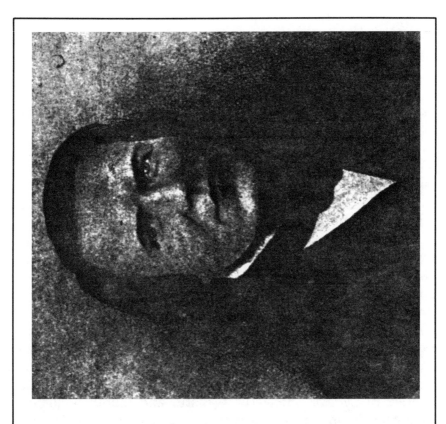

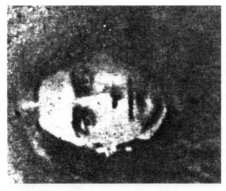

William Henry Eddy (1817-59) and spouse Eleanor Priscilla (c1821-47). William Eddy led fifteen members of the Snowshoe Party out of the camps of entrapment in December 1846. Of the eight who perished, seven were eaten, including two who were murdered for food. By the time Eddy returned to the mountain camp with the third relief, his wife and two children had died. Photos from daguerrotypes taken in Illinois and published for the first time in *The Pony Express*, August 1946.

The four men of the third relief took with them the four children left alive at the lake – Simon Murphy, and Frances, Georgia, and Eliza Donner. Along with them went Trudeau, barely able to walk, and Nicholas Clark, who had been in the mountains long enough to be considered a survivor of the Donner Party. Clark carried a heavy pack of Donner valuables, clearly with the permission of Tamsen. It apparently had not occurred to Eddy or the others to accompany Tamsen Donner back to Alder Creek, to see if George Donner were still alive. They had spent only two hours at the lake before starting back to the valley.

The four men of the third relief arrived in the valley with the four children, and with Trudeau and Clark, without casualty. Later, Trudeau, acting as their nurse, accompanied two of the Donner children to the naval hospital facility in San Francisco.

Trudeau, because of Thornton's and Stewart's accounts of events, became one of the villains of the saga. "More than once, it appears, [Trudeau] wished or even attempted to escape on his own account and leave the Donners in the lurch," wrote Stewart in *Ordeal*. Stewart's scenario and moral judgments went considerably beyond where the documents at his disposal should have allowed him (see critique of *Ordeal* in Chapter 15). Stewart relied almost wholly on Thornton, while disregarding the testimony of others, including Nicholas Clark and John Baptiste Trudeau himself.

Clark was another villain, in Stewart's view. He carried "a pack of forty pounds in booty and two guns," wrote Stewart, "while content to leave the child to perish." The truth was that no child was left to perish, and the alleged booty was sold by the administrator of the estates of the Donners on behalf of the Donner heirs. Clark paid the administrator $28.75 for the goods he carried out.

Chapter 11

CAPTAIN FALLON AND THE FOURTH RELIEF

Remaining at the high camps now were only Mrs. Murphy and Lewis Keseberg at the lake; and Tamsen Donner with her husband at Alder Creek.

The fourth relief was slow in being organized in the California valley. Few people expected anybody to be alive. The fourth relief was principally a scavenging expedition, headed by a huge mountainman with a reputation for ferocity, one Captain William O. "Le Gros" Fallon, sometimes called "Big Fallon." Fallon and two others, John Rhoads and Joe "Sailor Jack" Sels made a deal with John Sinclair, the alcalde at Sutter's Fort, who was acting on behalf of the children of the Donner brothers. The document was signed by the alcalde and by William Fallon, John "Rhoades" (x mark), and "Josephs Sel." It was agreed that the three rescuers would receive equal shares of half the property they recovered of the late Jacob Donner, including gold and silver, the other half going to the surviving Donner children; and that, if Jacob's brother George and his wife Tamsen were found alive, they could make arrangements for recompense with both or either of them.

The three signers were joined on the fourth relief by William Foster, Reasin Tucker, Edward Coffeemire, and Sebastian Keyser. What arrangement was made with them is unknown.

Even before the fourth relief left for the high country, sensational reports appeared in the press about Donner Party murders and cannibalism. They were circulated worldwide. An example was a piece by Elbert P. Jones in the *California Star*, April 10, 1847. "Calculations were coldly made as they sat gloomily around their gloomy campfires," Mr. Jones wrote somewhat redundantly, "for the next and succeeding meals....various expedients were devised to prevent the dreadful crime of murder, but they finally resolved to kill those who had the least claim to human existence....so changed had the immigrants become that when the party sent out arrived with food, some of them cast it aside and seemed to prefer the putrid human flesh that still remained."

As to what Fallon and the fourth relief actually saw or found in the camps, the historian has to choose between the conflicting reports of Captain Fallon and Lewis Keseberg. What follows is the report of William O. Fallon:

The California Star, San Francisco, June 5, 1847
EXTRACTS from a JOURNAL Written by a Member of the Party Latest from the California Mountains
    The extracts which we give below are full of thrilling interest. Mr. Fellun, the writer, better known as "Capt. Fellun," set out for the settlements in April last with six others, to extend relief to the remaining sufferers of the emigration, still within the mountains, and also to collect and secure the scattered property of both living and dead. He succeeded in reaching the cabins, and with the exceptions of Kiesburg not a soul survived. They returned, bringing with them this man, and large packs of valuable property. Kiesburg was found in truly a lamentable situation; a long subsistence upon the bodies of his deceased comrades had rendered him haggard and ferocious-looking, and the unsatiable appetite of the cannibal displayed itself on frequent occasions, even after animal meat had been placed before him. This fondness for human flesh he had suffered himself to acquire in preference to the beef or horse meat of which he had an abundance. And it is to be feared that his conduct in the mountains was far from justifiable, and a hidden transaction of guilt remains yet to be brought to light.
    We commend this diary as being a plain though well written document, and we have published it in the writer's own language, abating nothing from it in point of interest. Mr. Fellun certainly deserves credit for his management of the affair, as it will be seen that he effected the desirable end.
    "Left Johnson's on the evening of April 13th and arrived at the lower end of the Bear River Valley on the 15th. Hung our saddles upon the trees and sent the horses back, to be returned again in ten days, to bring us in again. Started on foot, with provisions for ten days, and traveled to the head of the valley and camped for the night, snow from 2 to 3 feet deep.
    "15th. Started early in the morning and traveled 23 miles, snow 10 feet deep.
    "April 17th. Reached the Cabins between 12 and 1 o'clock. Expected to find some of the sufferers alive, Mrs. Donner and Kiesburg in particular.

Entered the cabins and a horrible scene presented itself, – human bodies terribly mutilated, legs, arms, and sculls scattered in every direction. One body, supposed to be that of Mrs. Eddy, lay near the entrance, the limbs severed off and a frightful gash in the scull. The flesh from the bones was nearly consumed and a painful stillness pervaded the place. The supposition was that all were dead, when a sudden shout revived our hopes, and we flew in the direction of the sound, three Indians, were hitherto concealed, started from the ground and fled at our approach, leaving behind their bows and arrows. We delayed two hours in searching the cabins, during which we were obliged to witness sights from which we would have fain turned away, and which are too dreadful to put on record. – We next started for 'Donner's camp' 8 miles distant over the mountains. After travelling about half way, we came upon a track in the snow, which excited our suspicion, and we determined to pursue it. It brought us to the camp of Jacob Donner, where it had evidently left that morning. There we found property of every discription, books, calicoes, tea, coffee, shoes, purcussion caps, household and kitchen furniture scattered in every direction, and mostly in the water. At the mouth of the tent stood a large iron kettle, filled with human flesh cut up, it was from the body of Geo. Donner, the head had been split open, and the brains extracted therefrom, and to the appearance, he had not been long dead, not over three or four days at the most. Near by the kettle stood a chair, and thereupon three legs of a bullock that had been shot down in the early part of the winter, and snowed under before it could be dressed. The meat was found sound and good, and with the exception of a small piece out of the shoulder, wholly untouched. We gathered up some property and camped for the night.

"April 18. Commenced gathering the most valuable property, suitable for our packs, the greater portion requiring to be dried. We then made them up and camped for the night.

"April 19. This morning, [William] Foster, Rhoads, and J. Foster [aka Joe Sels] started with small packs for the first cabins intending from thence to follow the trail of the person that had left the morning previous. The other three remained behind to cache and secure the goods necessarily left there. Knowing the Donners had a considerable sum of money, we searched dilligently but were unsuccessful. The party for the cabins were unable to keep the trail of the mysterious personage owing to the rapid melting of the snow, they therefore went direct for the cabins, and upon entering discovered Kiesburg lying down amidst the human bones and beside him a large pan full of fresh liver and lights. They asked him what had become of his companions, whether they were alive, and what had become of Mrs. Donner. He answered them by stating they were all dead; Mrs. Donner, he said, had in attempting to cross from one cabin to another, missed the trail, and slept out one night; that she came to his camp the next night very much fatigued, he made her a cup of coffee, placed her in bed and rolled her well in the blankets, but the next morning found her dead; he eat her body and found her flesh the best he had ever tasted! He further stated that he obtained from her body at least four pounds of fat! No traces of her person could be found, nor the body of Mrs. Murphy either. – When the last company left the camp, three weeks previous, Mrs. Donner was in perfect health though unwilling to come and leave her husband there, and offered $500, to any person or persons who could come out and bring them in, saying this in the presence of Kiesburg, and she had plenty of tea and coffee, we suspected that it was her who had taken the piece from the shoulder of beef in the chair before mentioned. In the cabin with Kiesburg was found two kettles of human blood, in all supposed to be over one gallon. Rhoads asked him where he had got the blood, he answered, "there is blood in dead bodies," – they asked him numerous questions, but he appeared embarrassed, and equivocated a great deal, and in reply to their asking him where Mrs. Donner's money was, he evinced confusion and answered, that he knew nothing about it, – that she must have cached it before she died – "I have'nt it" said he, 'nor the money, nor the property of any person, living or dead!' They then examined his bundle and found silks and jewelry, which had been taken from the camp of the Donners, and amounting in value to about $200; on his person they discovered a brace of pistols, recognized to be those of Geo. Donner, and while taking them from him discovered something concealed in his waistcoat, which on being opened was found to be $225 in gold.

"Before leaving the settlements, the wife of Keysburg had told us that we would find but little money about him; the men therefore said to him that they knew he was lying to them, and he was well aware of the place of concealment of the Donners' money; he declared before heaven, he knew nothing concerning it, and that he had not the property of any one in his possession; they told him that to lie to them would effect nothing, that there were others back at the cabins, who unless informed of the spot where the treasure was hidden, would not hesitate to hang him upon the first tree. Their threats were of no avail, he still affirmed his ignorance and innocence, and Rhoads took him aside and talked to him kindly, telling him that if he would give the information desired, he should receive from their hands the best of treatment, and be in every way assisted, otherwise, the party back at Donners' camp, would, upon his arrival and refusal to discover to them the place where he had deposited the money, immediately put him to death; it was all to no purpose, however, and they prepared to return to us, leaving him in charge of the packs, and assuring him of their determination to visit him in the morning, and he must make up his mind during the night. They then started back and joined us at Donner's Camp.

"April 20. We [*i.e. Fallon, Tucker, Keyser, Coffeemire, at Alder Creek, rejoining William Foster, Joe Foster, and Rhoads at the lake camp*] all started for Bear River Valley with packs of 100 cwt. each; our provisions being nearly consumed, we were obliged to make haste away. Came within a few hundred yards of the cabin which Kiesburg occupied and halted to prepare breakfast, after which we proceeded to the cabin. I now asked Kiesburg if he was willing to disclose to me where he had concealed that money; he turned somewhat pale and again protested his ignorance: I said to him, 'Kiesburg, you know well where Donner's money is, and d--n you, you shall tell me! I am not going to multiply words with you, nor say but little about it – bring me that rope!" he then arose from his pot of soup and human flesh and begged me not to harm him – he had not the money nor the goods; the silk clothing and money which were found upon him the previous day, and which he then declared belonging to his wife, he now said was the property of others in California. I then told him I did not wish to hear more from him, unless he at once informed us where he had concealed the money of those orphan children, then producing the rope I approached him; he became frightened, but I bent the rope about his neck, and threw him, after a struggle, upon the ground, and as I tightened the cord and choked him he cried out that he would confess all upon release; I then permitted him to arise. He still seemed inclined to be obstinate, and made much delay in talking, finally but with evident reluctance, he led the way back to Donner's camp about 10 miles distant, accompanied by Rhoads and Tucker. While they were absent, we moved all our packs over to the lower end of the lake, and made all ready for a start when they should return. Mr. Foster went down to the cabin of Mrs. Murphy, his mother-in-law, to see if any property remained there worth collecting and securing; he found the body of young Murphy, who had been dead about three months, with the breast and scull cut open, and the brains, liver and lights taken out, and this accounted for the contents of the pan which stood beside Kiesburg when he was found. It appears that he had left at the other camp the dead bullock and horse, and on visiting this camp and finding the body thawed out, took therefrom the brains, liver and lights.

"Tucker and Rhoads came back the next morning, bringing $273, that had been cached by Kiesburg, who after disclosing to them the spot, returned to the cabin. The money had been hidden directly underneath the projecting limb of a large tree, and the end of which seemed to point precisely to the treasure buried in the earth. – On their return and passing the cabin, they saw the unfortunate man within, devouring the remaining brains and liver, left from his morning repast! They hurried him away, but before leaving, he gathered together the bones and heaped them all in a box he used for the purpose, blessed them and the cabin, and said, 'I hope God will forgive me what I have done, I could'nt help it! and I hope I may get to heaven yet!" We asked Kiesburg why he did not use the meat of the bullock and horse instead of human flesh, he replied he had not seen them. We then told him we knew better, and asked him why the meat in the chair had not been consumed, he said 'oh! its too dry eating!' the liver and lights were a great deal better, and the brains made good soup! We then moved on, and camped on the lake for the night.

"April 21st. Started for Bear River valley this morning, found the snow from six to eight feet deep, camped on Juba River for the night – On the 22d., traveled down Juba about 18 miles, and camped at the head of Bear River valley. – On the 25th, moved down to the lower end of the valley, met our horses, and came in."

CAPTAIN WILLIAM O. FALLON

There are some problems with this "journal," but before going into that matter something should be said about the life of William O. Fallon. The son of a St. Louis carriagemaker and a longtime Rocky Mountain man, Fallon was variously described by his contemporaries as "a strong, athletic man, as spry as a cat, and a great horseman [weighing] 200 pounds" and as "the finest looking man in the mountains" with a "noble figure" and (especially in California) as "a big, bullying Irishman." On the records of the fur trade from as early as 1826, his name appears as Fallon, Fallen, Fellun, O'Fallon, etc., with the sobriquets "Big" and "Le Gros." In the summer of 1834 he was reported to have purchased two prisoners from the Snake Indians, to be kept as slaves. The prisoners, Ute Indians, tried to escape, whereupon Fallon threatened to horsewhip a Snake squaw who, Fallon suspected, had aided his slaves in their escape attempt. The squaw grabbed a gun, threatening to kill Fallon on the spot. He was obliged to apologize and plead for his life.

After more than a decade of exploits in the Rocky Mountain fur trade, Fallon continued to lead a remarkable life. In 1845 he participated in the bloodless Micheltorena War in which the *Californios* defeated a Mexican governor. John Sutter wrote United States consul Thomas Larkin in San Francisco that "O Fallon....marched against us with his gang for the sake of getting some horses." At Sonoma the following year he participated in the Bear Flag Revolt, and on June 14 signed a declaration of principles of the Bear Flaggers, asserting independence from Mexican rule and establishing the California Republic. He later served in Fremont's California Battalion. In 1848 he and a Scotsman named Guthrie, travelling from Fort Hall to California, became restless and decided to go ahead of their party. They were attacked by Indians. Their mutilated bodies were found on the trail by the main party.

Fallon is often confused with another self-styled "captain," Thomas Fallon of Santa Cruz and San Jose. Both served in the California Battalion and later their paths crossed frequently at

Sutter's Fort, where their names are occasionally confused in the records of arrivals and departures. Some historians, including Bernard DeVoto in *The Year of Decision* (1943), Eliza Donner Houghton in *The Expedition of the Donner Party and Its Tragic Fate* (1911), and Thomas McEnery in *California Cavalier: The Journal of Captain Thomas Fallon* (1978) erroneously credit Thomas Fallon as the leader of the fourth rescue to the Donner camps.

FALLON'S "JOURNAL"

Of one thing we can be sure: No journal from which the extracts were allegedly taken has ever been found. Surely the person who actually composed them, as measured by his vocabulary, was a sophisticated and educated person: "the supposition was....we searched diligently....he appeared embarrassed and equivocated a great deal....he evinced confusion....with evident reluctance." This is not the language of a rough mountain man. It is quite likely that the *California Star* account was composed by someone in the vicinity of Sutter's Fort. There is reason to suspect Sheriff George McKinstry, a lawyer from Ohio who took a lively interest in the Donner Party. He was, in fact, in possession of Breen's diary and was in charge of Sutter's Fort in Lieutenant Edward Kern's absence, with responsibility to report on rescue operations to American government authorities. McKinstry later published a highly edited and grossly inaccurate transcription of Breen's diary. That McKinstry enjoyed the scurrilous is evidenced in a note he wrote to Kern from Sacramento on March 4, 1847, when Kern was on the rescue mission: "I advise you both [*i.e., Kern and Woodworth*] to look out for those Man eating Women, from what I can learn from Glover they prefer that kind of meat in larger than Nine inch pieces too" (Eberstadt, *A Transcription of the Fort Sutter Papers*, MS No. 115, McKinstry's underscoring).

The introductory comment that the journal was being published in Fallon's "own language" cannot be taken seriously. Whoever actually wrote the extracts did not seem familiar with Fallon's first name, nor with the spelling of the surname. On the two signatures I have seen, the mountaineer spells his name "Fallon."

Nevertheless, the world was prepared to believe almost anything about the Donner Party by the time the lengthy extracts from the alleged journal of "Captain Fellun" appeared in the *California Star*. The journal was generally accepted as fact until McGlashan began research on the Donner Party in the late 1870s. McGlashan doubted its credibility, as did historian Hubert H. Bancroft. Yet it must be dealt with, because it has been accepted as fact in large part by both Thornton and Stewart.

Stewart restored the Fallon journal to credibility. He granted that the journal as it appeared in the *Star* is "almost the only original source," but adds that "such good judges as Bryant [*What I Saw in California*] and Thornton accepted it at face value." He says further that Foster and Tucker of the fourth relief gave it their "tacit support," which means very little. In 1879, McGlashan said that "Captain Tucker is about the only available witness and his testimony is far more lenient than the rumors and falsehoods usually published."

GENERAL KEARNY'S CLEAN-UP

On June 22, General S.W. Kearny, who was leading an expedition back to the East and who had William O. Fallon with him as guide, paused long enough at the mountain camps to do a hurried and incomplete clean up job, burying the bodies and parts.

THE DONNER MONEY

What happened to the money of the Donner brothers? James F. Reed was reported to have taken several hundred dollars in trust, to carry with him to the settlements after he was expelled from the company. The Fallon relief party claimed to have found only a few hundred of the more than ten thousand dollars that the Donner brothers were carrying with them. Did they actually find more? Did earlier rescuers, such as Stone, Cady, and Clark, carry some of it away and not report it? Was the largest part cached by Tamsen Donner and never found? How does one explain the following curious entry for Saturday, May 29, 1847, a month after the fourth and last relief, in a ledger of arrivals and departures kept at Sutter's

Fort? – "O Fallen arrived back again from the mountains." What was Fallon doing there in the Donner camps by himself?

Fallon and Ned Coffeemire of the fourth rescue had spread lurid tales about the Donner Party in general and about Lewis Keseberg in particular. Ned Coffeemire was telling people that Keseberg had murdered Tamsen Donner and also, possibly, Mr. Wolfinger. At Captain Sutter's suggestion, Keseberg sued for defamation in the court of John Sinclair, Justice of the Peace ("Keseberg vs Coffymere - Action for Defamation of Character. Damages $1,000. May 5, 1847"). Only a very small part of the record of the litigation survives, on a single sheet of paper. It notes that Mrs. Wolfinger was called as a witness for Keseberg. Everybody in the jury was doubtless acquainted with the blood-curdling newspaper accounts about this demonic "foreigner." Nevertheless, the jury agreed that Keseberg had been defamed, although they awarded him a judgment of only $1, not the $1,000 he demanded.

Perhaps it is best to let Keseberg tell his own story, the subject of the next chapter.

Chapter 12

KESEBERG SPEAKS FOR HIMSELF

In the ensuing years Keseberg was almost universally vilified, but a few people believed that he had been unfairly maligned. One of them was Eliza Donner Houghton, daughter of George and Tamsen Donner. Although only three years old at the time of the entrapment, she later did considerable research. In the late 1870s, having convinced herself that Keseberg was not a murderer, she brought her concerns to the attention of C.F. McGlashan, who was publishing articles about the Donner Party in his Truckee newspaper and preparing a book on the subject. They sought out and interviewed Lewis Keseberg himself. McGlashan became convinced, along with Eliza, that Keseberg did not murder Tamsen Donner.

McGlashan interviewed Keseberg for the first time on April 4, 1879. He urged Keseberg to make a statement in writing, which Keseberg was at first reluctant to do. "What is the use," he said, "of my making a statement? People incline to believe the most horrible reports concerning a man, and they will not credit what I say in my own defense. My conscience is clear. I am an old man, and am calmly awaiting my death. God is my judge, and it long ago ceased to trouble me that people shunned and slandered me."

Keseberg finally prepared the statement, which is quoted here almost in its entirety, from McGlashan's *History of the Donner Party* (1880):

My name is Lewis Keseberg. I was born in the city of Berleburg, Province of Westphalia, in the Kingdom of Prussia, on the twenty-second of May, 1814. I am therefore almost sixty-three years of age. I was married June 22, 1842, came to the United States May 22, 1844, and emigrated to

California in 1846 with the Donner Party. I never have made a statement concerning my connection with that Party to any one connected with the press. It is with the utmost horror that I revert to the scenes of suffering and unutterable misery endured during that journey. I have always endeavored to put away from me all thoughts or recollections of those terrible events. Time is the best physician, and would, I trusted, heal the wounds produced by those days of torture; yet my mind to-day recoils with undiminished horror as I endeavor to speak of this dreadful subject. Heretofore I have never attempted to refute the villainous slanders which have been circulated and published about me. I feel it my duty to make this statement, however, because I am convinced of your willingness to do justice to all who were concerned in that dreadful affair, and heretofore I have been treated with gross injustice.

If I believe in God Almighty having anything to do with the affairs of men, I believe that the misfortune which overtook the Donner Party, and the terrible part I was compelled to take in the great tragedy, was predestined. On the Hastings Cut-off we were twenty-eight days in going twenty-one miles. Difficulty and disaster hovered about us from the time we entered this cut-off.

One day, while we were travelling on Goose Creek, we saw so many wild geese that I took my shotgun and went hunting. Ordinarily I am not superstitious, but on this morning I felt an overwhelming sense of impending calamity. I mentioned my premonitions to Mrs. Murphy before starting on the hunt. Becoming excited with the sport, and eagerly watching the game, I stepped down a steep bank. Some willows had been burned off, and the short, sharp stubs were sticking up just where I stepped. I had on buckskin moccasins, and one of these stubs ran into the ball of my foot, between the bones and the toes. From this time, until we arrived at Donner Lake, I was unable to walk, or even to put my foot to the ground. The foot became greatly swollen and inflamed, and was exceedingly painful. One day, at Donner Lake, one of my companions, at my earnest request, lanced my foot on the top. It discharged freely, and some days afterwards, in washing it, I found a hard substance protruding from the wound, and obtaining a pair of forceps, succeeded in extracting a piece of the willow stub, one and a half inches in length. It had literally worked up through my foot. I mention this particularly, because I have been frequently accused of remaining at the Donner cabins from selfish or sinister motives, when in fact I was utterly unable to join the relief parties.

When we reached the lake, we lost our road, and owing to the depth of the snow on the mountains, were compelled to abandon our wagons, and pack our goods upon oxen. The cattle, unused to such burdens, caused great delay by 'bucking' and wallowing in the snow. There was also much confusion as to what articles should be taken and what abandoned. One wanted a box of tobacco carried along; another, a bale of calico, and some one thing and some another. But for this delay we would have passed the summit and pressed forward to California. Owing to my lameness, I was placed on horseback, and my foot was tied up to the saddle in a sort of sling. Near evening we were close to the top of the dividing ridge. It was cold and chilly, and everybody was tired with the severe exertions of the day. Some of the emigrants sat down to rest, and declared they could go no farther. I begged them for God's sake to get over the ridge before halting. Some one, however, set fire to a pitchy pine tree, and the flames soon ascended to its topmost branches. The women and children gathered about this fire to warm themselves. Meantime the oxen were rubbing off their packs against the trees. The weather looked very threatening, and I exhorted them to go on until the summit was reached. I foresaw the danger plainly and unmistakably. Only the strongest men, however, could go ahead and break the road, and it would have taken a determined man to induce the party to leave the fire. Had I been well, and been able to push ahead over the ridge, some, if not all, would have followed. As it was, all lay down on the snow, and from exhaustion were soon asleep. In the night, I felt something impeding my breath. A heavy weight seemed to be resting upon me. Springing up to a sitting posture, I found myself covered with freshly-fallen snow. The camp, the cattle, my companions, had all disappeared. All I could see was snow everywhere. I shouted at the top of my voice. Suddenly, here and there, all about me, heads popped up through the snow. The scene was not unlike what one might imagine at the resurrection, when people rise up out of the earth. The terror amounted to a panic. The mules were lost, the cattle strayed away, and our further progress rendered impossible. The rest you probably know. We returned to the lake, and prepared, as best we could, for the winter. I was unable to build a cabin, because of my lameness, and so erected a sort of brush shed against one side of the Breen's cabin.

When Reed's relief party left the cabins, Mr. Reed left me a half teacupful of flour, and about half a pound of jerked beef. It was all he could give. Mrs. Murphy, who was left with me, because too weak and emaciated to walk, had no larger portion. Reed had no animosity toward me. He found me too weak to move. He washed me, combed my hair, and treated me kindly. Indeed, he had no cause to do otherwise. Some of my portion of the flour brought by Stanton from Sutter's Fort I gave to Reed's children, and thus saved their lives. When he left me, he promised to return in two weeks and carry me over the mountains. When this party left, I was not able to stand, much less to walk.

A heavy storm came on in a few days after the last relief party left. Mrs. George Donner had remained with her sick husband in their camp, six or seven miles away. Mrs. Murphy lived about a week after we were left alone. When my provisions gave out, I remained four days before I could taste human flesh. There was no other resort – it was that or death. My wife and child had gone on with the first relief party. I knew not whether they were living or dead. They were penniless and friendless in a strange land. For their sakes I must live, if not for my own. Mrs. Murphy was too weak to revive. The flesh of starved beings contains little nutriment. It is like feeding straw to horses. I can not describe the unutterable repugnance with which I tasted the first mouthful of flesh. There is an instinct in our nature that revolts at the thought of touching, much less eating, a corpse. It makes my blood curdle to think of it! It has been told that I boasted of my shame – said that I enjoyed this horrid food, and that I remarked that human flesh was more palatable than California beef. This is a falsehood. It is a horrible, revolting falsehood. This food was never otherwise than loathsome, insipid, and disgusting. For nearly two months I was alone in that dismal cabin. No one knows what occurred but myself – no living being ever before was told of the occurrences. Life was a burden. The horrors of one day succeeded those of the preceding. Five of my companions had died in my cabin, and their stark and ghastly bodies lay there day and night, seemingly gazing at me with their glazed and staring eyes. I was too weak to move them had I tried. The relief parties had not removed them. These parties had been too hurried, too horror-stricken at the sight, too fearful lest an hour's delay might cause them to share the same fate. I endured a thousand deaths. To have one's suffering prolonged inch by inch, to be deserted, forsaken, hopeless; to see that loathsome food ever before my eyes, was almost too much for human endurance. I am conversant with four different languages. I speak and write them with equal fluency; yet in all four I do not find words enough to express the horror I experienced during those two months, or what I still feel when memory reverts to the scene. Suicide would have been a relief, a happiness, a godsend! Many a time I had the muzzle of my pistol in my mouth and my finger on the trigger, but the faces of my helpless, dependent wife and child would rise up before me, and my hand would fall powerless. I was not the cause of my misfortunes, and God Almighty had provided only this one horrible way for me to subsist.

[McGlashan's question: Did you boil the flesh?]

Yes! But to go into details – to relate the minutiae – is too agonizing! I can not do it! Imagination can supply these. The necessary mutilation of the bodies of those who had been my friends, rendered the ghastliness of my situation more frightful. When I could crawl about and my lame foot was partially recovered, I was chopping some wood one day and the ax glanced and cut off my heel. The piece of flesh grew back in time, but not in its former position, and my foot is maimed to this day.

A man, before he judges me, should be placed in a similar situation; but if he were, it is a thousand to one he would perish. A constitution of steel alone could endure the deprivation and misery. At this time I was living in the log-cabin with the fireplace. One night I was awakened by a scratching sound over my head. I started up in terror, and listened intently for the noise to be repeated. It came again. It was the wolves trying to get into the cabin to eat me and the dead bodies.

At midnight, one cold, bitter night, Mrs. George Donner came to my door. It was about two weeks after Reed had gone, and my loneliness was beginning to be unendurable. I was most happy to hear the sound of a human voice. Her coming was like that of an angel from heaven. But she had not come to bear me company. Her husband had died in her arms. She had remained by his side until death came, and then had laid him out and hurried away. He died at nightfall, and she had traveled over the snow alone to my cabin. She was going, alone, across the mountains. She was going to start without food or guide. She kept saying, 'My children! I must see my children!' She feared she would not survive, and told me she had some money in her tent. It was too heavy for her to carry. She said, 'Mr. Keseberg, I confide this to your care.' She made me promise sacredly that I would get the money and take it to her children in case she perished and I survived. She declared she would start over the mountains in the morning. She said, 'I am bound to go to my children.' She seemed very cold, and her clothes were like ice. I think she had got in the creek in coming. She said she was very hungry, but refused the only food I could offer. She had never eaten the loathsome flesh. She finally lay down, and I spread a feather-bed and some blankets over her. In the morning she was dead. I think the hunger, the mental suffering, and the icy chill of the preceding night, caused her death. I have often been accused of taking her life. Before my God, I swear this is untrue! Do you think a man would be such a miscreant, such a damnable fiend, such a caricature on humanity, as to kill this lone woman? There were plenty of corpses lying around. He would only add one more corpse to the many!

Oh! the days and weeks of horror which I passed in that camp! I had no hope of help or of being rescued, until I saw the green grass coming up by the spring on the hillside, and the wild geese coming to nibble it. The birds were coming back to their breeding grounds, and I felt that I could kill them for food. I also had plenty of tobacco and a good meerschaum pipe, and almost the only solace I enjoyed was smoking. In my weak condition it took me two or three hours every day to get sufficient wood to keep my fire going.

Some time after Mrs. Donner's death, I thought I had gained sufficient strength to redeem the pledge I had made her before her death. I started to go to the camps at Alder Creek to get the money. I had a very difficult journey. The wagons of the Donners were loaded with tobacco, powder, caps, shoes, school-books, and dry-goods. This stock was very valuable, and had it reached California, would have been a fortune to the Donners. I searched carefully among the bales and bundles of goods, and found five hundred and thirty-one dollars. Part of this sum was silver, part gold. The silver I buried at the foot of a pine tree, a little way from the camp. One of the lower branches of another tree reached down close to the ground, and appeared to point to the spot. I put the gold in my pocket, and started to return to my cabin. I had spent one night at the Donner tents. On my return I became lost. When it was nearly dark, in crossing a little flat, the snow suddenly gave way under my feet, and I sank down almost to my armpits. By means of the crust on top of the snow, I kept myself suspended by throwing out my arms. A stream of water flowed underneath the place over which I had been walking, and the snow had melted on the underside until it was not strong enough to support my weight. I could not touch bottom with my feet, and so could form no idea of the depth of the stream. By long and careful exertion I managed to draw myself backward and up on the snow. I then went around on the hillside, and continued my journey. At last, just at dark, completely exhausted and almost dead, I came in sight of the Graves cabin. I shall never forget my joy at sight of that log-cabin. I felt that I was no longer lost, and would at least have shelter. Some time after dark I reached my own cabin. My clothes were wet by getting in the creek, and the night was so cold that my garments were frozen into sheets of ice. I was so weary, and chilled, and numbed, that I did not build up a fire, or attempt to get anything to eat, but rolled myself up in the bed-clothes and tried to get warm. Nearly all night I lay there shivering with cold; and when I finally slept, I slept very soundly. I did not wake up until quite late in the next morning. To my utter astonishment my camp was in the most inexplicable confusion. My trunks were broken open, and their contents were scattered everywhere. Everything about the cabin was torn up and thrown about the floor. My wife's jewelry, my cloak, my pistol and ammunition were missing. I supposed Indians had robbed my camp during my absence. Suddenly I was startled by the sound of human voices. I hurried up to the surface of the snow, and saw white men coming toward the cabin. I was overwhelmed with joy and gratitude at the prospect of my deliverance. I had suffered so much, and for so long a time, that I could scarcely believe my senses. Imagine my astonishment upon their arrival to be greeted, not with a 'good morning' or a kind word, but with the gruff, insolent demand, 'Where is Donner's money?'

I told them they ought to give me something to eat, and that I would talk with them afterwards, but no, they insisted that I should tell them about Donner's money. I asked them who they were, and where they came from, but they replied by threatening to kill me if I did not give up the money. They threatened to hang or shoot me, and at last I told them. I had promised Mrs. Donner that I would carry her money to her children, and I proposed to do so, unless shown some authority by which they had a better claim. This so exasperated them, that they acted as though they were going to kill me. I offered to let them bind me as a prisoner, and take me before the alcalde at Sutter's Fort, and I promised that I would then tell all I knew about the money. They would listen to nothing, however, and finally I told them where they would find the silver buried, and gave them the gold. After I had done this, they showed me a document from Alcalde Sinclair, by which they were to receive a certain proportion of all moneys and property which they rescued.

These men treated me with the greatest unkindness. Mr. Tucker was the only one who took my part or befriended me. When they started over the mountains, each man carried two bales of goods. They had silks, calicoes, and delaines from the Donners, and other articles of great value. Each man would carry one bundle a little way, lay it down, and come back and get the other bundle. In this way they passed over the snow three times. I could not keep up with them because I was so weak, but managed to come up to their camp every night. One day I was dragging myself slowly along behind the party, when I came to a place which had evidently been used as a camping-ground by some of the previous parties. Feeling very tired, I thought it would be a good place to make some coffee. Kindling a fire, I filled my coffee-pot with fresh snow and sat waiting for it to melt and get hot. Happening to case my eyes carelessly around, I discovered a little piece of calico protruding from the snow. Half thoughtlessly, half out of idle curiosity, I caught hold of the cloth, and finding it did not come readily, I gave it a strong pull. I had in my hands the body of my dead child Ada! She had been buried in the snow, which, melting down, had disclosed a portion of her clothing. I thought I should go frantic! It was the first intimation I had of her death, and it came with such a shock!

Just as we were getting out of the snow, I happened to be sitting in camp alone one afternoon. The men were hunting, or attending to their goods. I was congratulating myself upon my escape from the mountains, when I was startled by a snuffling, growling noise, and looking up, I saw a large grizzly bear only a few feet away. I knew I was too weak to attempt to escape, and so remained where I sat, expecting every moment he would devour me. Suddenly there was the report of a gun, and the bear fell dead. Mr. Foster had discovered the animal, and slipping up close to camp, had killed it.

I have been born under an evil star! Fate, misfortune, bad luck, compelled me to remain at Donner Lake. If God would decree that I should again pass through such an ordeal, I could not do otherwise than I did. My conscience is free from reproach. Yet that camp has been the one burden of my life. Wherever I have gone, people have cried, 'Stone him! stone him!' Even the little children in the streets have mocked me and thrown stones at me as I passed. Only a man conscious of his innocence, and clear in the sight of God, would not have succumbed to the terrible things which have been said of me – would not have committed suicide! Mortification, disgrace, disaster, and unheard-of misfortune have followed and overwhelmed me. I often think that the Almighty has singled me out, among all the men on the face of the earth, in order to see how much hardship, suffering, and misery a human being can bear!"

Keseberg's statement continues with an account of his life after he arrived at Sutter's Fort. Captain Sutter, who had urged Keseberg to sue for defamation, befriended him and gave him employment for seven months, for which Sutter was unable to pay him. Keseberg went to Sonoma and worked for General Vallejo, who also trusted him. Later, he returned to Sutter's Fort to open a boarding house, and in 1851 he became proprietor of Sacramento's Lady Adams Hotel (leading to such bad jokes as, "Keseberg made only one mistake, he opened a restaurant!"). The following year he sold the hotel at auction, but it burned down before the transaction could be completed. He returned to Sutter's Fort and built a brewery. In this venture he was almost successful, getting an offer of fifty thousand dollars for the property. But there was more bad luck. Before the paperwork on the deal was completed, the great flood of 1861-62 destroyed everything. He was a partner of famous pioneer entrepreneur Sam Brannan in a distillery at Calistoga. Brannan spoke highly of Keseberg's honesty and business ability.

Heinrich Lienhard, a Swiss emigrant of 1846 (Hastings Party), became friends with Lewis and Philippine Keseberg at Sutter's Fort, and for a short time they rented a shack on Lienhard's sheep ranch near the fort. In his published memoirs, Lienhard gave this description of Keseberg:

....a tall, intelligent man of military bearing, a Prussian...who had served with the infantry. He also said he had once been a travelling salesman for a business firm, had often visited Paris, and spoke French and German fluently. Considering the short time he had been in America, his English was excellent; he also understood and could speak a few words of Spanish. Keseberg's greatest weakness was his unbridled temper, and one day he confessed that it was the source of considerable embarrassment to him. After his anger had subsided, he always realized his mistake and was extremely penitent. He gave every indication of being an honorable person; I preferred him to many men who had not been accused of having eaten human beings. His residence at the sheep ranch was a brief one lasting only a month or two. While he was there he often suffered from cold and fever, and at such times was restless and irritable.

Lienhard said that Keseberg was an expert hunter. Often wild goose was on his table, "cooked in the French manner, and was so underdone that the blood ran out when the bird was carved." Lienhard described Mrs. Keseberg as a "buxom young woman some twenty-three years of age [who] had several admirers," adding that "her husband, who was frequently away from home for a month or more, was unaware of her flirtations." This report may be mere idle gossip. The journals of Sutter's clerks often list Mrs. Keseberg as a passenger on the schooner her husband navigated to San Francisco.

Lewis Keseberg, 1879

Lienhard listened as Keseberg told him the story of his Donner Party experiences. He believed him and concluded that Keseberg "was the victim of tragic circumstances."

THE KESEBERG GENEALOGY

Joseph Pigney did considerable genealogical research on the Keseberg family for his book *For Fear We Shall Perish*. Lewis Keseberg was born Johann Ludwig Christian Keseberg on May 22, 1814 at Berleburg, Germany, the son of Friedrich Ernst Keseberg, pastor of the State Protestant (Lutheran) Church, and Juliane Ludevike von Asmuth, daughter of the noble-born Johann Ludwig von Asmuth of Stuthutte.

Westphalia was one of the strongholds of Catholicism, wrote Pigney. Keseberg married a Catholic girl, Elisabeth Philippine Zimmerman (born May 16, 1823), daughter of Christian Zimmerman and Elisabeth Kieseler. Zimmerman was a well-to-do member of one of the princely families. The marriage ceremony took place in the State Protestant Church at Berleburg on July 22, 1842. Possibly because Keseberg's wife was shunned by the Catholic community of relatives and former friends, the Kesebergs decided to emigrate, arriving in the United States on May 22, 1844, Keseberg's thirtieth birthday.

Pigney gives the following data on the eight Keseberg children born in California:

(1) *Amelia*, born October 18, 1848 at Sutter's Fort; married Richard Koenig late in 1869; children: Edna and Hulda; died giving birth to Hulda on March 12, 1873; (2) *Lilly*, born late in 1850; married Mathias Johnson in March 1869; died at San Rafael in 1880; (3) *Paulina*, born February 12, 1854; lived in San Rafael for a while but returned to Brighton, Sacramento County, in 1880; died of cancer on December 19, 1881; buried in New Helvetia Cemetery; (4) *Julia*, born January 9, 1855; married George F. Hartmeyer in May 1873; died July 17, 1877 in Sacramento; her son, Charles Hartmeyer, was a longtime gardener at Sutter's Fort; (5) *Matilda*, born November 1, 1857; married Frederick Kummerfeldt on March 16, 1873; died February 1874, two months after the birth of a daughter, Clara Matilda, who died in November 1874; (6) *Bertha*, born during the summer of 1859; epileptic with severe mental retardation; died 1880; (7) *Ida*, born December 8, 1861; died June 8, 1862; (8) *Augusta*, born August 10, 1863; mentally retarded and epileptic, like her sister Bertha; died April 26, 1889 in a convulsion.

Pigney notes that Mrs. Keseberg died January 30, 1877 of pneumonia, in Brighton, Sacramento County. Lilly and Paulina came from San Rafael for the funeral. Julia was living in Sacramento at the time. By 1879, when McGlashan interviewed Keseberg, only four of the girls were alive and none had long to live. Two were subject to fits and often were uncontrollable. Keseberg in his final years was poor and mostly unemployed. On September 3, 1895, at age eighty-one, he died in Sacramento County Hospital, leaving "no special message for anyone," said the hospital superintendent. In the notes to his novel *Wheels West* (1955), Homer Croy cites a document he located in the records of the county hospital:

Hospital Number	*11029*
Name	*Lewis Keseberg*
Nativity	*German*
Age	*80*
Sex	*Male*
Occupation	*Brewer*
When admitted	*June 7, 1892*
Disease	*[blank]*
When discharged	*September 3, 1895*
How discharged	*died*
Remarks	*A last survivor of the Donner Party*

Mr. Croy could find no obituary in the Sacramento newspapers, nor a place of burial.

In an appendix to *Ordeal by Hunger*, Stewart purports to examine fairly all the charges against Keseberg, the whole spectrum of offenses ranging from abandoning Hardcoop to murdering Tamsen Donner, George Foster, Mrs. Murphy, and Mr. Wolfinger. Stewart granted that there was no evidence that Keseberg murdered Wolfinger and that a few of the other charges were unlikely. In the final analysis, however, he says that "human testimony [is] always liable to err and become confused, but seldom [is] likely to be completely fabricated." Thus Keseberg is damned again, without evidence.

Like McGlashan and Bancroft, I find Keseberg's testimony much more credible than that of Captain Fallon and the sensational Thornton. In a long letter to McGlashan in 1879, John Breen wrote: "When I left the cabins [March 3] Keseberg had not eaten human flesh. I had not heard such a thing mentioned." Virginia Reed also remembered the Kesebergs. "Poor Mrs. Keseberg," she wrote McGlashan, "was a pretty little woman, very humble and unassuming." Virginia remembered that Mrs. Keseberg seemed to be proud of her husband although he treated her "like a brute."

The opinion has been advanced by Jeannette G. Maino (*Left Hand Turn: A Story of the Donner Party Women*), that Keseberg was insane. Her opinion is based on the experiences of surgeon Dr. Victor Fourgeaud, who twice booked passage for San Francisco with his family on Sutter's launch *Sacramento*, captained by Keseberg. Fourgeaud's story, as told to Dr. John Lyman and reported by Lyman in the *California Quarterly* (Vol. XI, No. 2), reads as follows:

He [Keseberg] couldn't forget that orgy of flesh....It was a nightmare that exerted a terrible fascination....Sometimes at night Dr. Fourgeaud would overhear him telling the crew of his horrible repasts, describing in minute detail the delicacy of what he considered the choicest bits. Hands with long fingers seemed to be favorite portions....sometimes he screamed in his sleep. Blood curdling yells would awake the doctor. The babbling kept the passengers awake.

One wonders how much trust can be placed in such a report. If Keseberg behaved as described by Fourgeaud, why did Sutter, a good businessman, continue to employ him? How could Keseberg have succeeded in his several business ventures (until calamities not of his making occurred) if he were insane? Why would Sam Brannan, a sharp businessman, take a crazy man as a partner? A daily journal kept by Captain Sutter and his clerks reveals that Sutter entrusted Keseberg with the captaincy of his launch on the San Francisco runs with a crew of as many as four, full cargoes of three hundred fanegas (about seven hundred and seventy-three English bushels) of wheat, and as many as seven passengers. In fact, on July 13, 1847, the *Sacramento* departed with William Foster and his wife. William and Sarah Foster, let us recall, were both members of the Donner Party, and William accompanied Captain Fallon on the fourth relief that brought out Keseberg.

Would the Fosters allow themselves to be navigated by a madman? Would Dr. Fourgeaud risk the lives of his family with such a person at the helm? On September 24, 1847, the vessel arrived at Sacramento under Keseberg's command with "Mr. Rhodes and his wife" among other passengers. John Rhodes (Rhoads) was a member of the first relief, Daniel of the first and fourth reliefs.

The testimony that Keseberg gave McGlashan in writing is not among the McGlashan Papers at the Bancroft Library. What I have quoted of it is from McGlashan's *History of the Donner Party*. Some of it appears to be what McGlashan elicited from Keseberg during a personal interview. During one interview with McGlashan, Keseberg answered the charge that he had indirectly caused the death of Mr. Hardcoop on the trail in Nevada. Keseberg said that he, his wife, and two children were afoot or being carried, just as everybody else was. He expected Hardcoop to walk too.

Nevertheless, there was no end to lurid stories about Keseberg and to the public humiliation of the man. Yarns were told by people who posed as members of the Donner company or the relief missions. An informant of mine told me that her grandmother, raised in Calistoga, recalled children taunting Keseberg in the streets.

A fine tribute to Lewis Keseberg came from Hubert H. Bancroft:

He [Keseberg] was a man of intelligence, good education, and much business ability; and his record in California except as affected by suspicions growing out of the affair of '46 was a good one....It is fair to state that the charges by Captain Fallon rest on no tangible evidence, and that Keseberg is entitled to be regarded as an unfortunate victim. [*History of California*, vol. IV, "Pioneer Register and Index"]

Chapter 13

SURVIVORS AND CASUALTIES

FIGURES ON CASUALTIES

Details not in Breen's diary have been filled in by memoirs of survivors and descendants of survivors, and by a host of books and articles about this most famous of overland parties to California. The only two families to survive intact were the nine Breens and six Reeds, both with Irish-born household heads. It is known that of the eighty-one persons – twenty-five men, fifteen women, and forty-one children – who reached the Donner and Alder Creek camps, over two-thirds of the men perished, most of them during the first two months of the entrapment. (The single adult men tended to die first.) About one-third of the children died, mostly in the beginning and middle of the entrapment, and boys in the highest ratio. About one-fourth of the women died, mostly toward the end of the ordeal.

Also very startling are the figures on the bachelors and a few other males without blood ties to families in the Donner company. Of fourteen men in this category who reached the high camps, twelve perished, only Noah James and John Baptiste Trudeau surviving. Prior to reaching the high camps, three men in this category perished: Halloran, Snyder, and Hardcoop.

Still alive in 1920, among the eighty-seven people of the original Donner Party, were eight of the women, no men. They were four of the Donners (Leanna App, Elitha Wilder, Frances Wilder, and Eliza Houghton), two Reeds (Martha Lewis and Virginia Murphy), Naomi Pike Schenck, and Isabella Breen McMahon, the last survivor, who died in San Francisco in 1935.

THE SURVIVORS (age of those under 18 given in parenthesis)

Those who left the train early: Walter Herron and William McCutchen. (Hiram Miller left before the party reached the Little Sandy.)

One who was banished: James F. Reed.

Those who survived the Snowshoe Party in December: William H. Eddy, William Foster, Sarah Murphy Foster, Sarah Graves Fosdick, Mary Graves, Amanda McCutchen, Harriet Murphy Pike.

Those brought out alive by the first relief expedition in February 1847: Edward Breen. (13), Simon Breen (9), George Donner Jr. (9), Elitha Donner (14), Leanna Donner (12), William Graves, Lovina Graves (13), Eleanor Graves (15), Noah James, Mrs. Philippine Keseberg, Mary Murphy (13), William Murphy (11), Naomi Pike (3), Mrs. Margaret Reed, James Reed Jr. (5), Virginia Reed (12), Doriss Wolfinger, Eliza Williams.

Those brought out alive by the second relief expedition in early March: Thomas Reed (3) Martha (Patty) Reed (8), Solomon Hook (14).

Those brought out alive from Starved Camp by one section of the third relief in mid-March: Patrick Breen, Margaret Breen, John Breen (15), Patrick Breen Jr. (11), Peter Breen (7), James Breen (5), Isabella Breen (1), Mary Donner (7), Jonathan Graves (7), Nancy Graves (9), Elizabeth Graves (1, but died at Sutter's Fort).

Those brought out alive from the high camps by another section of the third relief in mid-March: Eliza Donner (3), Frances Donner (6), Simon Murphy (10), John Baptiste Trudeau.

Survivor of the fourth relief in mid-April: Lewis Keseberg.

THE CASUALTIES

On the trail: Luke Halloran, Mr. Hardcoop, William N. Pike, John Snyder, Mr. Wolfinger.

At the camps in December: Charles Burger, Jacob Donner, Joseph Reinhardt, Samuel Shoemaker, James Smith, Baylis Williams.

With the Snowshow Party in December/January: Antonio, Patrick Dolan, Jay Fosdick, Franklin Graves Sr., Lemuel Murphy (12), Luis and Salvador, Charles Stanton.

At the camps in January and February: Eleanor Eddy, Margaret Eddy (1), Milford Elliott, Lewis Keseberg Jr. (1), Landrum Murphy (15), Harriet McCutchen (1), Catherine Pike (1), Augustus Spitzer.

On the first relief expedition in February: John Denton, William Hook (12), Ada Keseberg (3).

At the camps in March: Elizabeth Donner, George Donner, Tamsen Donner, Lewis Donner (3), Samuel Donner (4), James P. Eddy (3), George Foster (4), Lavinia Murphy.

On the second relief expedition in early March (died at Starved Camp): Isaac Donner (5), Elizabeth Graves, Franklin Ward Graves Jr. (5)

No deaths on the third and fourth relief expeditions.

WILLIAM EDDY

William Eddy had a failed second marriage, to Mrs. P. Alfred at Gilroy in 1848; they were divorced in 1854. Two children were born of this marriage, James and Eleanor (Mrs. S.B. Anderson), who were living in San Jose in 1880. Eddy took a third wife in 1856, Miss A.H. Pardee. He died at Petaluma on December 24, 1859, apparently still indebted to the estate of George Donner for one silk handkerchief ($1), one blanket/overcoat ($10), and one "plain Casinet pants" ($6); and to the estate of Jacob Donner for eighteen yards of calico ($1.12½), one pair of shoes ($1), one pair of boots ($3), and two yards "domestic" ($1). (See "Sutter's Fort Documents Collection: Reed Family," files 422 and 423.)

THE REEDS

A biographical sketch of James Frazier Reed is given by John Carroll Power in *History of the Early Settlers of Sangamon*

County, Illinois (1876). According to the sketch, Reed was
born November 14, 1800 in County Armagh, Ireland; his
paternal ancestors were of "noble Polish birth" and the original
name was "Reednoski"; his mother was a Frazier of Clan
Frazier, Scotland; he was brought to America by his mother;
they settled in Virginia; at age twenty he left for the lead mines
of Illinois where he remained until 1831 when he came to
Springfield. His name appears with those of Abraham Lincoln
and Stephen O. Douglas on the muster roll of the Springfield
Militia that served in the Black Hawk War.

Like Eddy, Reed lost almost all his worldly possessions on
the trail east of the Sierras. But his wife and four children survived. Reed settled in San Jose, where he quickly succeeded in
business and political office.

Reed was a complex man – proud, brave, intelligent, energetic, and extremely loyal to family and friends. He was also
rash, acquisitive, deceitful, and quite capable of using questionable and even illegal means to achieve his ends. He forged
the signatures of members of his family and his servants on petitions for San Francisco properties, when they were at the
time entrapped in the mountains. He may also have forged
other documents (see Appendix E). He repeatedly lied in his
published accounts about the real reason he left the Donner
Party in Nevada. In fact, as late as 1872, in a legal deposition,
he said,

About the 17th of October, 1846, fearing that we should be late in getting in,
and chiefly with a view to get in ahead to California and send relief to the
Company if they should be overtaken by snows, about 60 miles from the old
sink of Humbolt River, I left the Company, distant from the old Sutter's Fort
about 300 miles, which I traveled mostly alone....

Nevertheless, his killing of Snyder was well known and
made Reed a feared man. That reputation no doubt made it
easier for him to serve in late 1846 as guardian of Mission
property at San Jose, later as sheriff of the District of Sonoma
(to which position he was appointed in June 1847), then custodian (again) of property at Mission San Jose, at the same time
acquiring much property in and near the mission and becoming
a highly successful producer of figs, pears, and apples.

James Frazier Reed and Margaret Reed. They and their four children were survivors of the Donner Party.

Virginia Reed Murphy, 1880.   Martha (Patty) Reed, 1854.

William McCutchen, 1880

Nicholas Clark, 1879

William C. Graves, 1879

Mary A. Graves Clark, 1879

Eliza P. Donner Houghton, about 1879

Georgia Donner Babcock, 1879

Photo engravings for C.F. McGlashan's *History of the Donner Party* (1880)

Reed served as a member of the first town council of San Jose in 1851 and as chief of police. He gave active support to the construction of a Methodist seminary that was to become the College of the Pacific, established first in San Jose, then moved to Stockton.

By 1851 in San Jose, the Reeds had two more children, Charles and William. Margaret Reed died in 1861, and James Frazier Reed in 1874.

Virginia Reed wrote with delight to a cousin back East about receiving, at age thirteen, her first proposal. It came from Perry McCoon, a ferryboat operator, as soon as she was brought out of the mountains, but she spurned the offer in favor of some schooling. Her stepfather, as staunch a Freemason in San Jose as he had been in Springfield, Illinois, was unhappy when Virginia announced her intention to marry Catholic John Murphy in January 1850 and become a Catholic herself. "I'll kill John Murphy," he roared, according to a family report. Perhaps Reed was disturbed as much by the fact that Murphy had had a marriage of sorts to an Indian girl in the gold fields, as he was by Murphy's "popery." Virginia and John eloped, and found refuge from Reed at Mission Santa Clara. Virginia, who was sixteen at the time, later wrote McGlashan (folder 48, bound letters, McGlashan Papers, Bancroft Library) that she was born on June 18, 1833, and married on January 26, 1850. "I was married twice," she wrote, "first by the Lieutenant Governor John McDougal, and then again in the Catholic Church." Reed forgave all when Virginia presented him with his first grandchild. The couple settled in San Jose and had nine children.

Martha J. (Patty) Reed married Frank Lewis at Santa Cruz on December 25, 1856, and they had eight children. She became one of McGlashan's valuable informants and, like her step-sister Virginia, a lifelong friend after he began his research on the Donner Party in 1878. When told she was only eight or nine years old at the time of the ordeal, John Breen wrote McGlashan, "I was under the impression that she was older. She had a wonderful mind for one of her age. She had, I have often thought, as much sense as a grown woman."

Of the other children of James F. and Margaret Reed, Thomas Reed never married; James F. Reed Jr. married Sarah

Adams in San Jose in 1879, and died in 1901 without issue; Charles married Imogene Bergler, and their grandson was Frazier O. Reed of San Jose; William died young.

The Reed's cook, Eliza Williams, found a husband, something of a surprise to Virginia Reed who obviously thought Eliza unmarriageable. A letter Virginia wrote about Eliza's catch appeared in an Illinois newspaper. On September 20, 1847, her father wrote to James W. Keyes in Springfield about Eliza's marriage: "Eliza Williams was married 5 days ago to a German. A fine fellow."

CHILDREN OF GEORGE AND TAMSEN DONNER

These were Frances, Georgia, and Eliza; and, by George's earlier marriage, Elitha and Leanna. From bits and pieces of information, we learn that Georgia and Eliza were taken in by a Swiss couple, Christian and Mary Brunner, at Sutter's Fort. The Brunners moved to Sonoma, and the two Donner girls spent seven years with them there. Meanwhile, their big half-sister Elitha, at age fourteen, married Perry McCoon, who had been rejected by Virginia Reed. Upon McCoon's death in 1853, she married Benjamin W. Wilder of Sacramento County. In 1854, Elitha and her husband gave Georgia and Eliza a home with them. Eliza and her sister Frances, and later Georgia, attended St. Catherine's Academy at Benicia and the public schools of Sacramento.

Leanna Donner, who married John App on September 26, 1852, had three children. Frances Donner, who married William R. Wilder on November 24, 1858, had five children. Georgia Donner, who married W.A. Babcock on November 4, 1863, had three children. Eliza, who married Sherman O. Houghton on October 10, 1861, had six children.

CHILDREN OF JACOB AND ELIZABETH DONNER

The survivors were George and Mary, and Elizabeth's son by a previous marriage, Solomon Hook. George married Margaret J. Watson on June 8, 1862. They had eight children. Mary married Sherman O. Houghton of San Jose on August 23, 1859. They had one daughter before Mary's death on June 21, 1860. In 1861, Houghton married his late wife's cousin, Eliza Donner.

The orphaned cousins Mary and Frances Donner seem to have lived at least for a time in the household of John and Priscilla Cottell in Santa Clara County. They so appear on the 1852 California State Census, enumerations dated October 19, 1852, p. 148. They are listed as orphans, born in Illinois, ages thirteen and ten.

Solomon Hook worked on the Wolfskill Ranch and was buried at Winters, in a cemetery off Highway 505, west of Davis, California. (No other information given in *Tour Guide Book*, Oregon-California Trails Association, 1991.)

MURPHYS, PIKES, AND FOSTERS

Mrs. Harriet Pike, whose husband was shot and killed accidentally by his brother-in-law, William M. Foster, at Truckee Meadows, married M.C. Nye at Sutter's Fort in 1847, and settled in Marysville. Her daughter Naomi Pike married John L. Schenck. She lived to be the next-to-last Donner Party survivor, dying in 1934 at the age of ninety. Sarah and William M. Foster, whose first child died at the lake camp, had at least five more children. Foster's Bar on the Yuba River was named for William M. Foster.

In June 1847 at the age of thirteen or fourteen, Mary Murphy married William Johnson, co-owner of the ranch which played such an important role in the rescue missions. The marriage was performed by Alcalde John Sinclair, who lived on a ranch across the Sacramento River and about two miles from Sutter's Fort. Shortly before her marriage, she wrote a very sad letter to relatives back east telling of her orphaned status and making it quite clear that she did not want to marry Johnson but had to do so in order to survive. She later wrote of her married life:

For several months I was busy serving to all of Mr. Johnson's wishes – doing his cooking and washing and trying to make a home out of a cattle ranch. I knew he was a crude man and I sometimes overlooked many of his faults; but I could not love a man who abused me with the rest of the ranch hands. He proved to be a drunken sot. Because of that I got in touch with the rest of the family and secured an annulment of my marriage from the church.

One of the problems Mary had with Johnson was that he refused to give up his two Indian squaws. She soon obtained a divorce and married Charles Covillaud, founder of Marysville (which was named after his young wife). According to the research of the Steeds (*The Donner Party Rescue Site: Johnson's Ranch on the Bear River*), Mary began life as a Baptist but was converted to Mormonism, probably in Missouri. After her civil marriage to Covillaud, she wanted to practice Catholicism. This posed an intricate problem for Bishop Eugene O'Connell, newly-appointed Catholic Vicar Apostolic of Northern California. When he arrived in 1861 in Marysville, a town of six thousand people, one-third of whom were Catholic, he was surprised to learn that the town was not named after the Virgin Mary but after the twice-married Mary Murphy Johnson Covillaud. Soon after his arrival, he wrote of his concerns in an amusing letter in which he posed some questions in canon law for his former colleagues at All Hallows College in Dublin, Ireland. In the eyes of the Church was Mary, a non-Catholic at the time of her marriage to Johnson (an Irishman but whose religion was unknown even to Mary), still married to him? Or was she truly married to Covillaud, who was born Catholic but was a Freemason? O'Connell noted that in 1854 the Holy See had communicated validity to marriages between Catholics and Protestants in California, the same as in Holland. In 1863, the Dublin Holy Office wrote O'Connell that the "external forms" of marriage (i.e., presence of the parish priest) could be dispensed with in the case of Mary and Charles. But even before he received the reply, it seems, O'Connell blest the union of Mary and Charles. She became a "very good Catholic and was noted for her universal charity and her interest in the progress of the Church," wrote Father Henry L. Walsh, S.J., in *Hallowed Were the Gold Dust Trails* (1946). Charles became a warm friend of the bishop, but Charles and Mary nevertheless were buried in different graveyards (both died in 1867), Mary in the Catholic cemetery, Charles in the nearby city cemetery. Julia Altrocchi in *The Old California Trail* (1945) wrote that Mary Murphy Covillaud of Marysville was the "ancestress" of author Kathleen Norris.

William G. Murphy attended law school in Missouri, practiced law at Virginia City, Nevada, until 1866, then joined his relatives in Marysville, California, where, in 1880, he held the position of City Attorney. At that time he and his wife had seven children. Simon P. Murphy went back to Tennessee, married, served in the Union Army, and died in 1873, leaving a wife and five children.

GRAVES, FOSDICK

Mary A. Graves married Edward Pyle in May 1847 at Sutter's Fort. A few years later Pyle was lassoed and dragged to death, and his body burned. Not long after, a suspect described as "a Mexican" was apprehended, from whom a confession was obtained after he was hanged and taken down alive a few times, as was the custom. He was then truly hanged, the first person so executed in California under the laws of the United States. In 1851, Mary married J.T. Clarke, a sheepman, and they settled in White River in Tulare County where they raised seven children. In 1887 Mary moved to Visalia in the same county to be near her son, Robert. She died on March 8, 1891, and was buried in Visalia Cemetery in a grave that remained unmarked until a ceremony was held at the grave site in 1991. At the ceremony, local historian Joe Doctor recalled that Mary's grandson, the late Gus Bequette of Visalia, said that he was told by his grandmother that she "ate human flesh for 20 days at one time and 10 days at another time."

Eleanor Graves married William McDonnell in 1849. They had nine children. Eleanor was residing at Knights Valley, Sonoma County, in 1880. Lovina Graves married John Cyrus in 1856 and they had five children. In 1880 they were living in Calistoga, California. Nancy Graves married Reverend R.W. Williamson in 1855. They had at least four children and settled at Los Gatos, Santa Clara County. William C. Graves practiced the blacksmith trade in Calistoga. An articulate man, he lectured back east on the Donner Party and later corresponded with McGlashan. In the late 1870s, he visited McGlashan in Truckee and prepared for him a valuable map indicating the relative locations of the cabins at the lake. He also prepared a lengthy account of the whole Donner saga (MS at Bancroft Library). His letters to McGlashan often tended to be embittered toward members of the party and of the rescue missions (his father, mother, brother, and brother-in-law were cannibalized). Eighteen years of age at the time he escaped the entrapment, William should have been the best of primary sources on the Donner Party, but unfortunately he wrote freely and with alleged authority on events that occurred after he had already left the high camp with the first rescue mission.

WOLFINGER

Mrs. Wolfinger, age about nineteen (if later census records can be believed) when brought out by the first relief in February, 1847, did not remain long without a husband. A June 20, 1847 entry in the journal kept by Captain Sutter and his clerks reads: "Mr. Zins got married with Mrs. Wolfinger." The civil marriage record is also extant:

Territory of Sacramento
Sacramento District

I do hereby certify that on Sunday the twentieth day of June A.D. 1847 George Zins and Doriss Wolfinger both of this District personally appeared before me and by me were lawfully joined together in the Holy Bonds of Matrimony. In witness whereof I have hereunto set my hand and seal this twentieth day of June A.D. 1847.

John Sinclair
Justice of the Peace

George Zins (aka Zinn) was a native of Lorraine, Switzerland, an overland immigrant of 1846, and an employee of Captain Sutter. George and Doriss (aka Doris and Dorothy on the records) set to work building what may have been the first brick house in California, on high ground at Sutterville, below the Sacramento embarcadero. Doriss mixed the mortar and carried the hod, while George laid the brick. They had two children, Rosa and Albert, before Doriss' death in 1861 at Nicolaus in Sutter County.

OTHERS

Big William McCutchen, who joined the Donners at Fort Bridger and who later rode ahead to Sutter's Fort and still later joined the second rescue, lived to old age in San Jose. In 1871, he and James Frazier Reed, also living in San Jose, were very unhappy about an account of the Donner Party by Frances H. McDougall that appeared in the *Pacific Rural Press* on January 21 of that year. McCutchen and Reed seem to have orchestrated their replies so that there would be no contradictions or embarrassments to Reed.

Selim E. Woodworth became very successful. In 1851, he was president of the Vigilance Committee in San Francisco, an organization that took over the reins of the city's government without the consent of the electorate for a few years, lynched four Irish rascals and deported to their native lands a score of others, mostly Irish. Woodworth must have been among those described by Professor James P. Walsh, writing of the "reforming" faction in San Francisco of the 1850s, who were motivated less by a desire to clean up corruption in politics than by their wish to destroy the political support of State Senator David G. Broderick, a Catholic Irishman. "Among those who cried the loudest for law and order," says Walsh, "were men of property who evaded their taxes and others who felt secure enough to negotiate with the city compromise settlements of unpaid taxes and their penalty fines." Woodworth wrote his own eulogistic account of his role in the Donner Party rescue missions for the *Annals of San Francisco* (1854). During the Civil War he achieved the rank of Commodore in the United States Navy. He died in 1870, one of San Francisco's most prominent citizens.

Rescuer John Stark, a native of Indiana, settled in Napa County, where he was sheriff for six years and, in 1852, represented the county in the state legislature. The father of eleven children, he died in 1875 at Calistoga, California, of heart disease, while pitching hay from a wagon.

Hiram O. Miller, who participated in two of the rescue missions, settled in Santa Clara County, where he died in October, 1867. In January 1851, he wrote Reed from Pueblo de los Angeles about gold mining properties he had explored two hundred and thirty miles east of the pueblo, and suggested that Reed come down and take a look before investing.

Rescuer John Rhoads, born in Kentucky in 1818, first settled near Johnson's Ranch and later moved to Sloughhouse in Sacramento County, where he died in 1866.

Rescuer Nicholas Clark, born in Massachusetts in 1816, settled in Honey Lake Valley in Lassen County, California. He was alive in 1885 and was the subject of a long article in the *Truckee Republican* (October 24, 1885) about his career as a sailor, adventurer, and pioneer settler

May 24, 1946 was the occasion of the 100th anniversary luncheon sponsored by the California Pioneers of Santa Clara County, to honor the memory of the Donner company and their rescuers. Breen descendants at the luncheon were Harry J. Breen of Hollister, J. Edwin Breen of King City, Barbara Breen Cornell, Edwina Breen Kump, and William Andrew Breen Jr. Reed descendants present were Frazier O. Reed and Frazier O. Reed II. William Eddy was represented by Virginia L. Eddy, Edyth Eddy Flagg, and James Eddy, and Augustus Spitzer by Pearl Adair Pearson. Descendants of the rescuers included Dr. E.E. Rhoads, grandson of Daniel Rhoads and grandnephew of John Rhoads; and Nancy Scherf and several others whose ancestor was Riley S. Moultry. Harry T. Pyle Jr. and Clyde Arbuckle represented Edward Pyle Sr. and Edward Pyle Jr., both of whom carried supplies from Johnson's Ranch to Mule Springs and Bear Valley.

The Donner Memorial State Park has maintained for the past few years index cards of visitors who are descendants of Donner Party members. Among more than one hundred and fifty cards with names and addresses and genealogical information is one that unfortunately contains no address: "Salvadore - Indian guide killed by Foster/long lost relative found in doing family tree - January 1987 Armando Noriega." Mr. Noriega added that "Salvadore['s] step brother settled in Colusa, Colusa County, Calif. 1856." That is all the information available at this time to perpetuate the memory of Luis and Salvador, who crossed the mountains with William Stanton, bringing food to the Donner Party in Nevada. However, research into the Mission registers may reveal baptismal entries for the two heroic Indians who have been more or less ignored by historians of the Donner Party.

Chapter 14

JOHN BAPTISTE TRUDEAU: AN UNSUNG HERO

John Baptiste Trudeau deserves special treatment. Although the role he played with the Donner families at the Alder Creek camp was spoken of kindly in the works of both McGlashan and Houghton, he was resurrected as a low and villainous creature in the pseudo-history created by Stewart, who pictured him as a "little mongrel" and a "little Mexican" with "bad qualities" who abandoned poor George and Tamsen Donner. Stewart's portrayal has been the inspiration for novels and poems and other histories of the Donner Party, as mentioned in Chapter 15.

Trudeau deserves to be presented through the eyes of those who actually knew him and, more importantly, by himself, as he did in an 1891 interview.

Eliza Donner Houghton was only three years of age at the Alder Creek camp, but her earliest memories were of John Baptiste. The memories, to be sure, were enriched over the years by her older sisters and cousins. In *Expedition of the Donner Party and Its Tragic Fate* (1911), she wrote:

> Oh, how we watched, hour after hour, and how often each day John Baptiste climbed to the topmost bough of a tall pine tree and, with straining eyes, scanned the desolate expanses for one moving speck in the distance, for one ruffled track on the snow which should ease our awful suspense.
>
> Days passed. No food in camp except an unsavory beef hide – pinching hunger called for more. Again John Baptiste and Noah James went forth in anxious search for marks of our buried cattle. They made excavations, then forced their hand-poles deep, deeper into the snow, but in vain their efforts – the nail and hook at the points brought up no sign of blood, hair, or hide....

John Baptiste Trudeau (c1828-1910), served the Donner families well but has been treated poorly by some historians and fiction writers; was only male capable of cutting wood and gathering food at the Alder Creek camp; later escorted two Donner children to medical facilities in San Francisco.

Sixteen-year-old John Baptiste was disappointed and in ill humor when Messrs. Tucker and Rhoads insisted that he, being the only able-bodied man in the Donner camp should stay and cut wood for the enfeebled, until the arrival of other rescuers. [*Author's note: Noah James was there, but he left with the first relief.*] The little half-breed was a sturdy fellow, but he was starving too, and thought that he should be allowed to save himself.

After he had had a talk with father, however, and the first company of refugees had gone, he became reconciled to his lot, and served us faithfully. He would take us little ones up to exercise upon the snow, saying that we should learn to keep our feet on the slick, frozen surface, as well as to wade through slush and loose drifts.

Frequently, when at work and lonesome, he would call Georgia and me up to keep him company, and when the weather was frosty, he would bring 'Old Navajo,' his long Indian blanket, and roll her in it from one end, and me from the other, until we would come together in the middle, like the folds of a paper of pins, with a face peeping above each fold. Then he would set us upon the stump of the pine tree while he chopped the trunk and boughs for fuel. He told us that he had promised father to stay until we children should be taken from camp, also that his home was to be with our family forever. One of his amusements was to rake the coals together nights, then cover them with ashes, and put the large camp kettle over the pile for a drum, so that we could spread our hands around it, to get just a little warm before going to bed.

When little Mary Donner, whose foot was badly burned by the fire at Starved Camp, was brought out by members of the third relief, John Baptiste was waiting for her at Sutter's Fort. In an April 1 report of recent events, Selim E. Woodworth said he had thought Mary's foot needed amputation, so he took her to the naval hospital in San Francisco with "her brother" [Solomon Hook?] who also needed medical attention. Accompanying him and acting as "nurses" for the children, Woodworth reported, were "the Spanish boy John Baptiste and Howard Oakly." This teenage boy still felt an obligation to the Donner children, even after he had been for many weeks the only person capable of gathering firewood at the Alder Creek camp and entertaining the children of the dead Jacob and the dying George Donner.

It was probably at the naval facility that John Baptiste encountered Lieutenant Henry A. Wise, who later claimed John Baptiste boasted to him about how he enjoyed eating human flesh.   (A critique of Wise's altogether unreliable reporting is given in Chapter 15.)

It is certain that Captain Sutter and others at the fort, who knew him as "Baptiste," trusted him. He was employed there in 1847-48 and, according to Bancroft, was "one of the earliest miners." The paths of Baptiste and James F. Reed met again after Reed, in April 1847, had been appointed sheriff of the District of Sonoma, on the northside of San Francisco Bay, and came to Sutter's Fort in pursuit of a thief. A May 31, 1847, entry in Sutter's journal notes that "Mr. Reed left with Baptiste in pursuit of a horsethief to the San Joaquin Tract." A June 1 entry reports that "Mr. Reed and Baptist arrived and brought the prisoner (Marris) and put him into prison." A June 5 entry notes that "the prisoner broke out of the prison but has been caught in the evening by Baptist, put in irons and in the prison again....Baptist received $5 cash from Mr. Reed for having caught Marris again." The July 23 entry lists several hands, including Baptiste, who left with Major Reading for the Cosumnes River. This would be Pierson B. Reading, who had held the rank of major in the California Battalion.

In the early 1850s, Eliza and Georgia Donner were living in Sonoma with Swiss immigrants Christian and Mary Brunner, whom the girls called "Grandpa" and "Grandma." One day they received a surprise visit from John Baptiste. He rode up and greeted the sisters with these words: "I heard at Napa that you lived here, and my pony has made a hard run to give me this sight of you." Sixty years later, Eliza wrote of the visit as follows:

We were surprised and delighted, for the speaker was John Baptiste who had wintered with us in the Sierras. We asked him to dismount, take a seat under the tree, and let us bring him a glass of milk. He declined graciously, then with a pleased expression, drew a small brown-paper parcel from his trousers pocket and handed it to us, leaned forward, clasped his arms about his pony, rested his head on its neck, and smilingly watched Georgia unwrap it, and two beautiful bunches of raisins come to view,—one for each. He would not touch a single berry, nor let us save any. He asked us to eat them then and there so that he could witness our enjoyment of the luxury he had provided for this, our first meeting in the settlement.

Never had we seen raisins so large, translucent, and delicious. They seemed far too choice for us to have, and John was so poorly dressed and pinched in features that we hesitated about eating them. But he would have his way, and in simple language told us that he wanted them to soften the recollection of the hungry time when he came into camp empty-handed and discouraged. Also to fulfil his assurance to our mother that he would try to keep us in sight, and give us of the best that he could procure. His last injunctions were, 'Be good little girls; always remember your mother and father; and don't forget John Baptiste.'

In the spring of 1884, Trudeau visited Eliza Donner Houghton at her San Jose residence. He had become a hop picker and fisherman in season. He continued to deny that any cannibalism had taken place at the Alder Creek camp, perhaps fearing that Eliza would think less of her mother if she knew that John Baptiste did the bidding of Tamsen Donner and that the children had eaten the flesh of both their father and uncle with their mother's knowledge and reluctant consent. But perhaps he had another reason for withholding the truth. He was still a "foreigner" in the eyes of the Anglos, and he knew what persecution another foreigner, Lewis Keseberg, had experienced for his cannibalism.

Trudeau was living at Ukiah in Mendocino County in the late 1870s when McGlashan was working on his *History of the Donner Party*, and was there as late as 1884 when Eliza Donner Houghton obtained the photograph of him which she reproduced in her book, published in 1911. She gave his surname as "Trubode," and this was copied by Stewart, DeVoto and others.

Aside from the unfortunate interview by Lieutenant Wise in 1847, Trudeau spoke for himself to the public only once in his lifetime. The Sunday, October 11, 1891, edition of the *San Francisco Morning Call* contained the account of an interview he permitted a correspondent of the *St. Louis Republic*. In the account, his name is given both as Juan Baptiste Truvido and Juan Baptiste Truxido. The article deserves to be quoted in its entirety:

ONE OF THE DONNERS

A Chat with a Survivor of the Ill-Fated Expedition to California

Up at Santa Rosa the other day I discovered another survivor of the famous Donner party who crossed the plains in 1849 [*sic*], writes a correspondent to the St. Louis Republic. The old gentleman was Juan Baptiste Truvido, one of the survivors of the ill-fated Donner party, whose heroism saved the lives of many members of his party, but who has been almost entirely ignored by the hands that have guided the lines of history. "It is true I am one of the few left of the unfortunate band," he said, "and I might give you columns of facts concerning it, but it would be too much, perhaps." When urged to repeat some [facts] of the ill-starred company, he brightened up and related the following:

"My name is Juan Baptiste Truxido, and I am 60 years old. My parents were of French birth and I was born east of the Rockies, not far from the Arkansas River. I spent my young days in the mountains and the plains and became, like most boys in those circumstances, an expert hunter and horseman. When Fremont and Kit Carson came along on their way to California I joined them and was with them until they reached the head-waters of the Green River. It was about that time I fell in with 'Jim' Hedgepath, who lives in this country [*James M. Hudspeth, who crossed with the Hastings Party in 1846 and settled in Sonoma County*]. After leaving Fremont's party I went to Fort Bridger, Utah, and remained there until July, 1846. The famous Donner party that had started from Springfield, Ill., in the spring of 1846, was at the fort and preparing to strike out to California. A new route had been laid out, or opened up rather, by L.W. Hastings, called the 'Hastings cut-off' and as it was said to shorten up the distance the party were anxious to go that way.

"Everybody familiar with the history of the expedition knows that if the company had followed the old Fort Hall road all would have been well, but owing to the advice of friends they took what they thought was the shortest way. I was sent along by the people at the fort as a guide and guard, and was with the Donners until rescued at Donner Lake.

"It was while struggling through the cut-off that the party was joined by W.F. Graves and wife and their eight children, Jay Fosdick and John Snyder. Snyder was the man who was afterward killed in a quarrel with James Reed, who was one of the originators of the Donner Party.

"Well, we struggled along through the mountains and after we had left Salt Lake a long ways in the rear things went fairly well until we got to Truckee. The party became divided by a terrible storm and never came together again until the rescue came at Donner Lake. The Reeds and Graves people were in the advance party, while the Donners, George and Jacob, and their families, were in the party left behind. Our little band worked bravely on until we came to Alder Creek Valley, where we had to stop, it being impossible to go further. The snow came on with blinding fury and being unable to build cabins we put up brush sheds, covering them with limbs from the pine trees.

"It was about the first of November, I think, that we went into that camp of snow and suffering, and we remained there until the latter part of February, when the Sutter party rescued us."

The old gentleman's story of the sufferings at his camp was graphic, indeed. At one time he was the only one in the party who was able to do anything. George Donner had an injured hand and had been laid up for some time. Death stared them in the face, and it was only by the most heroic efforts on the part of Baptiste that all did not freeze to death.

He kept the fires going through the long, weary hours of the night and worked with might and main to keep the little colony warm. Starvation they were face to face with, and Baptiste secured the meat that kept them alive with the greatest difficulty.

One day he had to kill a cub, and his escape from the infuriated bear mother was almost miraculous. In the number that lay huddled in the miserable camp were George Donner, wife and five children; Jacob Donner, wife and three children; a man named Shoemaker, Jim Smith, Mrs. Wolfinger, one Rheinhart, a Dutchman whom he called Charley, himself and two or three others whose names he could not remember. Sickness, the pitiless storms and starvation relieved Jacob Donner and wife and child, Rheinhart, Shoemaker, Smith and the Dutchman of their sufferings, and when the relief party—which Baptiste says consisted of two Indians and a white man, Rhodes, poorly mounted—reached them there was a mere handful of wretched, almost starved people left. George Donner's five children and two of Jacob Donner's children were among the saved.

Baptiste lives at Tomales Bay and is a widower. He has three sons and they make their living by fishing. He says that he never recovered from the effects of that four months' experience and that half of the story has never been told. No human flesh was eaten in the camp where he was; that occurred in the camp of the other party, which was about eight miles away, but which, of course, they knew nothing about. Not even a reference has been made to the noble part the old Frenchman took in saving the lives of his fellow-sufferers in anything that has been published, and it fills one with sadness to hear him speak of it.

This account of events forty-five years after they occurred is understandably inaccurate in spots, perhaps partly a consequence of the inventions of the newspaper reporter. It should be remembered, however, that Trudeau had viewed the events of the entrapment mainly in the isolation of the camp at Alder Creek. Accounts of Eddy, Reed, and William Graves also fall short of complete accuracy.

Trudeau should surely be forgiven for continuing to deny the cannibalism. Stewart thought otherwise. "When I consider such hypocrisy," wrote Stewart self-righteously, "I feel a longing for the society of an honest cannibal." For that harsh and unfair judgment, perhaps Stewart should also be forgiven. Tamsen Donner may have wished to die rather than leave her husband, but no one should have expected young and severely weakened John Baptiste to spurn the last chance to save his own life in favor of dying with George and Tamsen Donner.

John Baptiste Trudeau, who had a long life, marrying and raising several children, was a man of many surnames: *Trudo* on the Great Register of Voters (1868) for Marin County, where, as a resident of Tomales Bay, he registered to vote in April 1867; also *Trudo* on the 1870 United States Census (Tomales Township, Marin County, California) and on the 1880 Census (Table Bluffs Township, Humboldt County); *Trubode* in the reporting of Eliza P. Donner Houghton; *Trubador* on the 1900 Census (Tomales Bay). On his Marin County death certificate his name is given as John Baptist Truevido.

Why Trudeau had so many different surnames assigned to him is not clear. One reason may be that census enumerators and other official recorders spelled the name as they heard it. Or perhaps he preferred an incognito status to avoid being "Keseberged." The account of Lieutenant Wise in *Los Gringos* was the subject of discussion as late as 1879. In that year Martha Reed Lewis wrote C.F. McGlashan of her despair concerning Lieutenant Wise's account of John Baptiste, which had recently reappeared in a newspaper. At about this time his surname began to appear in the records as "Truvido," "Trubador," etc.

Trudeau died on October 9, 1910 of "senile debility" and was buried at Marshall on Tomales Bay. An obit entitled "Donner Lake Party Rescuer Passes Away," on the first page of the *Marin County Tocsin* (October 15, 1910), notes that "Truvido was an interesting character. His father and his grandfather before him had been French Canadian trappers and traders who roamed among the Indians in that vast empire lying west of the Mississippi river." The last paragraph reads, quaintly: "Truvido years ago settled among the Indians in Tomales and there among the half breeds he found congenial company. He married there and several dark skinned children bear his name."

John Baptiste was listed as a widower on the 1900 Census, when he was living in his son John's household. John Baptiste's wife's name was given as "Guadelupe" on the 1870 Census and "Ellen" on the 1880 Census. The death certificate for his son John, who died in 1913 at age forty in Marshall, gives John's mother's maiden name as Lupe DeMassano and his wife's married name as Josephine Truvido. Another son, Baptiste Truvedor, died on March 14, 1931, age "about 70" according to the death certificate, race "Indian." His death merited an obituary, headed "Pioneer's Son Taken By Death." The notice refers to him as "Baptiste Truvedor, 55, son of 'Little Baptiste,' hero of the Donner Party...son of a French Canadian trapper [who] was but 19 years of age at the time he joined the Donner Party" (unidentified newspaper clipping but dated March 19, 1931, Biography File, Kent Room, Civic Center [Marin] County Library).

THE ROOTS OF JOHN BAPTISTE TRUDEAU

Very little is known of John Baptiste's parents. His mother's birthplace is usually shown on census and other records as New Mexico. His father's birthplace is given variously as Missouri (1900 Census), New Mexico, and even France. John Baptiste's birthplace is given as Arkansas on the 1900 Census, but as New Mexico on other records, including the *Great Register of Voters* (Marin County, 1868). His obituary, with information no doubt supplied by one of his children, noted that Trudeau "never knew exactly where he was born [but] to the best of his knowledge he first saw the light of day somewhere in what is now the state of Utah."

An obscure document that did not come to light until the 1940s (see Appendix E) cites John Baptiste's proper surname, Trudeau, and gives a clue to the identify of his father. The document is a scrap of paper, on one side of which is a note signed by Jacob Donner and addressed to Milt Elliott, authorizing Milt to purchase mules, ponies, and other supplies. This note was probably entrusted to Elliott in November, during the beginning of the entrapment, when Elliott was among members of the Donner company who made a futile attempt to scale the pass and reach the Sacramento Valley. On the other side of this scrap of paper, in another hand, is the following note, only partly decipherable, over the signature of "John Trudeau":

> ...   ...*but a poor orphan*
> .....*with nothing*
> .....*dians killed my father*
> ...*I will give my rifle*
> *for a pony or a mule to ride*

It seems likely that Trudeau's father was among that hardy band of mountain men who plied the routes of the fur trade.* They travelled from Missouri southward to Santa Fe, or westward along the Arkansas River to the Rocky Mountains of Colorado and Utah, where the historic *rendezvous* of the trappers and traders were staged in the 1820s and early 1830s. Circumstantial evidence suggests that the man killed by Indians was the son of Montreal-born Jean Baptiste Trudeau, also spelled "Truteau" on the records (1748-1827), a distinguished pioneer schoolmaster and explorer of St. Louis (see Notes to Chapter 14).

*After this chapter was written and shortly before this book went to press, the author received information from two New Mexico sources: J. Richard Salazar, Chief of Archival Services for the State Records Center and Archives in Santa Fe, and genealogist Ralph Hayes of Corrales, New Mexico. The documents they sent indicate that a Juan Bautista Trudeau of Taos, who listed his age as 38, his occupation as farmer, and his birthplace as St. Louis, Missouri, applied for Mexican citizenship on September 13, 1830 and was granted citizenship on February 28, 1831. The name on the documents is variously given as Bautista Truido, Juan Bautista Truido, and Juan Bautista Trudeau, although it is unmistakably the same man. MANM film roll 13, frame 382, and roll 10, frame 685. Mr. Hayes also did a thorough search of the Archdiocese of Santa Fe church registers, 1823-1832, for a record of a marriage of Juan Bautista Trudeau and a baptism of a son by the same name, without success. It is possible that the mother of John Baptiste Trudeau of the Donner Party was an Indian woman, and that her marriage to Trudeau of St. Louis and the baptism of her children were never recorded on Roman Catholic registers. Such marriages of "squaw women" to trappers and traders on the Santa Fe Trail were quite typical. In the 1830s, with the decline of the beaver trade, it was quite usual for trappers on the Santa Fe Trail to seek land in New Mexico, for which Mexican citizenship was required. Such land was often contested by Indians, who raided the farms and killed the settlers. See David Lavender, BENT'S FORT (Lincoln, Nebraska, 1972); and Mari Sandoz, THE BEAVER MEN (New York, 1964).

Chapter 15

WHOM TO BELIEVE?

The great problem in writing a history of the Donner Party, as in writing any history, is that the testimony of first-hand observers of events is often in conflict. Survivors of the Donner Party and their rescuers gave conflicting stories to the press. Some of them also gave accounts of events at the high camps that occurred when they were not there.

After coming out with the first rescue and recuperating, William Graves participated in an aborted relief mission in late March that got only as far as Bear Valley. In later life he often reviled other survivors and rescuers. He had contempt for the testimony of William McCutchen of the second relief: "If you believe what McCutchen tells you," he wrote McGlashan in 1879, "you will have your *hands* and *head* full, for he never told the truth unless it was through a mistake." Based on what he heard from his sisters, Mary Graves and Sarah Fosdick, he was also critical, probably with justice, of William Eddy's account of himself and his unalloyed heroics with the Snowshoe Party. Graves faulted James Frazier Reed for caring for "nobody but himself" and Patrick Breen for the same reason. His general bitterness toward persons in the Donner Party is understandable, considering that members of his family, including his mother and father, were cannibalized by them. He published a version of Breen's *Diary* in which he deliberately falsified the record to protect his family.

Virginia Reed had a poor opinion of William Eddy. Responding to a letter from McGlashan in 1880, she said unkindly: "So you received a letter from the son of W.H. Eddy, a physician! I did not think a son of William H. Eddy would have brains enough to be a professional man, but it is not always the smartest parents that raise the smartest children." And about J. Quinn Thornton, to whom Eddy told his story, Virginia wrote: "Such a disconnected untruthful story. It sounds just like Eddy...."

TESTIMONY OF JAMES FRAZIER REED

Virginia's step-father, James Frazier Reed, gave an account of his trail experiences prior to being expelled from the company for killing Snyder, and also an account, in the form of a pseudo-diary, of the second rescue mission. His first recollections appeared in letters that were printed in two Illinois newspapers in 1846 and 1847, but he did not attempt to tell his story fully until 1871, in a long piece for the *Pacific Rural Express*, mentioned earlier in this book. His testimony is valuable to the historian of the Donner Party, but marked by serious omissions and errors. For example, in his earliest account, he failed to mention the real reason for his being exiled from the Donner Party, merely saying he decided to go ahead and obtain provisions at Sutter's Fort. Toward the Breens, he expressed only reluctant appreciation: "I thank Mr. Breen for giving shelter to my wife and children, but as to giving them of their *stores*, they never did" (*Pacific Rural Press*, March 25, 1871). That view was countered by his own two children, Virginia and Patty. They both remembered being fed by the Breens and expressed indebtedness to them for their own survival. Reed also wrote that "Mr. Breen was not sick at Starved Camp, neither was it feared that he would die." He was defending the decision of himself and three other rescuers to take out only three children, two of them Reed's own, while leaving seven Breens, fives Graveses, and Mary Donner in the snowpit, without food.

TESTIMONY OF WILLIAM EDDY

Stewart in *Ordeal* said of William Eddy that "no one excelled him in heroic endeavor, and yet his own story, as recorded through Thornton, is remarkably free of egotism." As should be evident by now, I do not share Stewart's opinion. Eddy's account of himself, at least as reported by Thornton, is invariably pure heroics, with others often falling short in matters of character and virtue.

Nevertheless, Eddy was surely one of the tragic heroes of the party. His wife and two children perished at the lake camp. He led the survivors of the Snowshoe Party to the safety of Johnson's Ranch after a month-long ordeal that defies description. He went part way with the first rescue, and all the way with the third. It is a pity that he could not limit himself to the truth, which reflected favorably on himself, when he told his story to Thornton. But he had a serious character flaw. He was a boaster and liar, and as a consequence he used Thornton, as Thornton used him, to construct many tall tales of the Donner Party that make fascinating reading but which have badly distorted the factual record for almost one hundred and fifty years and, in the process, severely denigrated members of the party.

OTHER PROBLEMS WITH THE EVIDENCE

The McGlashan Papers at Bancroft Library in Berkeley, California, contain over four hundred letters written to McGlashan by Donner Party survivors and rescuers more than thirty years after the entrapment. Reading these letters, one cannot help being struck by the notion that the testimony of many of the survivors had been colored by second and third hand accounts, often sensational and lurid, that they had read in newspapers and elsewhere over the years. This was especially true of the treatment of Lewis Keseberg. Survivors who were barely more than infants at the time of the entrapment were clearly repeating opinions that they had gotten from others, including secondary sources, although sometimes claiming them as the product of their direct memory of events.

FALLON

The extracts from the alleged diary of "Captain" William O. Fallon of the fourth rescue need to be treated with the utmost skepticism, for reasons already discussed in this book (see Chapter 11). The extracts need especially to be weighed against the detailed account by Lewis Keseberg himself.

BRYANT

Edwin Bryant's *What I Saw in California* was first published in 1848. Chapter XX contains the following items: (1) a copy of the long "Statement of John Sinclair Esq., Alcalde. District of Sacramento." Most of this is William Eddy's account of his own heroism with the Snowshoe Party; (2) a copy of an "Extract of a Letter from Mr. Geo. M'Kinstry" about the first and second rescue party; (3) "Copy of a Journal kept by a suffering Emigrant on the California mountains, from Oct. 31st, 1846, to March 1st, 1847," which Bryant obtained from George McKinstry, Sheriff of the Sacramento District. This is a version of Patrick Breen's diary heavily edited for both style and fact, and the author of it is not mentioned by name. It is very far from a "copy." Bryant also gives an account of the fourth rescue "as detailed to me by Mr. Fallon." The "facts" are essentially the same as had appeared in the *California Star* on June 5, 1847, purportedly from the "journal" of "Captain Fellun." Written so soon after the events, Bryant's account understandably lacked historical perspective. He was also an extremely poor judge of his few informants at a time when lurid tales were spreading all over the world and survivors had a strong need to remove themselves from any responsibility for the sordid and unheroic aspects.

THORNTON

Like Bryant, J. Quinn Thornton relied entirely too heavily on William Eddy as an informant. Thornton also branded Lewis Keseberg a demon for life. His version of events was published in 1849 by Harper & Brothers as part of a two-volume work, *Oregon and California in 1848*. McGlashan put some matters right in his own book in 1880, but Thornton's account has been a major wellspring of Donner Party mythology to this day. Thornton deceived the reader in his introductory remarks, stating that the "facts [of his narrative] were verbally communicated to me by survivors." Actually, in the course of the narrative, only Eddy is mentioned as having talked to him personally: "Mr Eddy informed me that....I was informed by Mr. Eddy....This, Mr. Eddy told me....Mr. Eddy, as he informed me...." The largest part of the narrative focuses on Eddy's heroics. Not once does Thornton mention any other survivor telling him anything. One is forced to the conclusion that Thornton got his information about events, especially those that occurred when Eddy was not present, from secondary sources, especially the wild accounts appearing in the press and being spread by people such as McKinstry and Bryant. Factual evidence regarding the unreliability of Thornton's account appears elsewhere in this book.

FARNHAM AND MARGARET BREEN

Eliza W. Farnham interviewed Mrs. Breen in 1849, obtaining her oral testimony and what appears to be the written testimony of her oldest son, John. Her account of the Donner Party, and in particular the experience as seen through the eyes of Mrs. Breen and her son, was published in a long appendix to *California, In-Doors and Out* (1854). Farnham was a zealous feminist. The main theme in her book, stated overtly and repeatedly, was to prove the *superiority* of women, including Mrs. Breen. For this reason, Stewart rejected her work completely, as "so sentimentalized and so obviously a defense of Mrs. Breen (who supplied the information) that it is not to be trusted." (Yet Stewart accepted Thornton as a "good judge," despite Thornton's heavy sentiment and acceptance of William Eddy's account at face value.) Farnham's account includes very long passages of John Breen's recollections, obviously provided for her in manuscript form and quite similar to what John provided almost thirty years later in an 81-page manuscript for McGlashan. Like his father, John wrote unornamented prose, without ego or sentimentality. Although not without minor errors, John's account of events on the trail, at the mountain camp, and at Starved Camp, is highly credible by any historical standards. When John cannot remember certain events clearly, he says so. His mother's account of the facts, as retold by Farnham, is also quite credible, except for the claim that only the children, not she, partook of human flesh. The denial of cannibalism, however, may not have come from the mouth of Mrs. Breen. It could have been Mrs. Farnham's invention, for her wording in the matter of the cannibalism is slippery and ambiguous, designed to fit her thesis: the superiority of women.

McGLASHAN

Soon after C.F. McGlashan took over the editorship of the *Truckee Republican* in 1876, he became interested in the his-

tory of the Donner Party. In 1878 McGlashan began
correspondence with survivors, and he interviewed many of
them. Articles about the Donner Party appeared in his
newspaper. In 1879 he published them in a book, and
continued his research. In 1880, his revised *History of the
Donner Party* was published in San Francisco by the A.L.
Bancroft Company.

McGlashan's object was to separate fact from the mythology accumulated over thirty years. In most ways, he succeeded.
He is surely more reliable than Thornton, yet the book suffers,
as does Thornton's, from a plethora of pious sentiment in the
florid style of the times. McGlashan established warm personal relationships with many of his informants and was careful
not to offend any of them. He therefore omitted evidence
from his interviews and in his correspondence that reflected
unfavorably on the informants or members of their families.
Even though McGlashan's book leaves much to be desired as
history, it was the first real attempt to dig deeply into as many
sources as possible and to organize the facts into a coherent
narrative of a significant California historical event. An historian today, attempting to write a history of the Donner Party,
conceivably could work without Thornton, Farnham,
Houghton, and Stewart, but could not do without the
McGlashan book and the McGlashan Papers at Bancroft
Library.

JOHN BREEN

John Breen's "Pioneer Memoirs," the original manuscript
of which is in the Bancroft Library, is re-printed in Appendix C
to this book. A most valuable source, slighted by George R.
Stewart, although John Breen had a reputation for honesty
(see Isaac Mylar's opinion of John Breen, in Chapter 15) and,
unlike William Graves and William Eddy, was not inclined to
report events that he did not experience at first hand.

VIRGINIA REED

The bright and witty Virginia Backenstoe Reed became
one of the major primary sources of information on the
Donner Party. Her account of the journey was first published
in the *Illinois Journal* (December 16, 1847). A longer account

was given in *Century Magazine* (July 1891), and published in book form under the title *Across the Plains in the Donner Party (1846)*. She corresponded frequently with McGlashan when he was writing his history, and after.

The letter to the *Illinois Journal* has an interesting history. McGlashan acquired a reliable version of the original letter, somewhat to the embarrassment of Virginia, who got an education when she came to California and wished to dissociate herself from the creative spelling, punctuation and grammar of her youth ("we come to Brigers Fort...they raped the children up....it was the couldes night you most ever saw the wind blew and if it haden bin for the dogs we would have Frosen." In California the family was getting "verry fleshey....Ma waies 10040 pon...Eliza weigh 10072" [that is, 140 and 172 pounds]. Stewart re-printed the letter in an appendix to the second edition of *Ordeal by Hunger*. It is a masterpiece of "folk literature" and is generally historically accurate.

Her many letters to McGlashan sometimes reveal much bitterness toward members of the party. Writing to McGlashan on November 3, 1880, after the appearance of the second edition of his history, she said:

....I am under no obligations whatever to the Donners. True, they were not present when my father was ban[i]shed, but after he had gone when we were being tossed from wagon to wagon like a football they took no more interest in our wellfare nor did they show us any more kindness than the strangers did who joyned our compina on the road. Naturally we expected more from them, old acqua[i]ntances and old friends. Freindship after all is as rare almost as Justice. You see, I am not in love with the Donner party. Why should I be? I know, there was some noble souls among them, but the majority were a miserable selfish *set.*

HUBERT H. BANCROFT

When Hubert H. Bancroft was preparing his six-volume *History of California* in the 1880s, he fully accepted McGlashan's account of the Donner Party. Like McGlashan, he rejected the demonizing of Lewis Keseberg. Bancroft's "Pioneer Register and Index," although not complete and not without errors, is a most valuable tool for Donner scholars.

ELIZA P. DONNER HOUGHTON

Although Eliza Donner, age three at the time of the ordeal, had little direct memory of events, she was a keen student of the Donner Party and was able to cut through the heavy accretion of fiction, especially concerning Keseberg. In *The Expedition of the Donner Party and Its Tragic Fate* (1911), she told of a May 16, 1879, meeting with Keseberg in a vacant room in a brewery adjoining Keseberg's house in Brighton, Sacramento County, where he lived as a widower with his afflicted children. She was accompanied by her husband and Mr. and Mrs. Mc-Glashan (McGlashan had interviewed Keseberg twice previously and had obtained his written statement of his experiences). The meeting confirmed what Mrs. Houghton had already been led to believe, that Keseberg was not the demon of the mythology. Regarding the reports of Captain Fallon and others, she posed some interesting questions: Why did not Fallon pursue the footsteps in the snow? Why did not the fourth rescue share their food with Keseberg? If Keseberg had been in a condition to walk to the settlements, why did the first relief permit him to remain in camp consuming rations that might have saved others? Why would Eddy and Foster of the third relief leave Keseberg with the helpless Mrs. Murphy, if they really believed Keseberg had murdered Jimmy Eddy and George Foster?

GEORGE R. STEWART

George R. Stewart's *Ordeal by Hunger: The Story of the Donner Party* was first published in 1936. It was the first major book exclusively about the Donner Party since McGlashan's *History of the Donner Party* appeared in 1880. In 1960, a revised and enlarged edition appeared, which has gone through many printings. It is the major, readily available source of information on the Donner Party for both scholar and general reader, but to the best of my knowledge it has never been seriously and critically reviewed by competent scholars.

Stewart was born in Pennsylvania, graduated from Princeton University, earned a doctorate at Columbia University in 1922, and taught at the University of Michigan and elsewhere before beginning a long career in the English Department at the University of California at Berkeley, writing many books about the American West and other subjects.

Stewart enriched his scholarship with a keen sense of how to tell a good story, full of suspense, employing many of the techniques of the novelist. He rightly saw the Donner company as "a microcosm of humanity, to be tested with a severity to which few groups of human beings in recorded history have been subjected, destined to reveal the extremes of which the human body and mind are capable."

This being said, one has also to remember that all history is written with a bias. Historians bring to their task their own backgrounds in time and place. Stewart, who died in San Francisco in 1980 at age eighty-five, never rid himself of the notion, still popular at the turn of the 20th century, that the White Anglo-Saxon Protestant was a morally superior breed of human being, thanks to both blood and culture. Today we label that attitude "racist." Stewart's *Ordeal* is laden with racism, especially regarding what we now call "ethnics." Indians are "cowardly," Mexicans are "mongrels," the Irish are "prodigal," and they all tend to "funk" when the going gets tough.

Stewart's initial error in fact, which helped shape his negative attitude toward Patrick Breen, was the belief that Patrick was only about forty years of age. From that mistake he drew the inference that Patrick was in "the full vigor of life" when actually Patrick was fifty-one years of age, a senior member of the Donner company, and in ill-health. Stewart notes further that the Catholic Breen family consisted "with true Irish prodigality of seven children." On the other hand, he describes Protestant George Donner as "having a gentle, charitable spirit" and his brother Jacob as "industrious and kindly." No prodigality, it seems, in the Donners, although George Donner had fifteen children by three marriages.

Stewart describes James Frazier Reed as an Irish-born Protestant, age forty-six. Reed clearly had the right stuff culturally and genetically:

There was a touch of the aristocrat about Reed – and properly, for he was sprung from the line of an exiled Polish noble. Reedowsky the name is said to have been originally. The fierce and haughty Polish nature had not been greatly subdued by having its blood mingled with that of the stiff-necked and restless Scotch-Irish. By virtue of both lines of descent Reed was a man for quick decisions and decisive action. At Fort Laramie when the old trapper had talked about the Fort Hall road, Reed had spoken up. "There is a nearer way!" It was like him – to choose the nearer way. It was like him also to own the best and fastest horse in all the company, to carry with him the full regalia of a Master Mason, and to hold in reserve for its impression upon Mexican officials a certificate of his character signed by the governor and duly stamped with the eagle, shield, and sun of the Great Seal of Illinois.

Not surprisingly, the mixed blood of John Baptiste Trudeau worked no such wonders. Instead, he is introduced as "a little frontier mongrel from New Mexico who claimed a French trapper for a father and a Mexican for a mother and probably had a strain of Indian from both."

Mrs. Breen is described as:

a big, raw-boned, masculine-looking Irishwoman....some people thought she was the man of the family anyway.

Where did Stewart get that description of Mrs. Breen? The question is worth answering in some detail, because the answer reveals the basis of Stewart's unflattering caricatures of both Mrs. Breen and her husband in his book, and in a score of books by authors who have accepted these caricatures on the authority of Stewart.

Stewart's undoubted source, although he did not cite it, was an account of a visit to San Juan Bautista in the summer of 1849 by John Ross Browne. Browne, born in Dublin, Ireland in 1822, was a Protestant and the son of a publisher who emigrated when John was nine years of age and settled in Louisville, Kentucky. At the time of his visit to the inn kept by the Breens in San Juan, John Ross was in the employ of the Revenue Service of the United States Treasury Department. He was travelling south on matters of import duties, and also to set up a line of post offices on the land route to Los Angeles. Later, he became a secret agent for the government in the mines. He was also a prolific author, writing many books about his travels. His great skill was in making routine experiences sound like high adventure. One might say that Browne was one of the great windbags of his day.

His visit to the Breens was described in *Crusoe's Island: A Ramble in the Footsteps of Alexander Selkirk with Sketches of Adventure in California and Washoe* (1872). The chapter is entitled "A Dangerous Journey: The Cannibal." Browne tells how he boldly left San Francisco on a perilous journey to San Jose and thence, with danger lurking all about him, to Salinas Valley and San Juan Bautista. (Surely one had to walk carefully, to avoid stepping on the heels of the throngs of gold-seekers heading for the mines on the crowded roads.) At the village of San Juan Bautista, he stopped for the night at what he called a "tavern" known as "The United States" and kept by an American and his wife in an old adobe house. After noting that the "woman seemed to be the principal manager," he had this to say, which later became the wellspring of Stewart's caricatures:

The woman....struck me as an uncommon person....tall, raw-boned, sharp, and masculine – with a wild piercing expression of eye, and a smile startling and unfeminine. The man was a subdued and melancholy-looking person, presenting no particular trait of character in his appearance save that of general abandonment to the influence of misfortune....In the course of conversation with the man, I found that he and his wife were among the few survivors of a party whose terrible sufferings in the mountains during the past winter had been the theme of much comment in the newspapers. He did not state – what I already knew from the published narrative of these adventures – that the woman had subsisted for some time on the dead body of a child belonging to one of the party. It was said that the man had held out to the last, and refused to participate in this horrible feast of human flesh....

Browne goes on like that and worse for three more paragraphs, focusing on the horror of being in the presence of a member of the "gentler sex who had absolutely eaten of human flesh." This act, in Browne's eyes, "invested her with a repellent atmosphere of horror. Her very smile struck me as the gloating expression of a cannibal over human blood." When Mrs. Breen handed him a plate of meat for his supper, "every morsel seemed to stick in my throat," said the traveller. "I could not feel quite sure that it was what it seemed to be. The odor even disgusted me. Nor could I partake of the bread...it was probably made by her hands – the same hands that had torn the flesh from a corpse and passed the reeking shreds to her mouth."

Browne could sleep "but little" that night in the room his hostess assigned him. In his bed he recalled a picture of an ogress with teeth long and pointed that he had seen as a child and now that terrible ogress "assumed a fearful reality, and became strangely mingled in my dreams with this woman's face." Browne was happy when daylight gave him an excuse to get up and "take a stroll in the fresh air" and continue southward for more high adventures.

Browne was writing in an age when serious people believed in physiognomy, the art of determining a person's character and intelligence from the shape of the body, especially the facial features; and in phrenology, the practice of studying character and mental capacity from the conformation of the skull. An observer less prejudiced than Browne might have described the same scene differently. He might have noted that the man of the house was subdued because he was tired, after a hard day's work on his farm, which after only two years, was flourishing with considerable cattle and numbers of horses, hogs, and sheep.. He might have guessed that the woman's sharp features and outward toughness hid a soft heart and belied the loving care she had given her own seven children and several others during the ordeal in the mountains.

Stewart eagerly latched on to the words "tall, raw-boned" for Margaret, and turned them into "*big*, raw-boned." Homer Croy in his novel *Wheels West* converted the phrasing into "*husky* Irishwoman" (Other fiction writers inspired by Browne/Stewart have made her "huge" and "coarse" and a veritable Amazon who intimidates her husband and the other men of the company.) At Starved Camp, Stewart's Mrs. Breen is "an enraged Irish virago" who unleashed "a torrent of cries upon the saints and the 'vargin'" because the men of the relief seemed to be dawdling. The stage Irish that Stewart put in her mouth was taken verbatim from Thornton.

With obvious reluctance, Stewart grants that the Breens were "a little more charitable" than the other families. But he quickly takes this small praise away. Regarding the Breens' hospitality toward the Reed family, Stewart says that "about all the Reeds got to eat were the leavings" and "when her husband was not looking, she [Mrs. Breen] would slip Virginia little pieces of meat." This is a mangling of Stewart's own source, Virginia Reed herself, whom I have quoted at length elsewhere in this book. The inference Stewart more fairly could have drawn from Virginia's being slipped a piece of meat on occasion is that Mrs. Breen did not want the three other, healthier Reed children to see this generosity. To give to them all would be to threaten the lives of Mrs. Breen's own seven children.

Stewart never misses an opportunity to take a shot at one or another of the Breens, often the cheapest of shots. After pointing up the historical value of the *Diary* and its reliability, Stewart manages to find a selfish motive for the writing of it: "the nearness to death....often gives men a feeling of importance." On Patrick's occasional references to his Maker in the diary, Stewart reminds us that Breen did not mention his God until a month after the beginning of the entrapment, when he began to fear for his life. Worse yet, on the occasion of the arrival of the first rescue party, Patrick "neglected to record his thanks to the God to whom he had so often called in time of trouble." Still more, Virginia Reed's account of accompanying the Breens in Catholic prayer every morning and evening and making a promise to God about embracing the Breens' Catholic faith inspired Stewart to comment on Virginia's "childish lack of logic forgetting that her own mother and many others were praying just as fervently and probably just as efficaciously in their Protestant fashion."

Stewart used Breen's February 11 and February 27 diary entries to suggest that Breen was constantly praying during these seventeen days while better men and boys were working:

....The Englishman John Denton, who was living with the Graveses, was in a bad state. The men and boys were so weak now that they hacked pitifully as they strove to fell trees for firewood. Patrick Breen's voice rose *almost continuously* in prayer; the others knelt beside him. Once *in a pause* they all heard from far above the faint honking of wild geese." [emphasis added]

The fact of the matter is that Breen's prayers were limited to a morning and evening ritual, as one of the Reed girls testified. Moreover, during the entire month of February, Breen alluded to God only four times in the diary, on the 1st,

10th, 12th, and 18th. Stewart is writing "history" with a sharp fictional edge.

Also troublesome is Stewart's almost complete lack of understanding of some of the subtle but important reasons for the survival of the entire Breen family. In the months of crisis the Breens exercised a daily discipline lacking in the other families. Every morning and evening Patrick Breen led his family (and the Reeds) in prayer. Almost every day he recorded events in his little book. He was ever hopeful. Even during the worst of times he could express confidence that the sun would soon break through, and he could express appreciation when it finally appeared. His wife stashed away the meat for even worse times, while the family survived mainly on hides. Patrick played the fiddle. He knew that man does not live by bread alone. Music and prayer uplift the human spirit.

Peculiarly, Stewart made the puzzling comment in his introduction to a facsimile edition of Breen's *Diary* that the document reflected "little evidence of deep religious feeling." Also puzzling was his contention that religion could hardly have been one of the motives for the Breen family's emigration to California. Stewart did not understand the faith, simply stated in the diary, of a man of little education, lacking the flamboyant soul-searching of New England Puritans such as Cotton Mather or Jonathan Edwards.

In a streak of insight into the minds of the men of the second relief, Stewart even managed to turn Patrick Breen's fiddle-playing into a fault: "To the men of the relief party it must have been a little irritating. Why couldn't Breen put some more energy into helping push the children along and not scrape so much on that damn fiddle?"

A serious human weakness in Stewart's view was to "funk" (to shrink or quail in fear). White Anglo-Saxon Protestants did not funk; others did. At Starved Camp, says Stewart, rescuer Brit Greenwood, whom he described as the "half-breed" son of the old trapper Caleb, "began to funk, and joined Patrick Breen at praying." That night, as the storm continued to rage, "the scared half-breed prayed womanishly [with Breen], when he should be carrying the wood." Again, this is fictional stuff. Stewart himself admits to the fiction in his own notes: "The experiences of this night are....confused in the various accounts.

My own account is something of a synthesis put together in the attempt to present clearly what most likely happened." Such fictionalization is frequent in *Ordeal*. Regarding the words he puts in the mouth of an old trapper at Fort Bridger, Stewart says candidly in his notes, "I have reshaped the quotation after my own opinion of what Bill would have said."

Unblemished by funkiness such as that of the Irishman and the half-breed was John Denton, who had weakened and been left to die on the trail by the first rescue:

Denton the Englishman died true to the best traditions of the common race. He did not whine or funk.

Trudeau is treated even worse than the Breens. Stewart's characterization of this young man bordered on fanaticism, as is indicated in this bit of understatement:

...The reader may have noticed that throughout the book [*Ordeal by Hunger*] I have been at difficulty in restraining a dislike for this character; I introduced him under the term "mongrel," and by so doing I intended not only to refer to his mixed blood, but also to indicate that he possessed the qualities conventionally ascribed to dogs of that sort.

Although Trudeau was the rock of support for the Donners for over four months, after others had died or had been brought out by the first and second relief, Stewart condemns him for attempting to "leave the Donners in the lurch." Worse, Stewart cites a report by Lieutenant Henry A. Wise of the United States Navy, which reveals Trudeau boasting about his cannibalism: "eat baby raw, stewed some of Jake [Donner], and roasted his head, not good meat, taste like sheep with the rot." The account by Wise first appeared in *Los Gringos; or, an Inside View of Mexico and California* (New York, 1849). In the preface, Wise states his purpose: "to compose a pleasant narrative, such as may please or interest the generality of readers." Chapter XI is entitled pleasantly "The Cannibal Emigrants, and the Dutchman's Appetite with Baptiste's Remarks thereon." Wise then proceeds to speak of Donner Party parents eating their own offspring. Further horror, "one Dutchman actually ate a full grown body in thirty six hours! another boiled and devoured a girl nine years old, in a single night."

One woman made "soup of her lover's head." The naval officer goes on to say that there were thirty survivors [not even close to the mark] and "a number of them without feet, either frozen or burnt off, who were placed under the care of our surgeons on shore."

Now, *everything* in Lieutenant Wise's account of the Donner Party was either badly skewed or false. If the misinformation did come from Trudeau, perhaps he was "putting on" the *gringo*, much as Benjamin Franklin enjoyed teasing the ladies of Paris with tall tales about America, like the one about fish swimming up a mile-high Niagara Falls. In any case, Wise's report is irresponsible as history. Equally irresponsible is Stewart's use of it against Trudeau, who later denied (probably for reasons suggested in Chapter 14), that any cannibalism had taken place at Alder Creek.

Stewart's claim that Trudeau and Clark left a living child at Alder Creek is especially irresponsible: "Th[ornton] states....that one of Jacob Donner's children was living at the time of Eddy's arrival at the lake, and Star [*California Star*] confirms this. I see no reason to doubt this contemporary testimony." The absurdity in scholarship here is that Thornton got his information from Eddy and from the *Star*, which almost certainly got it from the same Eddy; further, neither Eddy nor the other men of the third relief visited the Alder Creek camp; therefore, they had *no way of knowing* whether Sammy Donner was still living.

Ordeal by Hunger is not satisfactory as a history of the Donner Party from the perspective of late 20th century scholarship and values. History from a strongly racist point of view is no longer tolerable. But in any case *Ordeal* should be considered not as history but as fiction, heavily researched indeed, but a fictional account nevertheless. That it has received universal praise as history, in its original and revised forms, can be explained by the fact that a reviewer would find it necessary to read just about all of Stewart's sources before seeing how he blurred the line between fiction and history.

THE INFLUENCE OF STEWART

Nevertheless, *Ordeal by Hunger* will doubtless remain a classic in its field. It has been in print for more than half a century, and will continue to be an inspiration for poets and novelists, as well as historians and teachers. That, I think, is not the least reason why a new book about the Donner Party and a critique of Stewart's work are long past due.

Writers tend to accept Stewart's view of Patrick Breen as a lazy, prayerful lout, and his portrayal of Margaret Breen as an Irish harridan. They build on those caricatures. One such work is *The Mothers: An American Saga of Courage* by Vardis Fisher (1943). Fisher's Patrick Breen is "crippled or pretended to be." He "disliked everybody but his own family." His eyes are "cunning and cold" as he takes part in James Frazier Reed's "trial" after Reed slays Snyder. Again he is "cunning" in refusing a horse for the search for Hardcoop. He is one of the avengers who cries "Kill Jim Reed!" William Eddy is open, resourceful, and generous, while Breen is "a shrewd Irishman" who, with "crafty and hard" eyes, asks help from Eddy. Fisher assigns eight, not seven, children to Patrick on the trail. As to the Breens' supply of water on the desert (when they allegedly turned down Eddy's request for some of it), "Peggy Breen had *several* casks of water" [*emphasis added*]. Fisher labels the Breens "greedy," "superstitious," and "malicious." Patrick is "dishonest....all winter he had pretended to be a delicate invalid." He will not share with others the meat left him by his friend Dolan. He drives starving people from his cabin, even as he feeds an ox-head to his dog. Fisher is even more vicious in characterizing Lewis Keseberg.

In *The Ungodly* (1973), Richard Rhodes finds it difficult to say anything good about Patrick and Margaret Breen. Breen "*grudgingly* loaned the Germans [the Kesebergs] a horse." Rhodes has a satanic and lust-crazed Keseberg crushing the skull of the weakened Tamsen Donner with an ax, then raping the dead woman in his bed, before devouring joyfully both Tamsen and her husband!

The Donner Party, a poem by Robert Keithley, is hard to match for inaccuracy and banality. Portions of this long narrative "poem," published as a book in 1972, had previously been printed in several magazines, including *Harper's*. Keithley's story is told from the point of view of George Donner, husband of Tamsen. It is not verse, at least in my view, but rather 174 pages of plain prose sentences, occasionally spiced with a self-conscious metaphor, arbitrarily divided into three-line stanzas (although Keithley, cleverly, begins and ends each chapter with a four-line stanza).

The story wanders along with little regard for historical accuracy:

> *We met poor Patrick Breen*
> *who sailed from Ireland a year ago*
> *with his wife and six boys and a baby girl.*

Narrator George Donner is no admirer of the "foolish Irish....who would do well to sell all their livestock and start home, but they won't." Margaret Breen is given the name "Mary." Her husband Patrick, a greedy and suspicious sort, demands that George Donner show him and Graves the paper entitling George to the deceased Luke Halloran's money. At Pilot Peak, a hen-pecked Patrick sneaks off to get away from a complaining spouse, lies flat on his back under a cottonwood, and falls asleep with "the black book [Bible] propped on his chest as though a huge crow crouched upon his shirt and lifted its wide wings in rhythm with his breath" (one of the rare occasions when Keithley soars into metaphor, in a manner sure to please professors of English, especially those of a secular bent). Later, Breen raises the price on his oxen, "but he won't sell many."

Keseberg is predictably a demon in Keithley's hands. During narrator George Donner's final moments, Keseberg hobbles around with his walking stick, a veritable Lucifer at large, "crouch[ing] over the corpses [and] turning them this way and that with one end of his staff," then picking up a skull, plucking the brains, and tucking them carefully" in his lap while he breaks a breast apart and hunts with one hand for the heart."

Left Hand Turn: A Story of the Donner Party Women by Jeannette Gould Maino, published privately in 1987, concerns the struggles of five females of the party, of whom Margaret Breen is not one. The heroines chosen for focus are Tamsen Donner, Margaret Reed and her two daughters, and Mary Graves. Margaret Breen, however, is mentioned often, and she comes off fairly well compared to her husband. She is presented as a coarse and "hardened" woman with "huge arms and legs" and a "rough voice," but her "heart was kind." She is "more like a man than a woman," Margaret Reed says, but "I trust her with children; she seems to love them all, her own and every one else's." While heroine Tamsen Donner's voice is "surprisingly soft," Margaret Breen, in the next paragraph, "snorted aloud." She is occasionally petty, as when commenting on the unmarried Mary Graves ("ugly as sin or she'd be spoken for long afore this"). She is also capable of deprecating femininity itself, "the curse of Eve....God made us that way."

Margaret's' greatest problem, however, is her own husband, who has no redeeming feature whatsoever. He is lazy, prayerful, ineffectual, fatalistic, selfish, and unloving. Crossing the desert, Patrick says "God will get us through, put yourselves in his hands, pray" and Margaret responds angrily, "Shut your blatherin' mouth, Patrick Breen." Later, when personal property is being cached to lighten the load, Margaret says, "I ain't goin' to California without my silver dish, and that's that, Patrick Breen. You put down your Bible and I'll leave the dish." Patrick responds handily, "All right....we'll stay right here and let the Good Lord provide for us." On the attempt to climb the pass, Margaret admonishes Patrick: "You'd better be doin' something besides dependin' on the Lord. He's got his hands full this day." Patrick's fiddle-playing is also a great fault, and one of the relief party threatens "to bust that damned fiddle over Breen's head....he'd best help his family through the snow." Earlier, when the Reeds came to the Breen cabin, Patrick's welcoming comment is, "ivery family for himself, and mind you don't touch any Breen food."

Maino's fictional narrative is often broken by long italicized passages of historical narrative, based on an enormous amount of research. An impressive bibliography and extensive and quite valuable notes are included. This could have been a much more convincing book were it not for the caricatures of the Breen family and for its acceptance as fact of so many of the mythological elements to which Eddy/Thornton gave birth and which Stewart perpetuated.

Homer Croy in *Wheels West* (1955) employed James Frazier Reed as his narrator. "John Baptiste" is "the beady-eyed little Mexican"; Patrick Breen "when the danger was over....forgot God"; and his wife is that "husky Irish woman who so bravely slaughtered the oxen."

Joseph Pigney's *For Fear We Shall Perish: The Story of the Donner Party Disaster* (1961) is a peculiar book. It probably should be classified as fiction, as Jeannette Maino wisely noted in the bibliography of *Left Hand Turn*, but was published by E.P. Dutton & Co. as history, with a Notes and References section. Pigney uses the techniques of the novelist – extensive conversations, detailed settings provided by the author's imagination, and so on. Breen and Trudeau are portrayed harshly in a re-hash of their treatment in Stewart's *Ordeal*, or worse. But what makes this book different from the usual Donner Party fantasies is that there is a sympathetic focus on Keseberg from the beginning of the book (in fact Keseberg is the major character), and the narrative indicates strongly that the author has done considerable research on Keseberg, even if not on other aspects. The Notes and References section indicates that the genealogical information on Keseberg has come from a search of German records and, for the period after 1846, from California records. No book contains more factual information on Keseberg's life, before and after the Donner Party tragedy. Like McGlashan and Bancroft, Pigney sees him as a victim, not as a monster. Pigney correctly notes that Thornton's account drew heavily on wild stories in the *California Star*, much of them inspired by the unreliable Eddy.

DeVOTO

Substantial sections of Bernard Devoto's *The Year of Decision, 1846* (1943) have to do with the Donner Party. He examined no documents, depending almost wholly on Thornton and Stewart and adding some bold flourishes of his own. Reed's diary was "written by firelight in fifteen feet of snow" (he actually wrote it later, having been blinded during much of the storm). Virginia Reed, "before the year [1847] was out....married" (DeVoto confuses Virginia with Mary Murphy). The Reeds and the Breens all came through the ordeal, he thinks, because they had "the most complex nervous systems....and the simplest." DeVoto further confuses matters by crediting Captain Thomas Fallon of Santa Cruz and San Jose, not William O. Fallon, with heading the fourth rescue.

DeVoto's story contains the standard villains and ne'er-do-wells, John Baptiste "Trubode" ("worthless"), Keseberg ("a mere sac of bestiality," who had "probably" killed "little George Foster"), and, of course, Patrick Breen. DeVoto draws on Eddy's and Thornton's tales about Breen's hardness of heart. He takes Stewart's account of Breen having *some* water to spare in the desert and enhances it: "Old Patrick Breen, whose casks were *full*, refused [the Eddys] water." He states categorically that Reinhardt and Spitzer murdered Wolfinger. He absolves Keseberg of complicity in that act, but quickly adds that it "was the one offense Keseberg refrained from committing." His supreme hero, predictably, is William Eddy. DeVoto's account is almost worthless as history, but interesting if read as fiction, full of cliff-hangers ("It was up to William Eddy now") as his narrative moves from one 1846 emigrant party to another and back again.

BIRNEY

Even before the appearance of *Ordeal by Hunger*, fiction writers inspired by Eddy/Thornton were busily demonizing Patrick Breen and Lewis Keseberg. Hoffman Birney in the novel *Grim Journey* (1934) tells of the muster roll on the Little Sandy when Keseberg's "lips curled in a defiant sneer beneath his closely trimmed and curling beard....it was an odd coincidence that Keseberg's deep gutterals, which marked every *w* and *v* and prolonged the sibilants into a *hiss*, should have been followed by a shrill Irish brogue so thick that it seemed flavored with peat-smoke....'Breen is the name,' he answered [Birney follows this with a spiel in stage Irish]...a good natured laugh ran through the group." Birney quickly adds that it was a laugh less frequently heard as the company's "misfortunes augmented and [they] became better acquainted with the man." The novel is full of attacks on Breen's character. He is a "hypocrite" in religion. He quarrels incessantly with leader George Donner. He is totally selfish: "It's Paddy Breen I'm helpin,' he said grimly. Don't be forgettin' that." However, in a moment of generosity, Birney has "Paddy" arguing *not* to hang Reed after the Snyder killing.

STOOKEY

The last major history of the Donner Party was Walter M. Stookey's *Fatal Decision: The Tragic Story of the Donner Party* (1950). While offering nothing new about the experiences in the high camps, and unfortunately accepting a great deal of the mythology of Thornton/Eddy, Stookey presents the freshest and most accurate description of the trail of the Donner group through the Wasatch Mountains and across the Great Salt Desert to water below Pilot Peak.

Chapter 16

THE BREENS IN CALIFORNIA

The Breens were guided only by John Stark as they left Starved Camp. Food was waiting for them at Woodworth's advance camp in the Bear Valley, but it was another ten miles and a day or two to Mule Springs where horses were waiting. (Mule Springs is accessible today almost seven miles out of the village of Dutch Flat on the Lowell Hill Road.) John Breen recalled going from Mule Springs to Johnson's Ranch, another thirty miles, on horseback. What a luxury that horse must have been! John later wrote touchingly of his arrival at Johnson's:

> It was long after dark when we got in the valley at Johnsons Ranch, so that the first time I saw it [it] was earlie in the morning, the weather was fine, the ground was covered with fine green grass, and their was a very fat beef hanging from the limb of an oak tree, the birds were singing from the tops of the trees above our camp and the journey was over. I [kept] looking on the scene and could scarcely believe that I was alive, the scene that I saw that morning seems to be photographed on my mind; most of the incidents are gone from memory through the lapse of years, but I can always see the camp near Johnsons Ranch [*April 20, 1879 letter to C. F. McGlashan from Topo Ranch*].

SUTTER'S FORT

The family was then taken to Sutter's Fort at "government expense," John said, and greeted by the "generous" Sutter and, even more importantly, by John's younger brothers, Edward and Simon Breen. John was much impressed by the company of Indians on guard duty. Some were mounted, he remembered, and they "drilled every day."

Sutter's Fort, on the site of present-day Sacramento, must have seemed like a metropolis to John, as it did to many other

165

Sutter's Fort, 1847, and Captain John Sutter.

emigrants whose long trek invariably led them to this outpost of civilization established by John Sutter in 1839. In his "Personal Reminiscences" (1876), a manuscript at Bancroft Library, Sutter testified that he was born in Baden, Germany, in 1803 of Swiss parents; that they moved to Switzerland, where he became a cadet at a school in Bern; and that he served as an officer in the Swiss Army before emigrating to America in 1834. He traveled westward to Vancouver, meeting exploring parties and trappers of the American Fur Company. He voyaged to the Sandwich Islands, from where he took passage on a trading vessel to Sitka, Alaska, and thence by ship to Monterey, California. He made a favorable impression on Governor Alvarado and obtained the right to settle in the remote Sacramento Valley. After exploring the area he determined to settle there and took possession of the countryside. He quickly established friendship with the Indians, and with their labor began construction of his fort in 1839. He called his isolated fiefdom "New Helvetia."

He acquired more land from Alvarado and negotiated the purchase of Russian-owned lands known as "Ross and Bodega." From 1844, when the first wagons began arriving, Sutter's Fort became the great terminal point of emigration. Yet when John Breen arrived in March 1847, it was still very much a frontier outpost. Among the documents filed with the *McKinstry Papers* at the Bancroft Library is a census for Sutter's Fort for November 1846. The white population consisted of 160 males and 47 females, for a total of 207. Additionally, there were five Sandwich Islanders (one of them female), one negro, fifty "Indian servants (tame Indians)," and ten "half breed children." Cattle numbered 2,000, horses about 2,500, mules 70, sheep 2,000, hogs 1,000. There were three horse-driven mills, two water mills, one sawmill, one tannery, and about sixty houses in addition to the fort itself.

Sutter was undisputed lord of the valley and points beyond. Although he had become a Mexican citizen, after the outbreak of hostilities between Mexico and the United States he was appointed United States military commander of the district, Indian agent, and alcalde. He was generous with the newly-arrived, who needed his employment as he needed their labor. His fiefdom collapsed in 1848 when gold was discovered at a sawmill he had erected near Coloma.   Immediately his mechanics and laborers, white and Indian alike, deserted him for the gold fields.   His mills were abandoned, and he was unable to hire labor to herd his cattle or to plant and harvest his crops.

AT THE MURPHY RANCH

The Breen family stayed only briefly at the fort. Martin Murphy Jr. of the 1844 overland party offered the destitute Breens the hospitality of his ranch home on the Cosumnes River, south of the fort. The fact that both Murphy and Breen were born not far from each other in southeastern Ireland, that both were Catholics, and that both had experienced entrapment by the snows of the Sierras must have made it easy for them to become fast friends. Murphy was doing a thriving business selling cattle and grain from his ranch to John Sutter, as he would later to prospectors heading for the goldfields.

According to the recollections of two of the Breen boys, they and their father, along with Martin Murphy Jr. and some friends, went up to the high camp to retrieve what they could of the Breens' personal possessions. The retrieval missions may be reflected in the journal kept by Sutter and his clerks at the fort. A June 25, 1847, entry reads, "Shadden & Breen left for home" [*i.e., Murphy's Ranch*]. "Shaddon" is doubtless Jared Sheldon, who built a grist mill on the Cosumnes, not far from Martin Murphy. An August 18 entry reads, "Breen, Shadden, Buzzel, & Murphy here, Murphy fell severely sick." "Buzzel" may be G.W.P. Bissell who, with W.H. Aspinwall, purchased Mare Island in Sonoma County in 1851.

Harry J. Breen, a son of Edward, wrote: "When the men and big boys went back in the spring of 1847 for the wagons and property left at the Lake, my father said he would like to have something for a keepsake, so he brought back a knee joint and a hoof of one of their oxen that had helped sustain their lives. These are now [1950] at Sutter's Fort."

The Breen scavenging party also succeeded in retrieving a number of items that had belonged to the late Patrick Dolan. In 1847, Patrick Breen applied to the Justice of the Peace of the Sacramento District Court for authority to administer Dolan's estate. Attached to the petition was a list of over twenty items, mostly clothing, estimated value $360.29, a considerable sum at that time ["Sutter's Fort Documents Collection: Reed Family," file 471].

When archaeologist Don Hardesty did his digging at the site of the Breen cabin in the 1980s, the only artifacts he found were pins, a sewing awl, a darning needle, and fragments of glass tumblers.

The Breens remained at the Martin Murphy Jr. ranch until September 1847, when they headed for Mission San Jose. They stopped at the ranch of "Thomas Pile [Pyle] on the Mokelumne river," John Breen remembered. Then they made their way westward to the Amador Valley, where they were put up for a time at the ranch of Robert Livermore, an Englishman who had married Josefa Higuera and embraced her Catholic faith. John also said that Livermore "gave [the Breens] a quarter of a steer, saying that he never charged an emigrant for beef."

At Mission San Jose, the Breens were greeted by other '46-ers Jerry Fallon and Michael Murray, who soon were to settle in what came to be known as the community of Dublin in Alameda County (then part of Contra Costa County). Also at the mission was Leo Norris from Kentucky, another Catholic, who was to become a founder of the community of San Ramon, north of Dublin.

SETTLING AT SAN JUAN BAUTISTA

Patrick Breen, looking for a place to settle his family, visited San Juan Bautista. The first person he met was Father José Anzar who urged him to settle there. The priest offered him the use of his mission orchard, which was in a state of disrepair, without charge. He also provided temporary living quarters for the family in a partitioned section of the Mission building, and he introduced Patrick to General José M. Castro, who had been head of the Mexican Military District. Castro kindly gave the Breens the use of a two-story adobe house he owned but used only seasonally, accepting no rent. The adobe faced the plaza. "When [Castro] visited the next summer with his family," John Breen wrote, "he would take only a small part of his house."

In February 1848, the Breens were the first American
family to settle in San Juan Bautista.   They quickly made
friends with their Mexican-Catholic neighbors and with travellers, and all members of the family became fluent in Spanish.
The house was a natural stopping-off place for men trekking to
and from the Mother Lode.   The adobe unofficially became
"The Inn," as Patrick and Margaret opened the doors to way-
farers.   At first they had only the floor to offer, no beds, but
Margaret became famed for her hospitality, never turning away
a broken-down miner without funds.   Patrick and Margaret had
known unimaginable hunger and privation themselves, and
they never forgot it.

Judge James F. Breen, son of Patrick and Margaret, wrote
that his father was "absolutely without means" when the family
arrived at San Juan Bautista.   That condition was soon remedied when the oldest son, John, brought back a poke of gold
dust worth $12,000 from the Mother Lode.   In 1849, with part
of this new wealth, Patrick Breen purchased from Castro the
adobe house and four hundred and one acres adjoining the
Mission for two hundred pesos.   The transaction in Spanish
giving title to the property to "Señor Patricio Breen" was signed
by José and Modesta Castro on February 7, 1849, at the Court
of the Port of Monterey in the presence of Florencio Serrano,
Alcalde.   The 1850 assessment rolls indicated that Patrick had
20 milk cows, 6 saddle horses, 19 breeding mares, 30 wild
cattle, 30 sheep, and 4 hogs.   By 1854, his livestock had considerably increased: 16 horses, 30 mares, 460 head of cattle, 359
sheep, 75 hogs, and 1 mule, milk cows not cited.   A mare at the
time was worth $20, a mule $220.   During this period Patrick
increased his agricultural holdings in San Juan Bautista from
401 to almost 1,000 acres of good land and had fenced in 100
acres of it.

The infamous San Andreas Fault runs along the edge of
the property at the base of a little cliff below the Mission.   The
land can be viewed today from the gazebo of the Fault Line
Restaurant and Studio.   Looking northwest from there toward
the hills, Breen descendant Joe Cullumber of San Juan
Bautista pointed out to me the house where he was born, and
Breen Road about a quarter mile to the right of the restaurant.

In 1849 Patrick and Margaret had a son, William, baptized at the Mission. The Confirmation book for Mission San Juan Bautista in the 1850s contains the names of their seven oldest children, all confirmed by Bishop Joseph Alemany.

THE CHILDREN OF PATRICK BREEN AND MARGARET BULGER

John Breen (1832-1903). A sketch in the *History of San Benito County, California* (1881) gives John's birthdate as February 21, 1832, in Ontario, Canada. Thus he was only sixteen when he went to the gold fields, returning after a year from Mormon Island and Placerville with the fortune of $12,000 in gold, as mentioned above. In 1852 at age twenty, he married Leah Margaret Smith, the daughter of San Juan's first postmaster, Edward Smith. John built a fine adobe residence near the mission, within sight of the residence of his parents. He and Leah raised a family of ten children: Margaret Jane (Lillie), Patrick Edward, Adelaide, John Joseph, Thomas Frank, Mary Catherine (Kate), Isabelle, Gertrude, Charlotte, and Ellen (Nellie). A sketch in the county history notes that John had three hundred and thirty acres of grain and vegetable land in San Juan Bautista. He had another ranch of one thousand two hundred acres in the San Benito Valley where he kept two thousand sheep. In addition, he served on the Board of Supervisors, sometimes as chairman, for Monterey and San Benito counties.

On June 5, 1889, John Breen filled out a questionnaire concerning his San Juan properties (now in the Bancroft MS collection). He declared 1,200 acres of stock range and 300 tillable acres; 700 hogs, 50 cattle, 20 horses, and 28 acres of alfalfa, 180 of barley.

Isaac Mylar, whose father purchased 160 acres about one mile south of town adjoining the John Breen tract, had high praise for Breen in memoirs published in 1929:

A more honest and incorruptible man than John Breen never lived in San Benito Co. He was a very unassuming man, spoke but little, and when he did speak he talked directly to the point. He did not decide without due deliberation and once his mind was made up nothing could move him.

John kept up the diary tradition of his father. The little books in which he made his entries are at the Gleeson Library, University of San Francisco.

John's great-grandson, Harvey Nyland, a resident of San Juan Bautista, has served as sheriff of San Benito County since 1987.

Edward Breen (1833-1890). Edward was described as "tall and well-proportioned" and the "favorite of his mother." An agriculturist and stock-raiser, he farmed several hundred acres in San Juan. Later he acquired, by bequest of his father, one-seventh of 24,000 acres of Rancho San Lorenzo (Topo Ranch) north of King City, and, by bequest of his mother, her one-half share of that ranch. He married the spirited and attractive Catherine Sullivan of San Francisco and they had three sons, Eugene, Edward, and John Roger. Catherine died at the age of twenty-nine when two of the children were infants. In 1880 Edward married Mary Jane Burns in San Francisco. They had three children, Edwin, Harry, and William.

Edward's will, prepared on August 30, 1890, indicated his ownership of the 24,000-acre Topo Ranch; additionally, 350 acres in the San Juan Valley, 5,721 acres in Humboldt County, Nevada, lots in San Juan and Gilroy, and a mining claim in San Benito County, which, according to family folklore, Edward had "won in a card game." The Nevada property, his granddaughter said, was bought during the drought of 1862-64 and was valued then at $10,000. The estate was bequeathed to his children, share and share alike.

The Topo Ranch, or at least 15,000 acres of it, remained under family ownership until the hard times of the 1930s, when the Bank of America foreclosed on the mortgage. The bank then extended an option to buy to Swanson Meat Packing of Sacramento, but when Swanson failed to pick up its option, Montgomery Investment purchased "The Topo." Edwin Breen managed the ranch for its owners for many years, while his brother Harry handled the bookkeeping from his home in Hollister. Harry's great contribution, from an historian's point of view, was his interest in family history. He was active in historical circles and published "A Short Sketch of the Lives of Patrick and Margaret Breen and Their Family" for the *Pony*

Express Courier in March 1937 (see Appendix D). He also collected manuscript material, including letters from Ireland, Canada and elsewhere to the Breens.

Edwin retired to San Juan Bautista and died in 1960. Going south on Interstate 101 today, as one passes Greenfield, nearing King City, Topo Ranch can be seen to the left in the hills, east of the river and the railroad tracks. In 1991, the owner was Henry Singleton of Los Angeles.

Julius Trescony, a King City pioneer, was the subject of an oral interview published as *An Heir to a Land Grant* in 1978, part of an oral history project of the University of California at Davis. Trescony said that Edwin Breen "deserved most of the credit for starting the California Rodeo" in 1911.

Patrick Breen, Jr. (1837-1899). Patrick Junior was born on March 12, 1837, in Iowa, according to a sketch in the *History of San Benito County, California.* In 1864 he married Amelia Anderson, a native of Australia, after courting her in Dublin, Alameda County. She was the daughter of Foster Anderson and Mary Nash, Protestants of County Armagh who emigrated to Sydney, Australia, in the 1820s. Amelia had come alone to California in the 1850s, after her mother's death, to join an aunt in Dublin. Five children of Patrick and Amelia lived to adulthood: Mary (Molly), William, Peter, Eugene, and Amelia. Both Patrick and his brother John brought their brides into the Catholic Church. Patrick became a prominent sheep and cattleman in the San Juan and Salinas valleys. He also produced wheat and fruit. On June 5, 1889, he reported his San Juan properties as consisting of 1,300 acres of tillable land, but did not report the acreage of his stock range. He had 400 cattle, 140 horses, 125 goats, 50 hogs. Two hundred acres were in barley and 300 in wheat.

The property remains in the hands of Patrick Breen's descendants. In 1982, nineteen heirs (there are more today, I am told) were sharing the income from rentals on over 1,400 acres of Breen & Hudner lands.

A distinguished descendant of Patrick Breen Jr. is Dr. Peter Raven of St. Louis, botanist, Director of the Missouri Botanical Garden, Home Secretary of the National Academy of Sciences, author of twenty books and over four hundred articles. Another is Philip Hudner of Kentfield, California, a partner in the law firm of Pillsbury, Madison, and Sutro in San Francisco and a former head of the Society of California Pioneers.

Simon Breen (1838-1899). Simon inherited his father's love of music and, much like his father, played the violin skillfully. He seems to have been something of a family maverick, not interested in achieving the material success of his older brothers, but he certainly was far from poor and no one of the Breen boys enjoyed life more than he did. Sometime in the late 1860s or early 1870s, he purchased a Dubois and Seabury grand piano for his wife and daughter and the piano was brought around the Horn from New York to California. Simon liked to bring his pals home from the bar at the Plaza Hotel in San Juan, in the wee hours of the morning. He insisted on waking up his daughter, Mary Catherine Flint, for her to play the piano, accompanying his violin. The piano is now a fixture of the San Juan Bautista State Historic Park and Museum, donated by Joe Cullumber, a grandson of Mary Catherine.

Grace Flint Ordway was a grand-daughter of Simon, and her son, Ed Ordway, has passed on the following memoir to me: "My mother at eleven years old thought Simon's bright red hair was beautiful and after it was washed it would glisten in the sun as he sat outside to dry it and to pull it into tiny curls, after which he would go in the house to read by a window."

Simon stories abound in the family folklore. He was said to be one of the finest horsemen in San Juan Bautista in the years following the Civil War. One of his favorite tricks, it is said, was to ride a bucking horse into the plaza where he would place a gold coin in the stirrup and bet anybody that he could buck the horse around the square without the coin falling. Of course he never lost. He also served as a self-appointed cook for the vaqueros at the Breen ranch. He married Marie Constance Pedancet and their children were Mary Catherine and Geneva. Mary Catherine, born in 1868, married Benjamin Flint at San Juan Bautista in 1886. Geneva married Albert Beuttler, who owned a brewery in San Juan and did much hauling over Pacheco Pass to the San Joaquin Valley.

Simon had quite a temper, according to stories passed on to Ed Ordway. He lived with his daughter Mary Catherine in his late years. The Flint children liked to hear him swear, and would tease him when he was reading by the window to get him to give them a chase and a few swear words. When they did not want to eat their breakfast one morning and were making excuses, Simon told them about the Donner Party and how glad he was at one time to have his buckskin shoes to eat. To make his point, he poured coffee on his hot cereal, added syrup, stirred it up and ate it. "They got his point," Ed Ordway was told, "but weren't too impressed."

"He liked little kids, especially little Ray Flint," says Ed Ordway. Ed was also told the following touching story:

> In 1899, when typhoid fever was spreading across the Valley, little Ray Flint caught it and died. Simon himself was sick, although not of typhoid, and was moved to San Juan where two women looked after him. Simon kept asking how "little Gobbie" (his pet name for Ray) was, but they gave him no word of Ray's death. On the day of the funeral, however, Simon heard the procession coming and managed to raise up on an elbow to lift the curtain. He recognized some of the horses and certain rigs. This was enough to tell him his little Gobbie was gone; thereupon, he lay back on his pillow and died. (*Ltr. June 23, 1991, Ed Ordway to author*)

James Frederick Breen (1841?-1899). James was born January 21, 1841 near Keokuk, Iowa, according to a sketch in *The History of San Benito County, California,* although family records give 1842 as the year of his birth. The year 1841 is consistent with his age of nineteen given on the 1860 United States Census, in the enumerations for San Juan Bautista taken on June 6 of that year. He graduated from Santa Clara College in 1861, was licensed as an attorney the following year and then associated himself with a law firm in San Francisco. About 1863 he set up his own office in San Juan Bautista. When San Benito County was created in 1871, James was appointed superior court judge. Prominent as a Catholic layman, he served from 1882 to 1885 as president of the Alumni Council of the University of Santa Clara, succeeding in office Bernard D. Murphy, the Council's first president. He married Catherine McMahon, daughter of James McMahon, proprietor during the 1870s and 80s of the McMahon House, a well-known hotel in Hollister, San Benito County.   James and Catherine had a son Peter William, who died young, and two daughters, Margaret and Grace.

James was a Republican in politics.   In the elections of 1868, he was defeated for state assemblyman on a platform committed to the ratification of the Fifteenth Amendment to the United States Constitution, granting equality to all men, regardless of skin color. However, in the elections of 1876, he succeeded in winning a seat in the Assembly, where his record in opposing legislation to limit rights of workers to organize into unions commended him to the radical Workingman's Party, for which he served as a delegate-at-large at one time.

Isaac Mylar wrote that the James Breen residence was a "large commodious, handsome structure....built for him by Con Hickey, when James married James McMahon's daughter Kate." Mylar said that Judge Breen "owned, down on the river bottom, some 200 acres of land which he eventually set out to pears."

In July 1876, Judge Breen gave the welcoming address in Hollister on the occasion of the one-hundredth anniversary of the establishment of Mission San Juan Bautista.

Peter Breen (1843-1870). Peter, who attended Santa Clara College, died on July 3, 1870, his twenty-seventh birthday. On an errand for the nuns at the Mission at San Juan, he was kicked into unconsciousness when he fell from his horse at Pajaro Creek, and drowned. His funeral at the Mission was the largest San Juan had ever witnessed. Peter had planned to marry and toward that end had made a land claim in the valley.

Young Peter died intestate. On April 4, 1871, his brothers John and Edward filed a "Petition for Letters of Administration" with the Probate Court for Monterey County. The petition listed the following items: (1) tract of land in Monterey County (San Benito County had not yet been formed), about 170 acres, unimproved, $9,000; (2) an undivided one-fourteenth interest in the real estate of Patrick Breen, deceased, as described in inventory appraisement of Patrick's estate, $6,000; and (3) one-fourteenth interest in the personal property described in same inventory, $2,500; total value of Peter's estate not to exceed $20,000. The closest kin were listed as his mother Margaret Breen and seven siblings. (For information on the estate of Patrick Breen, on which Peter's wealth was based, see the description later in this chapter.)

Among the papers in the possession of a Breen descendant is a poem addressed "To Peter E. Breen/From his Mother" and dated December 20, 1869 at San Juan:

> Preserve thy Mother's gift with care
> From moths and all consuming rust
> I know that the road to heaven is prayer
> The martyrs' shield, the Christians' trust -
> When years shall dim thy lustrous eye
> And thou wilt tent beneath the sod
> Then thou wilt have no fears to die
> For through this gift, thou hast known thy God.

It is written in a strong cursive script, definitely not her own (it is markedly at variance with her signature on her last will and testament), and is probably not her own composition. Curiously, on the same page, below the poem in a different and less firm hand, is an incomplete sentence: "Margaret [*long space*] My, dear this the last good I can" [*end of passage*].

[Margaret] Isabella Breen (1845-1935). Isabella was the youngest of the Breen children to have crossed with the Donner Party. She was given an education to equip her with the refinements of a Catholic lady of her "station." She studied at Catholic academies administered by nuns at Monterey and Benicia. In 1869, she married Thomas Morgan McMahon, brother of the Catherine McMahon who married Isabella's brother James, and they lived at Hollister in San Benito County. Isabella passed away in 1935 at the age of ninety, the last survivor of the Donner Party. In 1930, five years before she died, she spoke of her father's Bible, which her father passed on to his son, John, but which she now had in her possession. The Bible was a withered volume covered with buckskin. She remembered the time at San Juan when her father fashioned the cover because he feared the book would fall apart. Interviewed by a reporter not long before her death, Isabella recalled how the mothers in the high camps of the Sierras boiled the hides that formed the roofs of the cabins and made a glue to be eaten. "All their lives," she said, "none of the

Breens could bear the sight of calves foot jelly." She also said, "I suppose I had the smallest chance of them all to survive, and now I am the last to be living. How strange it seems to me!" Isabella's red hair was still evident in 1934, the year before she died, according to a grandniece, Isabelle Breen Raven of Walnut Creek, California.

William Breen (1849-1874). Born after the winter ordeal, William had a short life. He attended Santa Clara College and married Mary Zanetta, daughter of Angelo Zanetta, a chef and hotelman of Monterey and San Juan. He died in 1874, leaving his wife and an infant daughter, Mary.

LAST YEARS OF PATRICK AND MARGARET

During the last twenty years of his life, Patrick Breen had a record of much service to his community. He served as postmaster and school trustee. In the early 1850s he made a deposition to the court at San Jose on behalf of Father Anzar who was being cheated of rent money owed him by Captain Thomas Fallon on a small mission orchard at Santa Cruz. Breen countered the obviously perjured testimony of Fallon and a crony who claimed, in an earlier deposition, that Breen witnessed the priest's consent to a settlement of the claim on terms very favorable to Fallon.

The Fourth of July celebrations at San Juan were first held at "Breen's Grove." Isaac Mylar wrote that the grove was originally owned by his father "but by an amicable arrangement Breen bought the twenty acres from him upon which the grove was located."

Patrick and Margaret did not forget their relatives back east, with whom they corresponded regularly, nor the parish pastor of the chapel at Ballymurphy in Ireland. Two years after Patrick's death, Margaret received this letter dated December 30, 1869, from Father P. Carey, Parish Priest of Borris, County Carlow:

My dear Mrs. Breen

I received a few days before Xmas your esteemed note containing an order for £8 towards the erection of Belfry and Bell and also a Cross on your native Chapel [at] Ballymurphy. You of course never saw the present Chapel it is a plain and substantial building but it wants the Badge of Catholicity, the

Cross - Besides a bell (about 7 cwt, it will cost £60 in Dublin) will summon the people not only on Sundays and holidays to come and adore in God's House, but will ring at 6 in the morning, at noon and at 6 in the evening every day that all who hear may raise their hearts to God, and say the 'Angelus' in honor of the mystery of the Incarnation   Tho people already have made up with a good grace £80 but the contemplated improvements will cost £200.

I announced from the pulpit in Ballymurphy where you have so many relatives, your generous donation, that came 3,500 miles across the Continent of America and 3,500 miles across the Atlantic and asked the Congregation['s] fervent prayers for your family and also for your deceased husband - My request was piously responded to - I have said the number of Masses I promised and everyday I make a memento for you at the Altar.

Wishing your family health, happiness, and spiritual and temporal prosperity during the approaching New Year and many similar years and that we may meet in Heaven to enjoy countless years of Happiness.

> I am my dear Mrs. Breen
> gratefully yours
> P. Carey P.P.

Mrs. Breen
San Juan
P.S. I would have written sooner to gratefully acknowledge your donation but the hurry of Christmas prevented me. However time and space have been annihilated and this will reach you in nearly a fortnight I expect. P.C.

EPILOGUE

In Patrick's declining years, fiddle-playing was his favorite recreation. On Sundays, Margaret always expected her children to gather at the adobe after Mass. According to family tradition she was at times disappointed by Patrick Jr., when he was too busy with ranch work to join the family.

Patrick Breen died on December 21, 1868 at age seventy-three in his bedroom at the adobe in San Juan. His children and grandchildren and a priest were at his bedside. The following is a translation of an entry in Spanish made by Father Cipriano Rubio in the Mission register:

In the year 1868, 22nd of December, I gave ecclesiastical burial to the body of Patrick Breen, 78 years of age, married to Margaret Bulger, native of Ireland, County Carlow, died the day before, having received the sacraments of Penance, Communion, and Extreme Unction.

C.F. McGlashan wrote that Patrick was "a man of more than ordinary intelligence....his life furnishes a rare type of the pioneer Californian." The person George R. Stewart found so

Breen home (the "Castro Adobe") in San Juan Bautista, Wilt, Edwin and Harry Breen on porch. Circa 1890 photo, courtesy of Philip Hudner of Kentfield, California. "Old Dick" and carriage in foreground.

The Fault Line Shop in San Juan Bautista and view of Patrick Breen's
original 400 acre grant, looking north from the gazebo of the shop. 1991 photos.

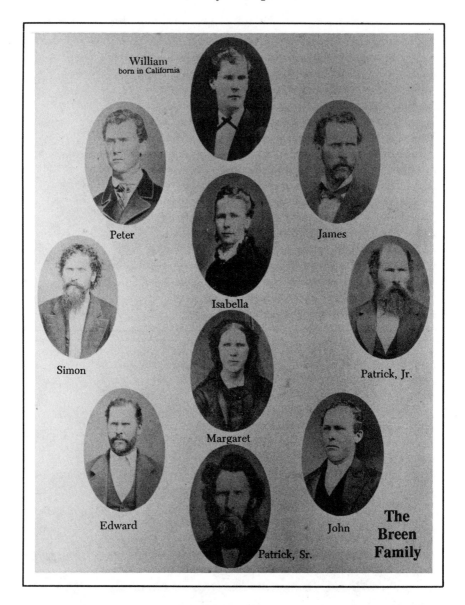

William
born in California

Peter

James

Isabella

Simon

Patrick, Jr.

Margaret

Edward

John

Patrick, Sr.

**The
Breen
Family**

(Margaret) Isabella Breen McMahon (1845-1935), less than a year old at the time of the entrapment, outlived all Donner Party survivors.

ordinary and even sluggish, except for a willingness to push a
pencil, play the fiddle, and pray, died a very wealthy man. His
will, dated December 6, 1868, indicated that he left one half of
his estate to his wife, and the other half in equal shares to his
seven sons, with the provision that they not sell any of the
property for two years. To his daughter Margaret Isabella
McMahon he bequeathed the sum of $3,000.

Patrick's property and personal estate was appraised at
over $110,000. The inventory included eleven items of prop-
erty: (1) the southwestern half of Rancho San Lorenzo north
of King City, 24,420 acres, appraised at $24,420; (2) a tract in
San Juan west of the Mission Orchard, 401 acres, $20,050; (3)
one "school land warrant located in the mountains near the
Round Springs," 320 acres, $480; (4) school land locations in
San Juan Valley in township 12 South Range 4 East, 461 acres,
$23,050; (5) a tract of land near Visalia in Tulare County
purchased from the government, 480 acres, $600;   (6)
possessory right to two pieces of government land near the
town of San Juan, 20 acres, $1,000; (7) lot 1 in block XVIII,
Smith's Map of San Juan, 130 x 134 ft. on the west side of the
plaza, occupied by the widow of the deceased, $3,500; (8) lot
2, block XX, 100 x 123 ft., $500; (9) lot 1, block XII, situated
on Second St., 103 x 207 ft., including saloon and frame house,
$4,000; (10) a lot in Monterey City southside of Decatur St.,
first lot east of William Malden's improvements, brick house,
$1,000; (11) a lot behind Hubbard's blacksmith's shop on First
St. in San Juan, $700.

The personal estate included (12) 1,500 head of cattle,
$30,000; (13) forty Spanish horses and mares, $800; (14) a two-
horse wagon, $60; and (15) household furniture, $200. The
papers that I examined did not include a statement of cash on
hand. Nevertheless, the estate as itemized was valued at more
than $110,000, a fortune in land and other wealth beyond the
dreams of the chieftains of old in County Carlow, Ireland.

The brick house on Decatur St. in the city of Monterey was
constructed in 1847 by Gallant D. Dickinson, an 1846 overland
immigrant. Some think it was the first brick house constructed
in California, a bit older than the George Zins house in
Sacramento built the same year. Patrick Breen purchased it in
1851 at a sheriff's auction. The bill of sale dated August 11,

1851 indicates he paid $1,376, of which $1,025 was for the lot with improvements; $66 for an adjacent lot; and $285 for a pile of 60,000 bricks at $47.50 per 1,000. The house was rented from 1852 to 1865 to the Davenport family. Long known as the "Breen Brick House," it was sold by Patrick Breen's grandson, Patrick William Breen, to R.M. Griffin in 1907, and in 1991 it was being restored by the California Department of Parks and Recreation

That Patrick had been zealous in acquiring and holding land was evident in a letter addressed to him by William J. Shaw on March 4, 1854, in reply to a letter from Patrick. The letter concerned "claim jumpers" or "squatters" who had settled on "school land warrants" claimed by Patrick Breen and which he had enclosed with fences. "What you did with the person[']s house and lumber," Shaw advised, "was perfectly right & you will without any reasonable doubt be held to have acted perfectly legally and properly." Breen employed attorney John Burke Phillips of the firm of Phillips and Ashley of Monterey to represent him on the school warrants. A receipt for $325 dated March 28, 1861 indicates that Phillips and Ashley received $315 for their services to Breen, $300 of it for the case of "Patrick Breen vs John Jordan" and $15 for the case of "Hollister *et al.* vs Patrick Breen." This was a litigious age in California, especially in the matter of land. (The school land warrants were in conformity with an act approved May 3, 1852, providing for the disposal of 500,000 acres of land donated to the state of California by the federal government.)

Margaret Bulger Breen died in 1874, six years after her husband. She surely ranks among the greatest heroines of the Old West. Without her strength, endurance and love, the Reeds, as well as her own family, would almost surely have perished at the camp by Donner Lake during the awful winter of entrapment. It is just as certain that, later at Starved Camp, nine children (five of her own and four others) and her husband would have perished, had she not been with them in that pit in the snow.

Margaret Bulger Breen was buried beside her husband on a hill in the district cemetery a short distance from the old Mission at San Juan.

GENEALOGY OF AN IRISH FAMILY

The genealogy of the Breens is worth studying, to show how a family of immigrants and their descendants became part of emerging and expanding Canadian and American societies. Toward that end, several appendices have been included. See also Notes to Chapter 1 in the Bibliography and Notes Section.

Patrick Breen, son of Edward (Ned) Breen and Mary Wilson, emigrated to Canada in 1828, according to family and other records. A younger brother, Samuel, married in Ireland and may have preceded Patrick to Canada by two years. (Samuel's oldest son, Edward, born in 1826, according to a Canadian baptismal record, claimed he was born very shortly after his parents' arrival in Canada.) By the early 1830s, Patrick, Samuel, two of their brothers (William and James), a sister, Charlotte, and their widowed mother were settled near today's city of London, Ontario. Another brother, Thomas, who later appears in Missouri, may also have joined the family earlier in Canada. Widow Mary Wilson Breen, whose husband Ned died in Ireland in 1816, was still alive at a great age in Canada in 1858, presumably living with her daughter Charlotte Burns. (See Appendix B, ltr. of March 3, 1853, to Patrick Breen from his brother William and nephew Patrick; also January 5, 1858 ltr. from John Canning to Patrick Breen.) Her death date and burial place have not been located. She had at least nine children, seven of whose baptisms are recorded on the registers of the Roman Catholic church at Borris, County Carlow (see Notes to Chapter 1). The nine known children of Edward and Mary Breen are:

Mary Breen (1793-1819), died in Ireland.

Patrick Breen (1795-1868), featured in this study.

William Breen (1798-1872). Married in Ireland to Mary Roche of Barnahashen Townland, County Carlow; they settled permanently in Canada. William died October 26, 1872 at the age of 74, Mary on October 24, 1890 at the age of 92. They are both buried at Holy Angels Cemetery in St. Thomas, Ontario. William and his son Patrick (called "Paddy") appeared on an 1848 list of tax assessments for Southwold Township, Elgin County, Ontario. Patrick had fifty acres (S-lot 7-LR) and his William had one hundred acres (N-lot 9-LR), both on Lake Road. Letters to Patrick Breen in California from William and his son indicate that they were not contented in Canada, and William's son wished to join his Uncle Patrick in California. That would not come to pass. Two children, both Irish-born, of William and Mary are known: William (1827-1851) and Patrick (1829-   ), who married Eleanor (aka Ellen) McGuire. Ellen died April 13, 1875 at age 43 after bearing at least ten children, several of whom settled in Michigan.

Samuel Breen (1800-1865). He married Margaret Murphy in Ireland. Their first child, Mary, was born there, year uncertain. Their second child, Edward, was born in Canada in 1826, shortly after the arrival of his parents. According to the recollections of Edward in old age, the family moved on to Burlington, Iowa, in 1833, and in 1837 to Tully, Missouri (near Canton). In 1840 and 1850, according to the censuses, they were residents of Jackson Township, Clark County, Missouri. In 1852, Samuel appeared on the California State Census, residing without family in the household of his brother Patrick in San Juan Bautista. It is evident that Samuel's wife and children arrived soon thereafter. On the 1860 United States Census for San Juan Township, Samuel was enumerated with his wife Margaret and several children: David (a blacksmith), Thomas, James, John, Margaret, and Catherine.

Old-timer Isaac Myler wrote that Samuel's oldest son, Edward, conducted a horse-shoeing business at Washington and Third streets in an adobe next to the Vache adobe. "Edward Breen was a happy-go-lucky chap," said Mylar, "who was forever playing tricks on the wights."

Samuel Breen and Margaret Murphy had thirteen children, eleven of whom are known:

(1) <u>Mary</u>, born in Ireland, married Patrick Daly at St. Marysville (now St. Patrick), Clark County, Missouri, arrived in California about 1853, and settled at Placerville. Two sons, Dennis, a widower, and William H., single, were living there in 1900 in households with several nieces, nephews, and cousins; (2) <u>Edward</u> (1826-1925) was baptized on July 17, 1828 at St. Thomas, Ontario, by missionary priest Fr. James W. Campion, his godparents being his uncle and aunt, Patrick Breen and Charlotte Breen (records of St. Augustine's Parish, Dundas). The baptismal entry indicates that he was born twenty months previously, on November 27, 1826. Edward married Elizabeth Ellen Simpson (1833-1915), whose father was a nephew of Daniel Boone, and they had nine

children. After working as a blacksmith at San Juan Bautista in the 1860s, Edward returned to Missouri where he died at Monticello on September 26, 1925, age 98, at the home of a daughter, Margaret Morrow. He had been converted to Protestantism some years before at a revival meeting and received a Protestant burial. A descendant of Edward is Troy C. Dacon, head of Omega-Epsilon Publications in San Diego. Another descendant is Vivian Breen Manka of Fort Madison, Iowa, the family genealogist;   (3) William (1830-   ) was born on February 7, 1830 and baptized at Yarmouth, Ontario, on May 26, 1830 by Fr. James W. Campion, his godparents being James Breen (presumably his uncle) and Bridget Brady (records of St. Augustine's Parish, Dundas), alive in Missouri in 1841;   (4) David, born January 1, 1832 in Canada, was working as a blacksmith in 1860 at San Juan Bautista, and died November 11, 1868 of smallpox. He was buried in the Catholic portion of the cemetery at San Juan Bautista;   (5) Thomas, born 1834 in Lee County, Iowa, married Matilda Boyle at Our Lady Help of Christians at Watsonville in May 1857, and they had six children. Thomas died July 3, 1872 in Ventura County, California, and was buried at the Old Mission Burial Ground. Matilda died March 22, 1920 and was buried in Long Beach, California;   (6) Ann, born 1838, died 1869, married Cornelius Hickey on November 8, 1854, and had three children, John, Mary Ellen (Nellie) and Annie. John Hickey married Mercedes Echeveria and had nine children. Nellie Hickey (1857-1919) married John Welch (1856-1922) on September 6, 1882 at Hollister, San Benito County, California, and they had six children, including Mary Welch who died in the spring of 1991 in San Benito County. Ann Hickey never married;   (7) Elizabeth, born 1840, died 1929, first married ___ Spitts, and after his death married Benjamin Cyrus Wilcox. She had four children, Mary, Julia, Sarah, Edward; (8) James, born about 1842, died 1887, married Fidella Sanford on August 19, 1868, and they had four children;   (9) Margaret, born March 12, 1848, died October 4, 1926, married Jose Gregorio Sanchez on July 10, 1865, eleven children;   (10) Catherine, born March 12, 1850, died June 3, 1934, married George Craig, one son, George, who never married; widowed in 1873, Catherine married Charles Peck, and they had two daughters, Margaret and Charlotte;   (11) John, born February 11, 1846, died June 13, 1867, never married, was buried in a Catholic plot at San Juan Bautista District Cemetery, San Benito County.

After Samuel Breen had raised his family, he left his wife at the home of a daughter in Hollister and went to live with another daughter, Mary Daly, in Placerville. Samuel died in July 1865 at Nigger Hill near Placerville. Samuel's wife, Margaret, died February 13, 1898 and was buried in the Catholic cemetery at Hollister.

Top: Margaret Murphy Breen (1800-98), who married Samuel Breen in Ireland in the 1820s. Their son Edward was born shortly after their arrival in Canada about 1826. *Below, L to R, four generations*: Celestin Leo Breen (1865-1951); Edward Breen (1826-1925); Clarence R. Breen (1892-1962), holding daughter Ruth (b 1915). Fort Madison, Iowa, October 1922. Courtesy of Vivien Breen Manka, Fort Madison.

George Breen (1803-   ), born at Ballymurphy, County Carlow (see Notes to Chapter 1), nothing else known.

Edward Breen (1805-   ), born at Barnahasken, County Carlow (see Notes to Chapter 1), nothing else known.

James Breen (1806-   ), born at Barnahasken, County Carlow (see Notes to Chapter 1), of whom very little is known. He was a witness at the wedding of his sister Charlotte to Patrick Burns at Southwold, Ontario, in 1828, and he was a sponsor at the baptism of his nephew William Breen, son of Samuel, at Yarmouth, Ontario, in 1830.

Thomas Breen (1810-   ), born at Barnahasken, County Carlow (see Notes to Chapter 1). He is doubtless the "Uncle Thomas" mentioned in an 1852 letter from Samuel Breen's daughter, Mary Daly, of Clark County, Missouri, to Margaret Breen, wife of her uncle, in California. She wrote that Thomas married "a bouncing widow, of Hardscrabble" in the fall of 1851. (See Appendix B, The Bathtub Papers.)

Charlotte Breen.   Born after 1810, she married Patrick Burns at Southwold, Ontario, on November 4, 1829, her brother James Breen being among several witnesses, Fr. Campion officiating. A son, Thomas, was baptized at Southwold on January 19, 1831, the godparents listed as "Patrick Breen and Peggy Breen," with missionary priest Fr. Cullen officiating (records of St. Augustine's Parish, Dundas). On October 1, 1839, a daughter Charlotte was baptized at St. Thomas, Ontario, according to the earliest records of St. Thomas Church. Charlotte married Bartholomew Coughlin in January 1855, with James Breen and Sarah McNiff as witnesses. Two sons, John William and Daniel, were born in 1856 and 1862.

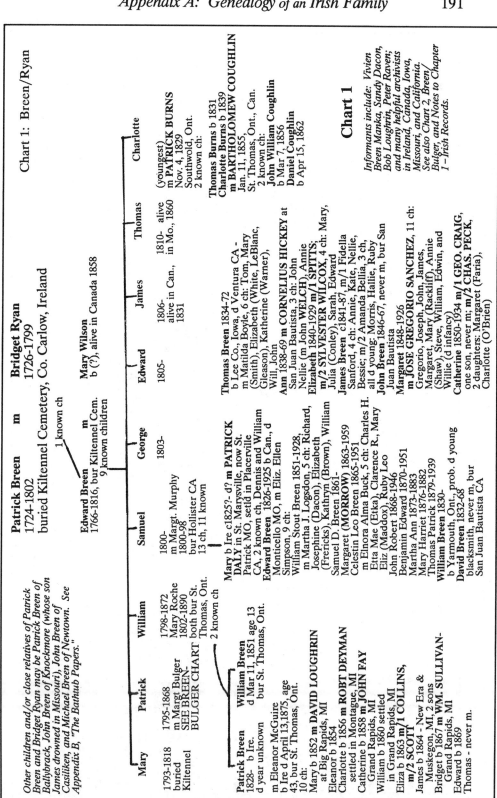

Chart 1: Breen/Ryan

Other children and/or close relatives of Patrick Breen and Bridget Ryan may be Patrick Breen of Ballybrack, John Breen of Knockmore (whose son James drowned in Missouri), John Breen of Casiliken, and Michael Breen of Newtown. See Appendix B, "The Bathub Papers."

Patrick Breen   m   **Bridget Ryan**
1724-1802   1726-1799
buried Kiltennel Cemetery, Co. Carlow, Ireland

1 known ch

Edward Breen
1766-1816, bur Kiltennel Cem.
9 known children

m

Mary Wilson
b (?), alive in Canada 1858

Children: Mary | Patrick | William | Samuel | George | Edward | James | Thomas | Charlotte

Mary
1793-1818
buried
Kiltennel

Patrick
1795-1868
m Margt Bulger
SEE BREEN-
BULGER CHART

William
1798-1872
Mary Roche
1802-1890
both bur St.
Thomas, Ont.
2 known ch

Samuel
1800-
m Margt. Murphy
1800-98
bur Hollister CA
13 ch, 11 known

George
1803-

Edward
1805-

James
1806-
alive in Can.,
1831

Thomas
1810- alive
in Mo, 1860

Charlotte
(youngest)
m PATRICK BURNS
Nov. 4, 1829
Southwold, Ont.
2 known ch:

Patrick Breen 1828- b Ire.
d year unknown
m Eleanor McGuire
b Ire d April 13,1875, age
43, bur St. Thomas, Ont.
10 ch:
Mary b 1852 m DAVID LOUGHRIN
at Big Rapids, MI
Eleanor b 1854
Charlotte b 1856 m ROBT DEYMAN
settled in Montague, MI
Catherine b 1858 m JOHN FAY
Grand Rapids, MI
William b 1860 settled
in Grand Rapids, MI
Eliza b 1863 m/1 COLLINS,
m/2 SCOTT
James b 1864 - New Era &
Muskegon, MI, 2 sons
Bridget b 1867 m WM. SULLIVAN-
Grand Rapids, MI
Edward b 1869
Thomas - never m.

William Breen
d Mar 11, 1851, age 13
bur St. Thomas, Ont.

Mary b Ire c1825?- d? m PATRICK
DALY in St. Marysville, now St.
Patrick MO, setld in Placerville
CA, 2 known ch, Dennis and William
Edward Breen 1826-1925 b Can., d
Monticello MO, m Eliz. Ellen
Simpson. 9 ch:
William Stout Breen 1851-1928, m
Martha J. Logsdon, 5 ch: Richard,
Josephine (Dacon), Elizabeth
(Frericks), Kathryn (Brown), William
Samuel D. Breen 1861-
Margaret (MORROW) 1863-1959
Celestin Leo Breen 1865-1951
Etta Mae (Etka), Clarence R., Mary
Eliz (Maddox), Ruby Leo
John Robert 1868-1946
Benjamin Edward 1870-1951
Martha Ann 1873-1883
Mary Harriet 1876-1882
Thomas Patrick 1879-1939
William Breen 1830-
b Yarmouth, Ont., prob. d young
David Breen 1832-68
blacksmith, never m, bur
San Juan Bautista CA

Thomas Breen 1834-72
b Lee Co., Iowa, d Ventura CA -
m Matilda Boyle, 6 ch: Tom, Mary
(Smith), Elizabeth (White, LeBlanc,
Gleason), Katherine (Warner),
Will, John
Ann 1838-69 m CORNELIUS HICKEY at
San Juan Bautista, 3 ch: John
Nellie (m John WELCH), Annie
Elizabeth 1840-1929 m/1 SPITTS;
m/2 SYLVESTER WILCOX, 4 ch: Mary,
Julia (Conley), Sarah, Edward
James Breen c1841-87, m/1 Fidella
Sanford, 4 ch: Annie, Kate, Nellie,
Bessie; m/2 Amanda Bellia, 3 ch,
all d young: Morris, Hallie, Ruby
John Breen 1846-67, never m, bur San
Juan Bautista
Margaret 1848-1926
m JOSE GREGORIO SANCHEZ, 11 ch:
Gregorio, Joseph, John, James,
Margaret, Mary (Rackliff), Annie
(Shaw), Steve, William, Edwin, and
Willie (d infancy)
Catherine 1850-1934 m/1 GEO. CRAIG,
one son, never m; m/2 CHAS. PECK,
2 daughters: Margaret (Faria),
Charlotte (O'Brien)

Thomas Burns b 1831
Charlotte Burns b 1839
m BARTHOLOMEW COUGHLIN
Jan. 11, 1855,
St. Thomas, Ont., Can.
2 known ch:
John William Coughlin
b Mar 7, 1856
Daniel Coughlin
b Apr 15, 1862

Chart 1

Informants include: Vivien Breen Manka, Sandy Dacon, Bob Loughrin, Peter Raven; and many helpful archivists in Ireland, Canada, Iowa, Missouri, and California. See also Chart 2, Breen/Bulger, and Notes to Chapter 1 – Irish Records.

Chart 1: Breen/Ryan

Chart includes 8 children, 31 grandchildren, 54 great-grandchildren, and 76 great-great grandchildren of Patrick Breen and Margaret Bulger.

Patrick Breen 1795–1868
b Barnahasken, Co. Carlow, Ire.
m
Margaret Bulger 1806–1874
b Rathgeran, Co. Carlow, Ire.
8 children

John Breen 1832–1903 b Can.

m Margt Leah Smith
12 ch (10 known):
Margt. Jane "Lillie" 1852–1915
Patk. Edward 1856-1938 the "Topo Pigeon" m Henrietta, no ch.
Adelaide c1858-1941
John Joseph 1860-85
Thos. Frank 1861-1946 m Kemp, 2 ch: Fran̄k, Blanche (Moore)
Mary Cath. c1865-c1957 m THOS. NYLAND 7 ch:
Edith (Macaral)
1 ch: Hazel (Laswell)
Bertha (Clark) 3 ch: Waldo, Gertrude (Orr) Virginia
Joseph Nyland, 2 ch: Peter, Betty
Adele (McConnell) no ch
Arthur Nyland 1895-1970
Mary Dorothy (Avila),
Harvey Nyland
Leah m Ralph Rosborough, 2 ch: Robert, Margt. (m/1 White, m/2 Gampell)
Agnes m Allen King, 1 ch: Marilyn (Neuterman) no ch
Isabelle 1867-1931 m Thos. F. Murray, 4 ch: Isabel C., Daniel J., Thomas F., Mary Madeline
Alice Gertrude 1870-1941
Charlotte A.(Obenchain) 1874-1931, 2 ch: Leo and John. Central Pt., Ok
Ellen (Eileen) A. (Stoddard) 1876-1937

Edward J. Breen 1833–90 b Can.

m/1 Cath. Sullivan, 3 ch:
Eugene 1859- no ch.
Jas. Edward 1871 d young
John Roger d young

m/2 Mary Jane Burns, 3 ch:
William A. Breen 1882- m Josephine Redmond 1 ch: Patk. William Breen Jr.
Jas. Edwin Breen 1884- m Charlotte O'Reilly 2 ch:
Barbara m WM. FRANKLIN CORNELL JR 5 ch:
Frank Cornell
Sydney (Curtis)
Gregory Cornell
John Patk. Cornell
Mari (Rossi)
Edwina m PETER KUMP 3 ch:
Peter E. Kump
Vicki (Englert),
Mary (Byrnes)
Harry Jos. Breen 1886- m Eileen Muder, no ch

Patrick Breen 1837–99 b Iowa

m Amelia Anderson, 6 ch:
Mary (Mollie) c1864- m JOHN L. HUDNER, 4 ch:
Paul Hudner m Mary Dooling, 3 ch: John, Philip (m Carla Raven), Stephen
Charles W. Hudner
Mary Amelia m NEIL DOUGHERTY, 2 ch:
Carol m WM. DOUGHERTY
Joan m HENRY J. GORIN
Helen Isabelle Hudner, unm.
William c1867-d young
Patk. Wm Breen 1870- m Charlotte Lenhart, 5 ch:
Elizabeth (Thornton), 3 ch: Anne (Fay), Marsha (Dawson) Mary (Doherty)
Josephine, unmarried
Anne, her twin, d infancy (2 wks)
Emily (Hecht), no ch.
James P. m/1 (Rita Campion); 2 ch: Mgt. Amelia (Thoming), Patrick; m/2 (Betty Hackett), 2 ch: Mary Amelia(Tipton) and Paul
Peter Breen c1874-m Laura Lenhart 2 ch:
John m Eileen Donohoe, 4 ch: John,Thomas,Peter,Anne(Solem)
Isabelle m WALTER RAVEN 1 ch: Peter Raven
Eugene Breen c1877- m Lillian, 3 ch:
John Robt, 2 ch: Mollie (Wilbur) and Nancy
Anne Breen of Pacific Grove
Paul, 5 ch: Paul Jr., Mollie (Kledzik), Anne (Becker) Patricia, Nancy (Apgood)
Amelia (Amy) 1880- m Tom O'Donnell, 3 ch: Tom, Clair, Amelia (Mimi) – no ch

---

Simon P. Breen 1838–99 b Iowa

m Marie C. Pedancet 2 ch:
Mary Catherine 1867- m BENJAMIN FLINT JR. 7 ch:
Benjamin Flint m Myrtle Cullumber
Grace Flint m EDWARD ORDWAY JR 2 ch: Grace (O'Connor) Edward Ordway
Raymond Flint, d young
Carolina Flint m JOSEPH CULLUMBER 7 ch:
Joseph Cullumber m Gladys Garratt
Gene Cullumber
Betty (Stephens)
Donald Cullumber
Lois (Schwartz)
Shirley (Maggini)
Wm. Alan Cullumber m Stella Franco
Eva Flint m/1 WALTER TOMLINSON, 3 ch:
Gladys (Hargous)
Ray Tomlinson
Robt. Tomlinson
m/2 PETER GALLI
Arthur Flint m Selma Swanson, 2 ch:
Jack Flint m Marie Raines
Marilyn m ROBERT HARRISON
Wm. Bradford Flint m Violet Moran, 1 ch: Wm. B. Flint Jr.

James F. Breen 1841–99 b Iowa

m Cath. McMahon, 3 ch:
Peter W. (d young), Margaret 1875-, Grace 1880- m Fjn Lund, Danish diplomat, no ch.
Geneva Breen 1866- m ALBERT BEUTTLER 10 ch:
John Louis, 1886-1900
Rose (Barrington), 2 ch: Mary Ellen, Jay
Albert (Jake) Beutler 3 ch: Francis, Zona, Wallace
Mary (Baldwin), 2 ch: Joie, Artie
George (Pilo), no ch
Margarete (Jones), 1 ch: Bonnie
Simon Beuttler, 3 ch: Doris, Agnes, Simon
Eva (Inns), 1 ch: Arthur Inns Jr.
Agnes (Johnson), 2 ch: Geneva, Bobby
Louis James, b 1906, 1 ch: Judy

Peter Breen 1843–70 b Iowa drowned in Pajaro Creek

(Margt.) Isabella Breen 1845–1935 b Iowa last Donner Party survivor
m THOS. MCMAHON 1 adop. dau.–Helena m Dr. ___ Smith; d young, no ch.

William Michael Breen b Cal. 1849–74
m Mary "Mariquita" Zanetta (who had 2nd m to Lupe Anzar) 1 dau: Mary (Mamie) Breen m JOHN KRAUSE, 2 dau: one d 9 mos; June m EMERSON LASATER, 2 ch (adop), Michael, John

---

c = circa, approximately

CHART 2: BREEN/BULGER

Informants include: Joe Cullumber, Ed Ordway, Marilyn Harrison, Phil Hudner, Isabelle Raven, Peter Raven, Elizabeth Thornton, Joan Gorin, Ann Breen, Barbara Breen, Edwina Avila, Harvey Nyland, Dorothy Avila, Leah Rosborough, Margaret Gampell, Jay Barrington. Other sources include civil and church records in Ireland, Canada, Iowa, and California.

THE BATHTUB PAPERS

"The Bathtub Papers" have survived because forty-five years ago a great-great-grandson of Patrick and Margaret Breen, only fifteen at the time, recognized their historical value. That descendant is Philip Hudner of Kentfield, California, long a partner of the law firm of Pillsbury, Madison and Sutro in San Francisco and a former president of the Society of California Pioneers.

Mr. Hudner took a keen interest in Breen family history early in life. His grandmother's first cousin, Harry J. Breen (a son of Edward Breen), was an avid collector of Breen folklore and documents. Among the documents in Harry's possession were five letters dated from 1852 to 1860 to the Breens from relatives in Canada and from a friend and another relative in Missouri. The letters were long and filled with priceless genealogical and other information about Ireland, Canada, and Missouri. Young Phil Hudner took on the difficult job of making very accurate typewritten transcripts of the letters. Were it not for a few clues in these letters, I would not have been able to acquire the Irish records on the Breen family (e.g., baptismal records, tithes, headstone inscriptions).

The originals of these letters and two letters from the parish priest in County Carlow remained with Harry until his death in 1960. His files were found in his bathtub in great disarray and were removed to the priest's house at the old Mission. It seemed that the papers were about to be thrown out when Hudner got word, made a fast trip to San Juan, and managed to retrieve them. In recent years he has loaned the papers to the Bancroft Library in Berkeley, because this library, as he wrote in a letter to the director of Bancroft, "is the preeminent library of Western history and already has Patrick Breen's diary and naturalization papers...I am concerned only with their safekeeping and availability to researchers and scholars." Mr. Hudner has given me permission to print the letters, which he calls "The Bathtub Papers."

To Mr. Hudner, I am also grateful for permission to print the 1826 letter testifying to Margaret Bulger's good character, and the 1869 letter thanking her for her contribution to the chapel construction fund, from the parish pastor of Borris in County Carlow. Those letters appear in Chapters 10 and 16. The letters that follow are presented without editorial correction, except for occasional paragraph divisions for the Canada and the Canning letters in the interests of clarity. For the identity of persons mentioned in the letters, see Appendix A: Genealogy, Chapter 1, Notes to Chapter 1, and Chapter 16.

Letter from Mary Daly of Clark County, Missouri, March 12, 1852, to Margaret Breen in San Juan Bautista, California. Mary is the wife of Patrick Daly and the oldest daughter of Samuel Breen, brother to Patrick.

My dear Aunt: – –

It is useless for me to attempt to describe my feeling when I read the numerous letters from your family to my parents, and find that my name is past and forgotten. It really appears as though you never let your imagination wander back to bygone days – to days that we have passed in "converse sweet", whilst I might say, in the United States, for I do not consider California one of them.

Edward and David have been talking of seeking their fortunes on the "golden shores" of the Pacific, but I think they have given out the notion, which I consider a very pious idea. – – David is now erecting him a shop at home for the purpose of commencing work at his trade. He is said to be a pretty fair workman.

Uncle Thomas – as you have long since heard – undoubtedly was married last fall to a widow, or as the saying is, to a "Bouncing Widow" of Hardscrabble. Upon an average he has married and parted once per week ever since. As for a farther history of his life you shall have upon demand. My husband is still in California, I recd. a letter from him dated December 24th. He wrote that he would be at home or would start home this month or next. I look for him, or will fondly anticipate his return in May or June.

I have but one child living a fine three year old boy, who says he wants to see his pappa very badly. My first child a boy now lies in our church-yard three miles below this.

I was truly gratified to hear of the marriage of your son, John Breen. I might say it was with mingled feelings of pleasure and regret. It was a pleasure to me to think he had found a lady on the Western shores of the United States, upon whom he could place his affections, a regret because I had warmly anticipated his return to Mo. for the purpose of finding a "better half" as David would term it. Tell him I hope he will be blessed with a namesake for me soon. Tender him and his wife my warmest love.

Mrs. Cowgill and Elisha bid me tender their regards to yourself and family. She is going to quit housekeeping for the purpose of educating Elisha.

Uncle Thomas says that he received a letter from Uncle Patrick some time since, stating that if he would go out to California he would give him all the money he wanted. I think it is dangerous to make such propositions as he is a man that would have a heart to take a consideration. In fact, such propositions are dangerous to make to any of us. The poet says –

'In vain our blocks and fields increase our store
When our abundance makes us wish for more.'

It might be so with him, but if you have really made him any such proposals I hope he will not want more than you can afford to give him.

I must come to a close. I have drawn my unprofitable scroll to a much greater length than I thought when I commenced. Write immediately,

And I am, as ever

Your Affectionate Niece

Mary Daly

Letter from William and Patrick Breen of Southwold Township [Ontario, Canada], November 2, 1852, to Patrick Breen in San Juan Bautista, California. The envelope bears Port Stanley and London [Ontario] postmarks. Letter writer William is Patrick's brother; letter writer Patrick is William's son.

Dear Brother   I received your leter which gave me great pleasure to hear that you and family were well which this leaves us all here at present thank God for it.

We are not able to give you any information as yet concerning James Bulger as we sent two leters to Toronto and was returned, the Priest was in Toronto twice this summer and made all inqureas [inquiries] both times of the Priest in Toronto & got his name in the papers   on the first of October and if he is anywhere in the vicinity of Toronto or in Upper Canada we will be able to give you an account in our next leter which will be as soon as we get any acount from him.

You wished to know who lived in the old house at home   from what I can find from a leter from Edward Doyle Kyle, it is Norwegeons lives there at present   they are people from Norway   minors   this is a changable world   I little thought once in my lifetime such people would live there. John Corry is got the land. [See note below.]

Concerning Ireland the birthplace of us all and many thousands beside us is got to be a poor distressed country by poor law and the failure of the potatoe crop two thirds of the inhabitants is broke. Patt Breen of Ballybrack is dead   John Breen of Knockmore his family is most in America   James his son came to America last summer   him and his wife was going to Missouri & got drowned on the Mississippi river. John Breen of Caselikin and family is well & desire to be remembered to you all, James Fenlon and family is well, Hugh OByrne I do not know I believe lives in the Detroit. [See note below.]

Prices of produce here this year Wheat 5s 6d per bushel – corn 50 cents – Potatoes 2s per bushel – Pork 4 to 5 dolors per hundred   Beef 3 to 4 dollors per hundred – Butter 1 to 1s – 3d per pound. Labouring men from ten to twelve dollors per month   there is a vast diffirence between the prices here and in California   I would like to know the prices of land in that country.

Mother enjoys pretty good health at present　she begins to look pretty old though　she is as smart on foot appearantly as she was ten years ago. We have got no account from Missurie now in three years, Burns and family is well. Myself and family is well and wishes to be remembered to you all. When you receive this send me an answer as soon as possible.　No more at present but remain yours

Affectionate Brother William Breen

[*postscript*]　Dear Uncle　You dont seem to encourage a person to go to that country　the object of my views was this, I intended to rent the farm & go to that country　I thought the quickes way to earn the money to raise the deed　Sir if it would not be to great a favour for me to ask if you could send me to the amount of three [or] four hundred dollors as I have got to pay the past payment on my land in fifty four, do not think that I want you to make a present of it　By no means, if you have riches you dearly earned it.　But if you could let me have to that amount it will oblige me in most wonderfull manner immaginable.　And I would send it back in two years with interest so as to have you satisfied.

Your nephew　Patrick Breen

Author's note:　John Corry is the John Curry who appeared on the c1850 *Griffiths Valuations* as leaseholder of most of the County Carlow land occupied by the Breens before their emigration in 1828 (see Notes to Chapter 1). It seems that a family of Norwegian miners was occupying the Breen house in County Carlow in 1852 or thereabouts.　Hugh O Byrne was clerk of the committee, which included Patrick Breen, that addressed a petition for a resident priest to Bishop Macdonnel of Kingston in September 1830.　He is listed as a warden for the church at St. Thomas in 1831, 1834, and 1836 on the "Church Wardens of St. Thomas Church Account & Memorandum Book," Diocese of London Archives.　With Dennis O'Brien, he was western agent for the weekly newspaper *The Catholic* in 1830, published at Kingston.

Joint letter from William and his son Patrick Breen of Southwold Township [Ontario], March 3, 1853, to Patrick Breen in San Juan Bautista, California. The envelope bears the postmarks of Port Stanley and London, Ontario (March 5, 1853) and Stockton, California (April 18), and carried fifteen cents postage. The letter and postscript are in the same handwriting, probably that of Patrick Breen.

Dear brother

　I received your leter the first of March & now answer it to let you know that father [and] all the family are well, hoping this will find you & family the same　you seem to speak pretty hard of California　I dare say that all your statment is correct it must be so where so many go & dont seem to know where they were going to Cal to get rich diging I knowed people that left Canada to go diging for gold that had never a spade in their hands or any other implemet of labouring work, broke down store keepers and half broke that would not work here nor there or any other place them was principally the people that went from those Countrys & perhaps the same from other places, the murder and robries there would not daunt me not in the lease if it is a mans fate to hapen so I suppose he cant help it. But when I am going there I shall bring such articles as would defend my life from such action it is nothing but right to warn a man of like danger it shows that you are a man of wisdom and understanding as I have often heard you were but knowing little of it till lately But this villiany will be stoped ther[e] I suppose in a short time now.

With regard to this country I suppose you are pretty well acquainted with the climate & say nothing of the goverment. I am now worth about 8 or 9 hundred dollars by selling of all property and stock I have I had a miss crop of wheat which trowed [throwed] me about 2 hundred dollors behind last year the winters here so long and the summer season so short that a man have to hire to get his work done in any season them prices dolors that it is pretty hard to make payments it will take me 3 or 4 years yet to get my land paid for & then in 20 years to come I dont expect to be much better than is people here 25 years & not no better of[f] now than they were 20 years ago some of your old neighbours hard industrous people A man can make a living here I know by being industrious and carefull but for makeing property I neednt mind it it will take a man six months to rake up hay in summer then six months in winter to trow to cattle to keep them from starving you dont do that in California dont you think a man by being indu[strious?] in California could make a home in course of 5 or 6 or 10 years the rest of the family choped and cleard 100 acres in Dunwich & will not have to pay at the rate of twelve dollors per acre you have not sent the price of land in that country I should like to know in your next letter about it

With regard to James Bulger I have got no account as yet [see note below] I got it in the Toronto paper stating that you want to hear from him that he was to write to me & got no account as yet perhaps you have You say that Unkle Samuel arived in that country I wish him luck and prosperity in his undertakings you said for me to show the leter I received from you to my father I never got a leter from you but I showed to him nor wrote one to you without his abrobation it is his wishes to go to see you but I suppose he never will unless all the family goes you need not encourage any person to go there but your prety good judge between both places & you can state in your next leter how an industrous person could make a living in that country We are all an industrous family & dont expect to make a living any other way we have to do that in Canada and would just as soon do it in California

as here   I do not expect to stop in cold Canada all my lifetime except it thor--
[sense of "unless it thaws"?]

   my father and mother & all the family send our love to you all   Grandmother & Burns & family is well. When you receive this send an answer as
soon as you can quickly if we are far distant it will be pleasure to hear from
you & family & Samuel and his family. No more at present. But remain
yours

William Breen   Patrick Breen

Author's note: James Bulger is most likely a brother or uncle of Margaret
Bulger Breen. Uncle Samuel is the brother of Margaret's husband, Patrick
Breen. "Grandmother" is Mary Wilson Breen, mother of Patrick, William,
Samuel, *et al.* "Burns and family" are Patrick Burns, his wife Charlotte
Breen, and their daughter Charlotte.

---

*Letter from John Canning of Sugar Grove [Fairfield County, Ohio], January 5,
1858, to Patrick Breen of San Juan Bautista, California.*

Dear Friend   I have received two letters from you one dated Oct. 9th. the
other Nov. 18th. both came here nearly at the same time, they raised feelings
in me that I thought were long since deadened by age and time, for several
nights whenever I closed my eyes I was in the "Bonnie Glen where early we
sported" and when awake I could think of nothing but the incidents of our
early days, many things I had long since forgot came vividly to my recollections and in imagineation I was young again.

   I need not tell you how happy it made me to hear from you and to find
that you are in easy circumstances. The last account I had from you was a
letter dated Oct. 17th. 1833 in which you mentioned an intention of going to
Illinois with Sam and M. Noddy   although I wrote to you several times afterwards I got no answer which I suppose was owing to both of us changing our
residence nor have I had any word from my mother   much later I wrote to
her in the spring or summer of '34 and sent her 40 sence. since that [then] I
never heard from her.

   I got married in August '34 and the spring following moved to Morgan
Co. Ohio and from there to Adams Co. Ohio where I bought 50 acres of land
and had a prospect of doing well when I lost it by the rascality of a man I
thought my friend and trusted too far.

   I afterwards went to the State of Indiana and lived about 60 miles below
the falls of Ohio for 4 years, that would be an easy place to live but for the
sickness, myself and family were scarcely ever free from Bilious diseases and
an ulcer had broke out on me after a severe attack of fever (called by Doc-
tors Fistula in Ano).

I went back to Pennsylvania where my health recruited but for several years the ulcer remained extremely painful at times and often making me unable to work and my family was increasing and all too small to help me any and it took harder work to live in Pen. than in Indiana. I worked mostly at a furnace cutting cord wood where I could work when I was able and rest when I was not, I went to live at a furnace in Lawerance Co. Ohio seduced by higher wages but found it as unhealthy as Indiana and moved back to Pen.

My oldest son (Patrick called after you) now began to be able to help me which made times a little easier. I had in the meantime got hold of 40 Acres of land where I now live and moved to it about three years ago, but I cannot do very well on it   the soil is very thin and in a bad settlement   mostly Germans and Virginians ignorant views and hoggish so that we are as much alone as if we lived in a Desert Island. There is a C. Church about 3 miles from us but the congregation is all Germans and the Preist attending it will not preach at all in English although often requested too as all the younger part of the congregation understand it, and he speaks it fluently. Drunkeness prevails amongst most of the Germans to an extent greater than I ever seen amongst the worst Irish.

My farm is not sufficient to support my family and a days work cannot be had without going 10 or 12 mil after it to the prairie or river bottoms where it is sickly   I will leave as soon as I can sell.

My son has been over most of the country west as far as the centre of Missouri and he found nearly all the Congress land that was worth any thing bought by speculators and held at high prices   all the Congress land in Ohio has been bought mostly by speculators for 12 1/2 cents per acre under the graduation law and although they got it by fraud and perjury they still hold it but it is not safe to buy from for the law requires 5 years settlement before making a deed.

I shall probably go to Pen. again where I can buy land in some of the new counties cheap still of a pretty good quality and at least in a healthy climate.

I have 3 sons and 4 daughters living   Patrick 22 years old   Mary 20 Margaret 18 Ellen 15 James 13 Thomas 22 and Jane 8   Pat and Mary live away from home   the others are still with me and are now going to school. I have been unable to educate them as I would wish, but thanks to God I have brought them up so far in Religion and morality, I do not believe that an oath or profane word ever passed the lips of any of them or that they ever spent a quarter of an hour in bad company   they are almost as eager as I am to hear from you for they have heard me spek so often of you that your name is more familiar to them than that of any of their relations

the little prayer book you gave me many years ago when you came to see me on the Maume [see note below] with your name written in it I still have though some what worn by constant use, often I have looked at it and at some old letters from you, and thought of our travels and adventures and the happy hours of friendship and sociability we spent together sometimes hoping we might meet again, I feel as I grow old a greater wish to see the friends of my youth and the "old sod" than I did.

I have met some Carlow men but none that I knew or that could tell me anything of them that I did know but as we are not likely to meet in this world I hope we will in a much better one and as you remarked the time cannot be long for we are both old. I am some what the youngest in years 57 last September but sickness and hard labour have made me probably older than you. I am unable to work very hard but my circumstances compel me to do all I can, my eyesight is failing but I can read without spectacles in clear weather. The fits I used to have gradually ceased on me and I have not had one in 3 years, my lungs are sound but my liver is very much diseased, and my stomach also so that I seldom or ever have a day of real good health.

I was much surprised to learn that your mother was still alive (she must be nearly 90) perhaps mine is also, you did not mention at what time my brothers and her were at Buffalo, if you have heard anything more of them do not forget to let me know, perhaps I may meet them yet,

tell me in what part of Missouri Michael Murphy is [see note below] and also where Thomas is. Sam you say is with you but where is James, and Charlotte she was married when you wrote to me from Canada, write to me and tell me the story of your life as I have done of mine.

Give my respects to your wife (I hardly thought she would remember me) and mother to all your family. To Sam and his family let me know how Sam is doing for I will be very glad to hear from him. Tell me something of the country for although I have heard enough about the mines I have heard little of the agriculture of it except its facilities for keeping stock what is the price of land, can a man with small capital do any thing at farming, what crops you raise can they be raised without irrigation, the price of produce wages and is the climate healthy, free from agure

I see in the C. Alm. that there is a priest in your town, you say you had no rain since February, we have had hardly a dry day since August the grain crops through all those states last season were the best ever known but a great deal of the corn owing to late planting on account of a wet spring did not get ripe and the fall and winter being warm and damp 1/2 of it is spoiled wheat is now selling here for 75 cts.   before harvest it was 1.50 cts.   the farmers of course unthankful to God for thier bountiful crops because they cannot get high prices for them, some of my neighbors who kept thier old wheat because they could not get 2 [cents] for it are now nearly crazy.

Business for some months has been nearly suspended. Banks suspending factories and public works standing still   everyone that has money afraid to let it out of his hands no credit. The great railroad and land speculation bubble has burst and thousands of rich men are beggars. Society seems rot-ten to the core, crimes of all kinds especially murder and robbery are committed with impunity, our government seems too feeble, the laws of the general Government are resisted by the state Authorities The state laws by organized mobs, or rendered inefficient by the neglect of officers or the partiality of courts perjury is hardly considered a crime.

It cannot well be otherwise not one in a hundred of the Protestants now even pretend to give their children the least religious or moral instruction and too many Catholics follow their example and a great many of our Clergy are fonder of building fine churches in cities than attending the scattered flocks in country places but these things cannot affect you or I long we will I hope soon meet where the wicked cease from troubling and where our friendship that time or distance has been unable to weaken will be prolonged through a blissful Eternity. (I suppose your son that is at college is intended for the Priesthood.)

Few men have seen more trouble than I have within the last 20 years a great deal of it from causes that I will explain to you in another letter. I have found warm friends amongst strangers and have been bitterly injured and deceived by those that from ties of affinity should be the last to injure me. Again remember me to you[r] Mother wife and family to Sam and his family, write to me all about them for they seem like my own relations.

I remain Dear Patrick your old friend and Comrade

John Canning

Author's note: "The Maume" is a river which flows from Lake St. Marys in Ohio northwest through Allen County and Fort Wayne, Indiana, then northeast through Ohio to Lake Erie. Michael Murphy must be the one who signed the 1836 subscription for the Parish Priest of St. Thomas, Ontario. Thomas is brother of Patrick Breen of this study. Charlotte is their sister. Samuel Breen is a brother.

Letter from John Canning of Cranberry, Venango Co., Pennsylvania, October 15, 1860, to Patrick Breen in San Juan Bautista, California.

Dear Friend I got a letter from you Dated Nov. 18th 1857 But although I wrote to you on the 5th of Jan. '58 and twice since come last March I have got no more letters from you.

I sold the land I had in Ohio and bought a much better place 8 miles from Franklin Venango Co. Pen. and about three miles from the Allegany River. I am in much better health and everything much more prosperous with me than when I wrote to you at first if you have written to me your letter must have been lost (too frequent an occurrence on the California route) for I have kept up a correspondence with the P. office where I formerly lived in Ohio and probably never reached you. I hope however that this will reach you and find you and your family and friends in good health. I have been unable to find my Mother Or brothers although I have searched a good deal for them. I seen a man from Kiltealy about two years ago   he was well acquainted with the Country about Kiledmond [see note below] but very little with the people, only he told me that Jack Kelly of Kiledmond had went to America and come home again afterwards   he was murdered and his house robbed.

The country is improved there of late years, ther is farms cultivated and slate houses built along the road through Scollagh Gap to Newtonbury, also a road opened through Neenuve Gap to Newtonbury and houses built along it. There is a farm made up in the gorge of the Mountains on the stream that runs past Connors Mills, times indeed as far as I can learn are good in Ireland, very little crime, less pauperism than in England or Scotland   the Orange faction entirely put down by Government, you will see in the papers how they were rebuked by the Prince of Wales in Canada.   Such news is cheering to us although we will never see the old sod again.

The place I have now I bought in the woods for 3 dollars an acre   I have now about 20 ac cleared and a house and small barn on it. last year '59 all the Grain fruit and even grass in this section of the country was killed by frost A frost in June killed wheat rye and [tim?] meadows...even the leaves on the oak trees   then an early frost in the fall killed corn B wheat and Pot. so that it was nearly a famine   farmers had to sell their stock for want of winter feed and to buy bread. The furnace owners took advantage of the hard times to get work done for almost nothing. Men worked for 40 cts. a day and boarded themselves. But this year we have had abundant crops of all kinds   even the potatoes are better than they have been any year since '44.

There is a great excitement on account of the discovery of great quantities of Petroleum or Rock oil at a depth from 20 to 200 feet below the surface of the earth   more than 100 wells have been sunk in this county some yeilding 20 barels of oil in 24 hours   if the oil continues saleable at 25 cents per gallon our oil wells will be as valuable as your Cal. gold mines.

The value of land is increasing here   I was offered 500 dollars for my place last week. The land here is better for grass oats and potatoes than for wheat   it would be excellent for corn only for the late vernal and early fall frosts to which those Mountain counties are subject. The range is as good as any in America in the same climate for cattle on account of the great quantities of land about that the timber has been cut off for cord wood for furnace use and which have grown up with excellent grass.

The great panic of '57 is now passed and business of all kinds is good but real estate generally through West Pen. Ohio is not worth more than 1/2 as much as it was five years ago.

Political excitement is greater than I ever seen it before. That scoundrel Douglass has split the Democratic party to forward his own ambition and now the Black Republicans are carrying their ends triumphantly indeed 2/3rd of our citizens seem to think that Negro Emancipation is the only subject worth thinking about of course it will soon die away as the Know Nothings did. No man will now acknowledge that he wanted Catholics or foreigners deprived of their priveleges 3 years ago.

Pride is making rapid strides in this country the line between rich and poor is getting as strongly marked as in Ireland. Hired hands men or women do not sit at the table with the family in towns or villages or even in the country at the wealthy farmers.

Write to me and let me know how you all are write to me at length as I have got none of your letters except the first two. Answer the queries I sent to you in the letter of Jan. '58 especially with regard to where Thomas is in Missouri, also where Michael Murphy of Myvally lives as through him I might find out something of my Mother or Ellen, likewise where James and Charlotte are as you mentioned nothing about them in your first letter, let me know all about Sam and his family.

Tell me more of the farming in California what chance there would be for me and my family there. The cost of the Overland journy I could leave this place with about 600 dollars, 3 boys 13, 16, & 24 years of age 4 girls 11, 16, 10 &22 years all as able and willing to work as any others in Pennsylvania, it would cost about 30 Dollars to get to St. Louis, the rest of the journy I know nothing about.

My family all join with me in sending our love to you and your family. Remember me to your wife to your mother and to Sam and his family. Direct to Cranberry Post Office Venango County, Pennsylvania I remain Dear Patrick your old friend as I was 42 years ago when we left the Shamrock shore together

John Canning

P.S. I hope that letter will be more certain to and from Cal now as the U.S. is sending troops to subdue Prairie Indians. There is a Cath. church within 4 miles of me we have free schools in this State but they are managed so as to be worse than useless. The Catholics here are Irish or of Irish desent but unfortunately too many of them are no credit to their Country or Religion.

J. C.

JOHN BREEN'S "PIONEER MEMOIRS"

An 81-page handwritten manuscript, the original of which is in Bancroft Library, file C-D 51, copied in its entirety with the permission of Dr. Bonnie Hardwicke, Head, Manuscripts Division, Bancroft Library.

San Juan   San Benito Co Cal
Nov 19th 1877

H. H. Bancroft Esqr
San Francisco

At your request I write my recollections of my trips across the plains, in the year 1846 and 1847, and also something about what I remember of the early days in this state – Being born and raised on the frontier I have not had a chance to be educated in such schools as at this time exist all over the country so what I write, will not be elegant nor will it be very connected as I write only what occurs to my mind; the way the thing looks to me as I look back thirty years, I can only say that you are welcome to what I may send you –

My father and mother were born in Ireland, they came to America about the year 1828 where I the oldest of a family of nine was born in the year 1832, my father with his family, settled in the Teritory of Iowa in 1835 where he remained until the fifth day of April 1846. Then he with my mother and six brothers and one sister started for California   my father had for several years talked of going to California or Oregon.

The Mexican war I believe caused him to decide to come to this state.

We left our home in Iowa with three wagons drawn by seven yoke of oxen. – and some cows and horses. The horses were intended for the saddle, as at that time in Iowa, it was thought that horses were not suitable to draw wagons across the Rockey mountains as the country between Missouri and California was called –

Two of the wagons were loaded with provisions & the third a light wagon carried the small children and some beds. We crossed the Missouri river at Glascow [Glasgow] after a very tedious journey on acount of high water as the spring of 1846 was exceeding wet, in that part of the country. In due time we arrived at a camp called the Lone Elm, across the Missouri line This place was thought to be the limit of civilization, at this camp were some hunters returning with furs & they gave us some dried bufalow meat and told us that we had no idea of what we would suffer before we reached California. This prediction proved too true – At this camp was a Elm tree the only tree of any kind in sight. I shal never forget the loneliness of the scene boy though I was at time. What made the matter still more lonelir we were only one family not having yet been joined by any other parties crossing the plains that year. Still we were fairly on our way across the plains, and were afterwards joined by other parties. At one time the company consisted of about 1500 souls under the command of Col. Russel but after geting through what was called the Sioux country the company began to break up it being too large on account of wood and water. – About the head of the Sweet-Water as near as I can remember the company consisted of the families of George Donner who was generaly called the captain, Jacob Donner James F. Reed William Greaves, Rhinehart and Woolfinger, two Germans who were partners, one of them was a married man

Two men named Pike, and Foster, brothers in law, and both haveing wives and children and other relatives   A man named Eddie a man by the name of Keysburg, a man with[out] family named Patrick Dolan who traveled with my fathers family and my father and his family and two men who drove the cattle one of whom was called Allen, the name of the other I do not remember   There probably were others, but I cannot call them to mind at this time, nor do I remember the number of persons in the train, that it was stoped by the snow, near, what is now called Doner Lake – We got along without any unusual trouble until we left the old emigrant road that passed on the North side of the Great Salt Lake and by the advice of a man named Hastings undertook to find a rout by the south side.

Here our real troubles began, we were delayed for near a month in the timbered canions to the East of the lake, where there was little feed for stock. But when we got out on the valley where Salt Lake City now stands there was fine grass and water, and no one to molest us as the indians were not troublesome and the Mormons had not arived. We should have wintered here as the season was late, but there was no one in the company that had ever been to California and it was not supposed that we would be stoped by the snow – The next trouble was the long drives without water or grass over ground covered with salt, on these deserts some families lost most of their cattle, and the stock of the whole train got very poor, so that, many wagons were left on the road, still we pushed on as best we could

On the Humbolt river, J. F. Reed and a man named Snyder quarreled and Snyder was killed; some thought Reed was to blame others that Snyder was in the wrong   at all events Reed left the company on horseback and alone leaving his family with the company, I have always thought that this was a misfortune for the whole party as Reed was an inteligent and energetic Man, and if he had remained the party might of got through – He said that he would go before and endeavor to send help back as provisions were now geting scarce

About this time a man named Stantoun started ahead to Sutters Fort to send help back

He got from Captain Sutter some mules, and two indians to assist him, he packed the mules with provisions, furnished by Sutter and hurrieing back met the party near the sink of the Humbolt

He delivered the provisions to the people, but instead of returning to California he remained with the company to try to hurry them up as it was nearing the last of October and snow was liable to fall on the Siera Nevada but he could [do] but little as the teams and people were worn out and had little energy left, still the kind and brave Stantoun remained as did the two indians from Sutters Fort   This noble conduct lost him his life as the dreaded snow came, and in trying [to] cross the mountain with the mules and the indians, he and they were lost, and his unburred bones are bleaching in some canion of that mighty range of mountains.   He was one of the most disinterested men that ever lived   he had no rellative in the company [and] expected no pay of any kind; the only motive that he could have was the desire to help the worn-out wanderers with whom he had traveled most of the way from the Missouri river   I do not know, I never did know, his christian name nor what part of the States he was from but I am convinced that no more brave or generous man ever died in the endeavor to help his fellow man

He was a hero

After leaving the sink of the Humbolt the company as if by mutual consent disolved, or gradually separated, some wanted to stop and rest their cattle   others in fear of the snow were in favor of pushing ahead as fast as possible, as provisions were geting short which fact greatly increased the danger of delay – My father and some others after geting on the Truckey river concluded to travel as fast as they could, as there began to be heavey clouds on the high range of mountains to the West, and this from what we had learned from Captain Fremont was a certain sign of snow on the mountains About the first of November 1846 we arrived at what proved to be the first of the main ridge, and camped at the foot of what is now called Doner Lake, It was raining when we stoped, but before morning their was some snow on the ground, we started at daylight, but soon found that the snow increased in depth as we advanced, and after traveling about two miles, it was so deep that the cattle could go no further and to make matters worse another storm began, so we retraced our steps to the camp of the night before at the lake, in a day or two the weather cleared, and some persons went to examine the road on the mountain to see if the cattle could cross, at night they returned and reported six feet of snow, two miles from camp   this report put an end to the further effort, of crossing with the wagons, which, made the prospect, for men with families of small children & looking to them for relief gloomy in the extreme.   The company were now scattered along the Truckey river for several miles, the family of Doner I believe were the lowest down the river, each family built some kind of house, and killed all their cattle, as they could not live; the ground being covered with snow; There was no salt among the little stores of provisions now left, but the meat did not spoil as it soon got frozen and so remained until it was consumed. A short time after the heavey fall of snow, a party of about twenty, or perhaps more, started on snowshoes across the mountains. The party consisted of both men and women but I do not know how many of each, nor do I remember many of the names, among them were two Greaves father and son, and two daughters, of the old man, one being married, I do not remember her husbands name. Foster and a man named Eddy, also a man named McCutcheon, Patrick Dolan was of this party

They took only a small share of provisions expecting to get into the Sacramento Valley soon if ever, but it was never for most of them, as a heavey storm began the day after they left   The Valley of the Truckey which lasted several days, and as not one of them had ever, been in such a place before they did not know the course, and so could make no progress; The result was that most of the party was lost,

A curious feature of the disaster was that the women stood the hardship better than the men.

I believe none of the women of their party died.

Some time in the month of February Several men, with Jas. F. Reed who had left the company on the Humbolt, came over from Sutters Fort with what provisions they could pack on their back, to assist the emigrants into the Sacramento Valley

They thought best not to try to take all at this time,

Two of my brothes went over with their party, In the course of two or three weeks another party came out, and all of my fathers family, got over into the Valley, but there were still some at the camps on the Truckey, among them were some of the Doner family and a man named Keysburg befor the next party went to their assistance many of them
died

With the party which was made up of my fathers family and some of the Greave children, and I think some of the Doner children, was a man named Stark   I think his name was John Stark, he came with a company from the valley to help to get the emigrants over. The stoutest of the emigrants were taken charge of by some of the men from California who immediately started to a station on Bear River, low down in the mountains, where there were provisions

Their was left behind all my fathers family but my two brothers, who had gone over with the first relief party   also some of the Greaves children and I think some of the Doner children, all of whom were weak and unable to travel far each day;

With this little party Stark remained and had he not done so probably not one of them would have got out of the snow as the other men were not willing to wait for the weak children to get along, as they feared another snow storm. But Stark was brave and intelegent and of great bodily strenght, he said that he would take them all to Bear Valley if they would only live long enough.

From the start he cheered the children telling them that they would soon be out of the snow, and have all the fat meat that they could eat, and when one of the children would fall unable to go farther, he would carry it until it was a little rested   in fact he caried some one of them almost constantly while traviling and sometimes had two at a time along with a heavy load of provisions; still he never uttered a word of complaint or got out of temper

He would laugh and say it was no trouble to cary the children that they [were] so thin that they were very light, that we would soon be out of the snow when we would have enought to eat and take a long rest

In this way he succeeded in geting all into Bear Valley where there was but little snow, and some provisions; and in a day or two we got to a camp called "Mule Springs", where there was no snow, and here there was a pack train in charge of Selim E Woodworth a government officer, Here was an end to hunger and cold, and here the great task of noble Stark was at an end

Were it not for him I would probably not be here today.

Few men have the resolution and physical strenght that he had, and if he had less of either he could not have done what he did. He was what I will call a perfet man, perfect in both body and mind.

I saw him but once since I came to California. He lived I think in Sonoma County and had a family. He died three or four years ago.

All honor to your memory, brave and generous honest Stark [*John's double underscoring*] From Mule Springs we went on horseback to Johnsons Ranch, on Feather River in the East edge of the Sacramento Valley.

This was in the fore part of the month of March 1847. –

Johnson the owner about a year – after maried one of the Doner party, A young girl named Mary – Murphy. I will ever remember the appearance of the country about Johnsons ranch   the grass was forward, and many flowers mingled through it, the weather was warm and clear, which gave a sensation to the tired emigrant that I can not describe

From Johnsons we were taken to Sutters Fort, at government expense;

This place was thought to be the end of the trip in those day. The emigrant did not stop until he got to the Fort   then he began to look about for something to do. – At the fort was Captain Sutter, a fine looking man; attending to a large business. He was a good friend to the emigrant in those days   every member of the Doner party has good reason, to remember kindly generous Captain Sutter; Their was at the fort a company of native indian soldiers, about seventy or eighty, They mounted guard and drilled every day so as to be ready for an attack of an enemy, either indian or Mexican; the war being still going with Mexico, but their was [no] sign of war here; all was peace

There were about a dozen whitemen at the fort at this time among them, Sutter, Folsome, Neal, Marshal, Weimer, Selim–E Woodworth, Col Mc–Knstrey and others   From Sutters Fort I went to the ranch of Martin Murphy on the Macousumne river about twenty miles south of Sutters Fort, here lived Mr Murphy with his family farming and raising stock, He treated my father and family very kindly. Mr. Murphy now lives near, Santa Clara in Santa Clara county   He came to this coast I think in 1845. His father and four brothers and sister came at the same time, He has two sons members of the State Senate at this time. –   From Murphys ranch I moved in September 1847 to Mission San Jose, on the way we stoped at the ranch of Thomas Pile on the Mokelumne river   he had just located   he had no neighbor nearer than Murphy on the Macousumne and Livermoor in the Livermoor Valley on the San Joaquin or in the San Joaquin Valley no one had as yet settled – on the way to Mission San Jose, we camped on the ranch of Mr Livermoor   He was making a riata

I told [him] that we wanted [to] buy some beef   he gave a quarter of a steer, saying that he never charged an emigrant for beef.

I here saw the first Spanish family   there were two or three families of Native Californians liveing on the ranch

There [was] no land in cultivation on the ranch, but there were great members [*sic*] in sight. –

The next day we arived at the Mission San Jose   Here were several American families. Leo Norris, who now lives in San Ramon Valley Contra Costa County, John M. Horner who I believe still lives near the Mission   M. Murray now living in San Francisco, M– Welch now dead; he was murdered a year or two after, by whom is not known, Jerry Fallon now dead, and a man named Marshal now dead

The Californians treated us very kindly   Jesus Vallejo a brother of General Vallejo lived at the Mission, he had a large ranch about four miles north of the Mission, I am under obligations to him for many favors, Augustin - Alviso, had a large ranch between the Mission and the bay, was very kind to us, also Guilermo Castro who had a ranch North of the Vallejo ranch did us many favors

In the month of February 1848– we moved to San Juan Bautista where I am now, and have lived most of the time since that time

When we came here their were only native Californians   they treated us kindly although the United States, were still at war with Mexico, even General Jose Castro who was very much opposed to the American occupation of California was friendly, and let us have his residence here free of rent; he lived at Monterey at the time, The next summer he had occasion to come here a short time with his family, but he would take only a small part of his house, saying that he would stay but a short time, and did not want to disturb us

The next year my father bought the house. It has ever since been ocupied by my father and brother

General Castro is now dead; he was a fine man in appearance as well as in disposition; he was over six feet in hight and well built, his complection was that of a pure Spaniard, his wife Dona Modesta, was very fair skined as were his son and daughter   they looked like Americans and they were as amible as they were fair –

I will ever kindly remember good general Castro   At the time the General lived in this place, Colonel Mason and Lieutenant Sherman now General Sherman called to see him, Sherman after the interview said that Castro was an accomplished man

Some time in March I think 1848 a man passed through here on the way to Monterey   he had about two ounces of gold; he was going to show it to Colonel Mason, and get his opinion as to whether the stuff was gold   he said he was sent by Captain Sutter, he stoped on his way back and said that the government officers at Monterey pronounced it gold

This was the first gold found in California I believe. –

When we arrived here, the Californians were the most happy people I ever saw   they all appeared to have every thing that [was] required; There was plenty of beef, and it was easy to rais what little wheat and beans they needed, –

Father Anzar was in charge of the church here. He was a brother of Juan Anzar who owned the 'Ken Sabe' and Aromas ranches

Father Anzar remained here many years after I came, he then went to Mexico where he died; Juan Anzar is also dead. F.P. Pacheco lived on the since noted Pacheco ranch   San Philipi Mannell-Larros lived on the Santa Anna, Crux – Cervantes lived on the San Joaquin ranch noted as being the first ranch presented before the United States Land Commission, in which case several legal points were settled, Jose Maria Sanchez lived at the Mission, Gilroy lived on the San Isidio ranch near where the town of Gilroy now is

These old ranch owners are now all dead –

Monterey was only a small town, though it was the capitol in 1848, it has changed but little since--

I went to the mines in June 1848, I worked during the summer at what was called Mormon Island, Saml – Brannan had the only store here, he must have made a great amount of money as their were many people here mining, and gold was plenty, and many bought things that they did not need or sold their gold to Brannan for five or six dollars per ounce their being reports several times during the summer that the stuff was not gold, others thought that even if it was gold it would soon be so abundant that it would be worthless, and so they would give it for any thing that they saw for sale--

During the winter of 48 or 49, I mined and built a house, where Placervill now stands

I saw the men hanged to a tree, which tragedy caused the place for several years to be called Hang-town, The lynching even if the men deserved death was barberous, as it was first decided to flog them which was done, the next day some new evidence came out, and a great number of people collected and hanged them

I will never forget the day, the ground was covered with snow the skie with colouds   all nature seemed to mourn over the cruel act being done

But it may of been for the best, Their were no courts and the power to punish crime had to be with some one

This was a hard winter in the mines   every thing was enormously high, on act [account] of the soft condition of the ground, it was impossible to haul freight from Sacramento, I saw a Saloon keeper pay fifteen hundred dollars for sixty gallons of whiskey. I paid eight dollars per lb for pork

Their was no fresh provisions in the camp, and more than half the people had the scurvey before spring

In March I returned home to San Juan, and have mined none since

The next American family that came to this Valley was Edward Smith, he came to this state from Pike County in 1848. He had a family of a wife and five daughters and one son. All the girls are now living and married one of them is my wife. I married my wife in 1852, when I was twenty years old

I have eight children. Edward Smith died twenty years ago   He was the first Post Master at this place

My father died nine years ago, He was one of the three first Supervisors of Monterey County and was Post Master here after Smith died for many years.--Some one writing to the San Francisco Chronicle last December from Illinois said that Patrick Breen was killed, while crossing the plains by J.F. Reed; The writer probably refered to the killing of Snyder, but even then he stated what was not true as he said that 'Breen struck Mrs Reed with a whip, which so enraged Reed that he, plunged a knife into Breen, killing him

Now the truth is that the team was "Stalled" on a sand bank on the Humbolt river; it was Reeds team; Snyder was driving Greavs team next to Reeds behind Reed was on the off side of his team assisting his man to get the team to pull. Snyder came up on the nigh side also to assist. Soon there was an altercation between Reed and Snyder   When Snyder called Reed some name and attempted to strike him across the tongue between the oxen and the wagon, Reed jumped across the tongue and stabed him, Snyder died in a couple of hours.

Mrs Reed had nothing to do with the affair and if she had Snyder would not strike her, for he would not strike a woman at all; He was too much of a man for that.

Snyders loss was mourned by the whole company; Still Reed was not blamed by many – –

I do not remember any thing more that would be of any interes to you. – What I know about the early organization of the State & c. is a matter of history and has often been written about, and so you are better posted about those things than I am – I do not want to be understood by this, that I think what I have written is interesting but I know that I have done it willingly and I believe that what I have stated is true –

Hoping that it will be of some use to you, in your, History of California now being written – I am sincerely your friend

John Breen

Author's notes: Page 205 – "two men who drove the cattle one of whom was called Allen, the name of the other I do not remember." John is probably referring to teamsters employed by other families; however, there is none of record named Allen. Page 206 – "[Stanton] hurrieing back met the party near the sink of the Humbolt." Reports of witnesses vary as to exactly where Stanton and the two Sutter's Fort Indians met the company, but it may have been further west than John recalled, at Truckee Meadows or the lower Truckee Canyon. Page 207 – John's memory is wrong about Reed heading the first relief; he led the second relief. Page 209 – For an account of some of the people at Mission San Jose mentioned by John (Jeremiah Fallon, Michael Murray, and Leo Norris) and the settlements that became Dublin and San Ramon, see Margaret E. Fitzgerald and Joseph A. King, *The Uncounted Irish in Canada and the United States*, P.D. Meany Publishers, Toronto, 1990, pp. 213-27. Page 210 – John modestly fails to mention that the Castro Adobe in San Juan Bautista was purchased with part of the gold John himself brought back from Mormon Island near Placerville.

———————

HARRY J. BREEN'S SKETCH

The following paper was written by Harry J. Breen, a grandson of Patrick Breen Sr. and a son of Edward Breen. Its full title is "A Short Sketch of the Lives of Patrick and Margaret Breen and Their Family: Members of the Ill-Fated Donner Party of 1846." It appeared in the PONY EXPRESS COURIER, *March 1937, and a copy of it can be found in the Breen Papers at Bancroft Library.*

Patrick Breen and his wife Margaret, whose family name was Bulger, were born in County Carlow, Ireland; Patrick in 1790 [1] and Margaret in 1810 [2]. They married in Ireland [3] and came to Canada by way of the St. Lawrence River in 1828.

They settled in what was known as Upper Canada in the vicinity of Toronto [4] where their first two children were born. John in 1832 and Edward, my father, in 1833. Remaining in Canada till 1835 [5] They then moved down to Keokuk, Iowa Territory, and were engaged in farming and stock raising until 1846. During their residence in Iowa five more children were born to these good pioneers, who lived to reach California. Patrick, born in 1837, Simon, 1839, James, 1842 [6], Peter, 1843, and Margaret Isabella in 1845. Another son, James [1st], was born in 1835 and died in 1836. After reaching California another son named William was born in 1849.

Having lived five years in the United States, Patrick Breen applied for citizenship in 1840 and was granted his papers in the District Court at West Point, Lee County, Iowa, October 15, 1844.

Like many another Irishman in those days, Patrick Breen had the urge to go toward the setting sun and build a home for himself and his family in the new country of California that they were beginning to hear about. He had read Fremont's report of his first trip to the West and had talked to Jim Bridger in St. Louis, during a trip he had made there down the river from Keokuk. What he had heard and read about the Western country fired his imagination, but the Mexican War breaking out really decided the issue [6], and on April 5, 1846, Patrick Breen with his wife and children and all their worldly possessions struck out for California. It wasn't the Golden West then, as gold had not been discovered.

Their outfit consisted of three wagons, seven yoke of oxen and cows and saddle horses. A friend, named Patrick Dolan, and his family [7] traveled with them as well as two men [8] who drove the cattle and horses.

Their course was southwest to the Missouri River which they crossed at Glascow and then turned westernly. The little party continued a long way on the road before joining up with any of the other emigrants who afterwards formed themselves into what was known as the Donner Party.

Many accounts of the trials and the hardships of the party have been written, so I will not concern myself with these things here, as they are well known to readers of California history. Patrick Breen's manuscript diary written while the party was snowbound at Donner Lake is the only record of the party's sufferings, and is today one of the most valued possessions of the Bancroft Library.

Several fine accounts of the Donner Party have been written with information obtained from survivors, but other fanciful accounts have also been published that are no credit to the Donner Party and less credit to the authors.

All the family arrived safely at Sutter's Fort in March 1847, where they rested and retrieved their wagons and possessions from Donner Lake. My father and one of his brothers went back over the mountains with the men who brought the wagons over. They used stock loaned to them by good Captain Sutter for this purpose. After recruiting themselves, the family's next move was down the Sacramento Valley to the ranch of Martin Murphy on the Cosumnes River. Murphy and his brothers and sisters with their parents were the first emigrant party with wagons to come to California by way of the Truckee River and Lake route. The Breen family occupied a cabin left by the Murphys in 1844, during their stay at the Lake.

They left Murphy's ranch in September 1847 and journeyed across the San Joaquin and Livermore Valleys to Mission San Jose. They lived in the Mission until February 1848, when they began their last move and arrived at the Mission San Juan Bautista, which place was destined to be their permanent home. The Breen family were the first Americans to settle in the little Mexican pueblo, and the first in what was afterwards to become San Benito County.

The family made friends rapidly with their Mexican neighbors to the extent that Commandante-General Jose Maria Castro, military head of the district [9], gave them the use of his large two story adobe headquarters buildings facing the Plaza, to occupy as their home. Castro would accept no rent for the house and stayed with the family whenever he came to San Juan.

In 1849 Patrick Breen bought the house from Castro and at the same time bought about 1000 acres of valley land from him also. Recently the old adobe home was sold by the Breen heirs to the State of California to become a part of the State Park at San Juan. Being [that the Breens were] the only American family in the town, many persons of prominence in the early history of the state stopped with Patrick Breen and his family in their hospitable home. Sometimes government officials, business men, and other travelers on their trips from San Francisco to the capitol at Monterey or up and down the coast, would exchange their tired horses for fresh mounts and pick up their own animals on the return trip.

My father has often told of many men, who in after years became nationally famous, who had accepted his father's hospitality. Among them were Lieut. Wm. T. Sherman, Lieut. U.S. Grant, Col. Mason, General M. Vallejo, Thomas O. Larkin, and many others. The two men who carried the gold flakes found by John Marshall at Sutter's Mill to Monterey to show them to Col. Mason and have him test them officially, also stopped overnight with the Breens. My father said he was allowed to hold the gold in his hand, and always considered it an honor to have touched the first gold found in the West. My mother's mother, Mrs. Patrick Burns, came to California in company with Mrs. T.O. Larkin. My mother's aunt, Katherine Benson, married Michael Murry of the Livermore Valley who had come to California with the Martin Murphy family in 1844 [9].

John Breen, the oldest son, went to the diggings at Mormon Island in June 1848, and built the first house on the site of Placerville which was then called Hangtown. He witnessed the hanging of the two men whereby the town got its name. He continued to mine until 1849 and then came home.

The Breens were now established in their new home and engaged in farming, dairying, and cattle raising and prospecting. In a few years Patrick Breen and three of his sons bought 24,000 acres of the San Lorenzo Rancho in Monterey County. He was one of the first three supervisors of Monterey County and postmaster at San Juan Bautista for many years.

Henry Miller, the great cattle man and butcher of California, told my mother that the first herd of beef cattle he purchased when in business, was bought from Patrick Breen. I have Patrick's old account book in which this transaction is entered in his own hand writing.

James Breen, the fifth son, attended Santa Clara College and was one of the early graduates of that first school of higher learning in California. A classmate was the nationally famous attorney, Delphine M. Delmas. James studied law and became district attorney of Monterey County, and when San Benito County was formed he was made the first Superior Judge in which office he continued for many years until his retirement.

John, Edward, Patrick, and Simon were engaged all their lives in farming and livestock business. John and Edward at long periods were supervisors in Monterey and San Benito Counties.

Peter Breen was drowned in the Pajaro River from the back of a horse he was riding in 1870. His mother said the terrors of Donner Lake were as nothing compared to her sorrow when her dead son was brought home to her. William, the youngest son, who was born in San Juan in 1849, died in 1874 and left a widow and infant daughter. They are both alive.

Margaret Isabella, the only daughter and last living survivor of the people who made up the Donner Party, married Thos. McMahon, a business man of San Juan and passed to her reward at ninety years of age. She was educated at the old Convent in Benicia and with the Sisters of Notre Dame in San Jose.

All the other sons married and had large families and there are now many descendants of Patrick and Margaret Breen living in Central California. The entire family and their offspring have always held an honored position in the communities in which they live and have been true to the grand heritage passed on to them by their ancestors, of honesty, courage, and their trust in God.

Dates of Birth and Death:

Patrick Breen	1790-1868
Margaret Breen	1810-1874
John Breen	1832-1903
Edward Breen	1833-1890
James Breen [I]	1835-1836
Patrick Breen	1837-1899
Simon Breen	1839-1899
James Breen [II]	1842-1899 [10]
Peter Breen	1843-1870
M. Isabella Breen	1845-1935
William Breen	1849-1874

[children of Edward Breen]

Edwin Breen	Born 1884
William Breen	Born 1882
Harry Breen	Born 1886

Notes:

1. Patrick was actually born in 1795. See Chapter 1 and Notes to Chapter 1.

2. According to the same records, Margaret Bulger was baptized March 2, 1806, daughter of Simon Bulger and Margaret Bulger of Rathgeran Townland.

3. Patrick and Margaret were probably married in Canada, although no marriage record has yet been found.

4. They settled in Southwold Township very near St. Thomas in southern Ontario, one hundred miles southwest of Toronto.

5. 1834 is given in some family records as the year the Breens departed for the West. According to the same family tradition, they also seem to have

had a brief Springfield, Illinois, period, before moving further westward to Keokuk, Iowa.

6. The Mexican War could not have been a reason for the Breens' departure for California. The Breen family and Dolan left Keokuk with their four wagons on April 5, 1846. Congress did not declare war on Mexico until May 13, 1846. Several other errors of Harry are drawn from John Breen's manuscript "Pioneer Memoirs."

7. Patrick Dolan was a bachelor, traveling without relatives. Stewart in *Ordeal* gives his age as about 40, apparently a guess, but the 1840 United States Census, Township 65, Lee County, Iowa, gave his age as between 20 and 29, enumerated consecutively with Patrick Breen and James Ryan, and without family. If that is correct, Dolan was between 26 and 35 at the time of the entrapment.

8. John Breen in "Pioneer Memoirs" recalled two drivers, one named "Allen" and another whose name he could not remember. However, John may be referring to men who worked for others in the wagon train. In any case, there is no record of a teamster named Allen in the Donner Party, nor of any teamsters traveling with the Breen family in particular after they joined the Donners.

9. Michael Murray did not cross with the Murphy Party of 1844. He arrived in California by wagon in the fall of 1846 with his brother-in-law, Jeremiah Fallon. They were among the founding settlers of Dublin, Alameda County. See Margaret E. Fitzgerald and Joseph A. King, *The Uncounted Irish in Canada and the U.S.* (1990), pp. 213-27.

10. James may have been born in 1841, if a biographical sketch in a county history and the census of 1860 are correct (age 19 on that census).

THE REED AND MILLER DIARIES: A CRITIQUE

There are two important documents that have not been subjected to ad-
equate analysis by Donner Party scholars. The first of them I will refer to as
the Reed Diary, the second as the Miller Diary.

THE REED DIARY

James F. Reed kept a notebook/diary of the second relief expedition.
The original was among the many items from the Martha Reed Lewis Estate
donated to the Sutter's Fort Historical Museum in 1945-46. The custodian is
now officially the Sacramento Historic Sites Unit of the California Department of Parks and Recreation. The curator (1991) is Michael F. Tucker. The
diary is in folder number 85 of the Martha Reed Lewis Papers (designated
"MRL" in the Bibliography and Notes Section of this book).

It is a well-worn notebook 7-3/4" x 6-1/2" with a gray cover of heavy paper. The document has been folded in half lengthwise many times, obviously
to fit a man's pocket. The entries are in pencil and pages are often stained
and smudged.

The document was begun as a notebook of Reed's expenses in helping
to organize the relief. The diary portion seems to have been an afterthought.
The inside front cover and the first ten pages are mostly notes of purchases
of provisions for emigrants and members of the relief. The last few pages
contain an accounting of the survivors and the dead.   The diary portion
begins with a February 7 entry on page 11 (following a February 10 entry for
provisions). The succeeding dates are not always clear, but the last is a long
entry for "6th Sunday" [March] describing events at Starved Camp during the
great storm.

Reed was dead by the time McGlashan began his research in 1878, but
the original diary or a copy of it was made available to him by Reed's
daughter, Martha "Patty" Lewis. McGlashan published most of the diary in a
highly edited form in the 1880 edition of his *History*. However, McGlashan
omitted or severely edited certain passages involving events that Reed could
not possibly have known at the time. This was the only version of the diary
available to George R. Stewart for his *Ordeal* (1936). It should have been
obvious to even the most innocent reader of western fiction that Reed could
not have made diary entries in the pit at Starved Camp, in the present tense,
during a raging storm, while he was blinded or unconscious; yet Stewart (as
did DeVoto in *The Year of Decision*) credited him with such a marvel with
pencil and paper.

In 1947, after the Reed-Lewis Papers had come into the possession of
the Sutter's Fort Historical Museum, the museum's curator, Carroll D. Hall,
published *Donner Miscellany*. The book included an accurate transcription of
the diary portion of the document, beginning with the February 7 entry. In
1960, the revised edition of Stewart's *Ordeal* appeared, which included in an

appendix Stewart's own transcription of the Reed Diary, differing little from Hall's but containing diary entries only from February 21/22. In a preface, Stewart granted that there was no longer any reason to believe that Reed wrote down his words while he was huddled in the snow at Starved Camp, since he included information about simultaneous events in the valley and at the high camp that he could only have obtained at some later time. Reed, blinded or unconscious at Starved Camp during many hours of the storm, had to have obtained his information from someone else, such as McCutchen or Miller, yet Stewart neglected to mention this obvious conclusion, even in his notes to the second edition.

The diary portion of the notebook begins on page 11, February 7 entry, but on the preceding page, anachronistically, is a February 10 entry recording purchase of moccasins for members of the relief expedition and others. The diary seems to end with a March 4 or 5 entry (Reed did not always give exact dates), about the time of the arrival at Starved Camp. This last entry is a long *ex post facto* description of events during the storm at Starved Camp, and includes information about conditions elsewhere that he got from Woodworth and others later. (See also Chapter 10, pp. 84-88.)

Reed seems to describe events that occurred during only two full nights of the storm, not three (as given in Stewart and other secondary sources). If so, Reed left Starved Camp on the second day after the night on which the storm broke. He mentions nothing about the Breens being able to leave with him but refusing to do so, something he alleged much later.

Reed wrote in one diary entry, concerning when he was going up to the mountain camp, of the joyous meeting with his wife as she came down with the first relief, and of how "every woman and child e̶x̶c̶e̶p̶t̶-̶m̶y̶-̶w̶i̶f̶e̶" (Reed lined out the last three words) was begging pitifully for bread. Professor Stewart proceeds to garble this event and another one: "Reed is naturally the central figure of his own narrative, but he is not boastful. He records his incapacity during the emergency of the storm and the heroic labors of McCutchen. Apparently to spare the feelings of the other refugees he [Reed] deleted the words indicating that of them all his wife alone did not cry out for food." This borders on the mendacious. The events at Starved Camp – and the "heroic labors of McCutchen" during the storm – occurred a week later. Mrs. Reed was not at Starved Camp. But Stewart's fictional blending of two separate events enables him to present Mrs. Reed heroically, while indirectly casting less favorable light on Mrs. Breen.

THE MILLER DIARY

The second diary is certainly the most curious of all documents connected with the Donner Party. It came to light for the first time in the 1940s, among the Martha Reed Lewis Papers, more than seventy years after the deaths of Reed and Miller. Although, if genuine, it is the most valuable of all trail documents for the Donner company, it is not mentioned by McGlashan in his 1880 *History*, nor is it mentioned in the considerable surviving correspondence between McGlashan and Reed's daughters, Martha and Virginia, although he was in constant correspondence with them during the preparation of his book. It seems evident that (a) Virginia and Martha, for their own reasons, did not reveal the existence of the diary to McGlashan (they were zealously protective of their father's reputation, as evidenced by their constant insistence, in letters to McGlashan, that he portray him as an unalloyed hero); or (b) they did reveal its existence, but McGlashan, for his own reasons (a paramount one being not to write anything that reflected poorly on the families of his informants), chose to ignore it; or (c) the existence or location of the diary was not known at that time to the Reed family (a most unlikely possibility, given the fact that it was composed mostly, not by Miller, but by James F. Reed, and became part of his daughter Martha's estate).

This document purports to be a diary composed on the trail, from April 25, 1846, when the Reeds and the Donners left Springfield, Illinois, to October 5, when Reed was expelled from the company for the killing of Snyder. What follows is a series of facts, some of them curious, about the diary:

(1) The Miller Diary (in folder 51 of the Martha Reed Lewis Papers) is a little book in almost totally unworn condition despite entries allegedly made almost daily for five months on the trail. It is bound in black leather, 5-3/4" x 3-1/2" with an envelope-style flap, attached to which is a 22" long wrapping string, like a shoelace. It is evident that this string has seldom if ever been used. The inside back cover has a pouch for storage. The edges and spine of the book show absolutely no signs of wear, with the exception of about one-inch of one edge of the back cover, a consequence of jamming a number of other documents into the storage pouch (where they were found when the diary came into the possession of the Sutter's Fort Historical Museum).

(2) All entries are in pen and ink, except for some numerical notations on the last few pages. The pages have suffered no water or other damage, with the exception of two slight water stains on facing pages in the middle of the book.

(3) The handwriting in the diary has been analyzed by two experts, one at the request of Carroll D. Hall, the other recently at my own request. Hall's expert was Sherwood Morrell of the Criminal Identification and Investigation Division of California's Department of Justice. Mine was Dr. Duayne J. Dillon of the Criminalistics Services Center of Martinez, California, a person of national reputation with long experience in handwriting analysis. Dr. Dillon was not aware of Morrell's analysis or conclusions before he reached his own conclusions. They differ only slightly and not significantly from Morrell's.

Hiram Miller borrowed of me in May 1846 $ 1.50
in July 3.
15.50
17.00

July 3. he gave me in Silver $ 10.50
6.50

balance due me

First page, following a blank page, Hand B, unidentified. Perhaps Mrs. Reed?

Hiram C. Miller
April 20 1846
Elois Milford Elliott

Inside front cover, Hand A, identified by two experts as the writing of Hiram O. Miller

First two pages of diary entries. First two lines in Hand A (Miller): "Left Home __ 26 of April/May." Next ten lines (May 13-15) in unidentified Hand B, then Hand A (Miller) from May 16 ("twenty two miles from....").

we are now on the West means
and from then we
traveled a Bout 15
miles and camped on
a Creek their is plenty
2 of water and timber

3 We made this day 18
18 Miles and Camped
on Pawnee Crik here
is a Natural Bridg
1½ Miles above Camp
4 We Celebrated the glorious
4th on the Camp we
remaining here to this morning
this is the
6 We left Camp which
listed and our Oxen
moved off in fine style
and went 16 miles 1½
and encamped on the Beaver
Iy. GWR about

Little Banch
Wena

½ a mile from the South
fork of the Platt which
Strum in Streets about
6 miles from Camp when
their is a fine Cold Bank
left camp in good order
and moved up the Platt 15
and encamped on the
Beaver in a Beautiful
grove of Cotton wood
Sandhills Buffalo
went up the Platt 18

Weds

any Grofsour men and
Bpacamped Thyout
the up in crofsing 12
the up in Crofsing
be certain to come up
On the South side of
Crofs the road fter
is desirably the best.

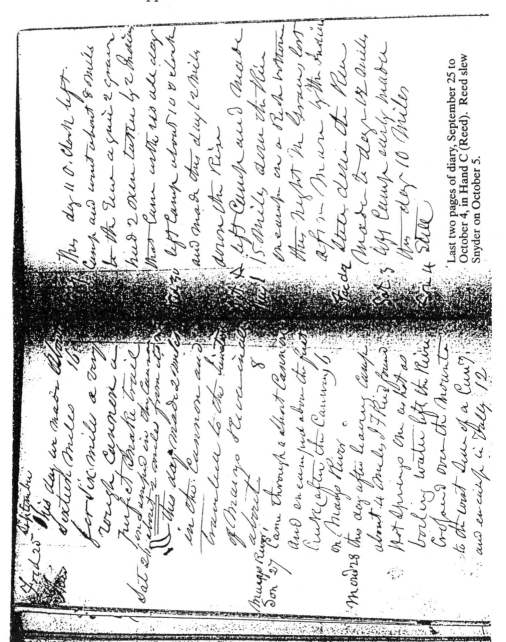

Last two pages of diary, September 25 to October 4, in Hand C (Reed). Reed slew Snyder on October 5.

(4) The diary is written in at least three different hands. On the inside front cover is the notation "Left Home,/Hiram O. Miller/April 16 1846/and Milford Elliott." This is in the hand of Hiram O. Miller.

(5) The next page, in an unknown hand, is this sole entry: "Hiram Miller borrowed/of me in May 1846 $1.50/in July 3d $15.50 [total] 17.00/July 3d he gave me/in Silver $10.50/balance due me $6.50." On the next page, where the diary actually begins, lines 3 through 12 are in the same unknown hand.

(6) Lines 1 and 2 of this first page are in Miller's hand; so are the last 8 lines, and all entries for the next 10-1/3 pages, through July 2. This is about the time, which we know from other sources, that Miller left the company of the Reeds and Donners. The entries are more of a log than a diary, most of Miller's entries reading like this one for May 22: "and from ther wee traveled a Bowt 15 miles and Campe on the wapalose" [Wapalusa].

(7) Reed's hand is at work exclusively on the last 23-2/3 pages of the diary, the entries generally five to ten lines, but containing considerably more detail than Miller's bare bones notations. Reed's last notation, for Sunday the 4th of October, is the briefest of all, one inscrutable word: "Still." We know from other sources that he slew Snyder the next day.

(8) Reed's entries are often in the third person: "Tues 11 [August] left camp and took the new rout [through the Wasatch] with Reid [*sic*] as Pilot" (the last three words in distinctly larger and heavier script). On the 14th and 16th of August, he refers to "Reeds Gap" twice (underscoring it the second time). Reed's entries indicate that it took only eighteen days to cross the Wasatch into the valley of the Salt Lake by the route he blazed, whereas other witnesses claimed it took at least a week more than that. In his September 4 entry, he blames his teamsters for the loss of his oxen on the drive across the Salt Desert, but takes no blame for the one week delay below Pilot Peak while he retrieved his huge wagon over twenty-five miles back on the trail and while the whole company turned out for an unsuccessful search for his lost oxen. The delay proved disastrous.

(9) Following the last diary entry are some blank pages, and then four pages with notes in pencil. One page consists of numbers and tallys, and some indecipherable handwriting. Three pages list purchases of items of clothing from Jake and George Donner on November 20, 1846, and January 30, 1847, e.g. "blanket coat - to be paid in California at California price," "1 pair Brogans for Jim Smith," "1 pair gloves," "1 pair pantaloons," etc. The writing is in at least two different hands, but not any of the three hands of the diary entries, according to analyst Duayne J. Dillon.

(10) Among the most curious things about this diary were some of the folded pieces of paper which Curator Hall found stuffed in its pocket when he took custody of the Lewis Papers. Hall transcribed some of these items for *Donner Miscellany*. At the same time, since Hall was a scholar with integrity, he raised several disturbing questions: Did Reed write his entries in after years? Why did he write in the third person? Can his dates be trusted? Why has the diary remained seemingly unknown? "Here is something," wrote Hall, "for the avid historian to mull over." George R. Stewart did some mulling over, after he saw a transcription of the diary for the first time in *Donner Miscellany*. He wrote Hall, attaching lengthy notes. With regard to the questions Hall raised, Stewart wrote: "I see nothing to suggest that Reed wrote these entries in later years. And also nothing to indicate that he might have copied in his own handwriting something which someone else had written." Nevertheless:

(11) One of the folded pieces of paper contains a note signed "George Donner," dated at "Donners Camp, Nov. 18 1846," authorizing Milford Elliott to purchase supplies. On the back of this note is "A Statement of Breen & Halloran/Stock of Merch, etc., taken June 25th - 1845" [*sic*]. The items below that heading show the value of Halloran's stock ($1,435) and Breen's stock ($452.76), and their shares of the cash acquired by the sale of their goods. This note, including the date of it, makes little sense, and perhaps confuses "Breen" with "Dolan." That such a note was among Reed's papers is mystifying.

(12) On the back of the above item is a partly decipherable note over the signature of "John Trudeau," already quoted in this book (see Chapter 14). Hall, doubtless influenced by Stewart's description of Trudeau as "a little frontier mongrel," drew the mistaken conclusion that the note was "presumably not in Trudeau's handwriting [because] probably he could not write." Trudeau could read and write English, at least in 1867 when he registered to vote in California, literacy in English being a requirement. The 1900 census enumerator (Tomales Bay, Marin County) also noted his ability to read and write English.

(13) Included in the pouch were a number of receipts for clothing, horses, and food in connection with the second relief, organized by Woodworth and Reed. Many of these receipts appear to be in the hand of Reed, except for the signatures.

(14) Also, in Reed's hand: "A List of merchandise belonging to the Estate of Jacob Donner. Sold to Sundriee persons on the 2nd day of March 1847, by Hiram O. Miller." The list of purchasers of boots, handkerchiefs, jeans, shoes, cloth and other items includes Mathew Dofar, Henry Dunn,

Chas. Stone, Nicholas Clark, Chas. Cady, Joseph Jaundro [Jondro, Gendreau], Joseph Varo [Verrot], and "Keesberger," total purchases $118.81.

(15) Also in Reed's hand: the Donner Party account with Sutter for the relief mission of Stanton, Luis, and Salvador, compiled by Reed at Sutters's request. The arithmetic is confusing and not quite accurate: $364 owed Sutter for seven mules ($210) and 800 pounds of flour ($64), six pack and riding saddles ($84) and fifty pounds of dried beef ($3), the entire debt being pro-rated among James F. Reed ($52.81¼), Wm. H. Eddy ($30.68¼), P. Brinn ($71.37½), Wm. McCutchen ($22.12½), Graves ($89.93-3/4), Wm. Foster ($52.81¼), and "Keesbergher" ($44.25).

(16) In Reed's hand, except the signature, is a document over the name of "Edwin Bryant, Chief Magistrate, Dist. of San Francisco," authorizing Reed to administer the effects of the estate of Jacob Donner.

(17) In Reed's hand are several petitions for land over the signatures, clearly forged, of his servants and family members at a time when they were entrapped in the high camps: (a) Petition to John Burton, Alcalde for the Pueblo de San Jose, over the "signatures" of "Bailos William" and "E. Williams." The petition was approved by Burton on December 1, 1846, and by R.F. Pinkney ("Commg U.S. Forces at Pueblo San Jose") on January 26, 1847, more than a month after the death of Baylis Williams in the mountains; (b) another petition dated December 1, 1846, this one over the signature of Reed and the forged signatures of his wife and four children, for San Jose land, also summarily approved by Burton and Pinkney; (c) still another petition, same dates of submission and approval, over the signatures of "J.F. Reed" and "M.W. Reed."

(18) Two ""warning" letters entirely in Reed's handwriting. One of them reads: "To all whome it may concern   Notice is hereby given that any person taking tiles or timber or in any way disturbing the houses belonging to the Mission of San Jose will be punished according to <u>law</u>. /s/ James F. Reed, Mission San Jose, 20 January 1847/by order of R.F. Pinkney, Comd. Pueblo de San Jose." The other is identical, except that the name of James F. Reed is omitted.

Reed, until the end of his life, was always very sensitive about the Snyder affair. As late as 1871 he continued to claim publicly that his reason for leaving the Donner Party in Nevada was merely to ride ahead, voluntarily, to California to obtain and bring back provisions. The 1871 articles by Frances H. McDougall in the *Pacific Rural Press* aroused Reed and McCutchen to reply with articles in concert. Both handwritten and typewritten early drafts of their replies are in folders 461 and 462 of the Martha Reed Lewis Papers. One is a 49-page handwritten manuscript on legal-size paper (together with a

10-page single-spaced typewritten transcript). Most of it is in one firm, clear hand, but on p. 6 are two sections written in what seems to be the shaky hand of the elderly Reed. In this manuscript appears Reed's explanation of why he abandoned the Breens at Starved Camp: "He [Mr. Breen] and his family were all strong enough to travel....we remonstrated with him....finding that we could [not] prevail upon him I asked some of the men standing by to witness that. I then told Mr. Breen that if his family died there blood be upon his head and not on ours." Reed does not explain why he abandoned Mrs. Graves, the Graves children, and the Donner child.

Conclusion: The disturbing questions raised by Carroll D. Hall in *Donner Miscellany* can never be answered with certainty.

The almost pristine, unworn condition of the "Miller Diary" suggests that it was carefully protected on the trail and afterwards. If the entries, with pen and ink, were indeed made on the trail over a four-month period, that could have been accomplished on a small table in Reed's huge palace car, at first by Hiram Miller, later by James F. Reed. The third and rather fine hand could be that of Mrs. Reed, although I do not have a sample of her handwriting for verifying this hypothesis. Another possibility is that the portion of the diary in Reed's hand was composed sometime, even years, later, and that many of the dates were taken from published sources, such as Thornton, except where the delays reflected poorly on Reed himself. If so, Reed could have chosen the October 4 date for his last entry after consulting Thornton, who gave October 5 as the day Snyder was killed. In that case, the diary cannot be used to confirm Thornton, as Stewart did in the 1960 edition of *Ordeal*, in an attempt to prove that the killing could not have taken place at Gravelly Ford.

It seems evident, however, that at least some of the Reed documents from the Lewis estate were composed, and even forged, by Reed long after the events they describe, perhaps as late as 1871. Reed's intention may have been to construct what he thought would be a true record of events that he failed to record at the time of their occurrence. That he was not above forgery in a good cause is evidenced by the signatures on the petitions for land for his servants and family members. It is unlikely that his daughters, who developed a warm friendship with McGlashan that lasted a lifetime, were unaware of their late and beloved father's hand in the Hiram O. Miller Diary, and perhaps of the dubiousness of some of the papers stuffed into the pouch. If McGlashan was shown these documents, he was totally silent about them in his *History*, much as he was silent about many reports of witnesses in his voluminous correspondence. Although over four hundred of these letters from witnesses survive, McGlashan's daughter revealed that, before his death, her father destroyed the greatest portion of the correspondence in the interest of not compromising his informants.

NOTES

key:

MRL - Papers from Martha Reed Lewis's estate, "Sutter's Fort Document Collection: Reed Family."

BancMs - Bancroft Library, Berkeley, California, manuscript collection.

LDS - Church of Jesus Christ of Latter-day Saints genealogical collection, Salt Lake City.

Notes to Chapter 1: Ireland to the New World

Ireland. In 1990 and 1991, at my request Father Nicholas Moore, P.P., Borris, County Carlow, searched the old registers from about 1790 to 1810 and found the following entries for baptisms (sps = sponsors or godparents):

June 30, 1793. Mary Breen. Ned Breen & Mary Wilson, Barnahasken Townland. Sps Luke Nowland & Margaret Byrne.

June 11, 1795. Patrick Breen. Ned Breen & Mary Wilson, Barnahasken Townland. Sps L. Moore & Elizabeth Wilson.

December 11, 1800. Samuel Breen. Edward Breen & Mary Wilson, Barnahasken Townland. Sps L. Moore & Elizabeth Wilson.

January 24, 1803. George Breen. Edward Breen & Mary Wilson, Ballymurphy Townland. Sps Edmund Byrne & Mary Breen.

May 5, 1805. Ned Breen. Ned Breen & Mary Wilson, Barnahasken Townland. Sps Patrick Breen & Mary Breen.

July 24, 1806. James Breen. Ned Breen & Mary____, Barnahasken Townland. Sps Sam Nowland & Hariot Nowlan.

August 28, 1810. Thomas Breen. Edmond Breen & Mary Wilson (townland not given in data from Fr. Moore). Sps Pat Doyle & Betty Breen [?].

Additionally:

March 2, 1806. Margaret Bulger. Simon Bulger & Margaret Bulger, Rathgeran Townland. Sps Patt [Patrick] Bulger and Catherine Murphy.

No record of the marriage of Edward Breen and Mary Wilson was found. No record was found, despite a second search, of the baptism of William Breen, son of Edward and Mary, born about 1798 according to a headstone inscription, St. Thomas, Ontario. As for Charlotte, a daughter of Edward and Mary, a search for years following 1810 may produce her baptismal record; also record of the marriage of Samuel Breen and Margaret Murphy, about 1827.

The headstone inscription for the Breen grave is described in *County Carlow Tombstone Inscriptions* (Kiltennel Cemetery), copy in LDS Archives.

> *[IHS. With a cross on top of the H.] Erected by Patrick Breen in memory of his wife Bridget Breen, also Ryan [maiden name], who Departed this life December 29th 1799 aged 73 years also lieth the body of Patrick Breen who Departed this life January the 1st 1802 aged 77 years. Also his son Edwd. Breen who depd August the 9th 1816 aged 50 years. Also Edwd Breens daughter Marry who dept January 2, 1819 aged 23 years. Reqt in Pace, Amen.*

Mary was actually twenty-five years of age. The error is a quite usual one, perhaps owing to the fact that Mary was approaching the age of spinsterhood.

The *Tithe Applotment Book*, year 1826, for Ballinvally and Barnahasken (adjoining townlands), Civil Parish of Kiltennel, Barony of Idrone East, is on film at the LDS Archives in Salt Lake City.

Ballonvally [sic] Townland - Parish of Kiltennel

	Occupier	Acres	1st qual.	2nd qual.	3rd qual.	Tithe
1.	Breen, Patt	21	6	11+	3+	£0.12.5½
2.	Breen, widow	13/2/21	7+	3	3+	£0.9.8
3.	Breen, widow	24/3/0	18+	3	3+	£0.18.0½
4.	Breen, Samuel	37/3/39	6	18+	13	£0.15/10
		97	38	36	23	

Barnahasken Townland – Parish of Kiltennel

	Occupier	Acres	1st qual.	2nd qual.	3rd qual.	Tithe
1.	Breen, Mary, wid.	26/0/30	7	4	15	£0.16.1
2.	Breen, William	38/2/0	18	16	4	£1.2.10
		64	25	20	19	

Total for family	161	63	56	42	£4.14.11

The "townland" is an ancient land division, the smallest unit by which head landlords measured their holdings. Sizes of townlands differed widely. Ballinvally (also known as "Ballinvally & Kiltennel Townland") comprised 265 Irish acres in 1826, twenty-six lots leased by twenty-three persons. Figures are in Irish acres, roods and perches. One Irish acre equalled 1.6 English or statute acres, 4 roods to the acre, 40 perches to the rood. The 161 Irish acres occupied by the widow Mary Breen and her three oldest sons equalled about 257 English acres, most of it of first and second quality and tillable. The figure for the compulsory tithe to the established Protestant church is in pounds, shillings, and pence. The sum of £4.14.11 equalled what a landless cottier might earn for five or six months of hired labor.

The *Tithe Applotment Book* does not indicate lot numbers, nor the name of the head landlord or middleman. However, *Griffiths Valuations* of circa 1850 for these same townlands indicated that John Curry was then occupying the formerly Breen lots in "Ballinvally & Kiltennel" (lots 1a and 1b, Ordnance Survey Map 22) and that he and Laurence Lalor were the occupiers of the Barnahasken lots (1 and part of 2a, Map 22), on lease from the Earl of Courtown. No rates (taxes) have been charged on agricultural land since 1980, so I have been informed by James Kearney, Secretary of the County Carlow Council (ltr. April 24, 1991), but some of the ratepayers before 1980 are indicated on a sheet prepared in 1928. Rates were paid at one time or another on lots 1a and 1b in Ballinvally & Kiltinnel by John Flood, James Doyle, Michael Fogarty, and Samuel B. Little; and in adjoining Barnahasken, lots 1a and 2a, by Laurence Lalor and Mary Murphy.

The names on the baptismal register, tithe books, and valuations, when compared with the names on the earliest registers and other records for the Catholic Church at St. Thomas, Ontario, suggest strongly a pattern of chain emigration of relatives and friends.

For information on Catholic/Protestant strife in County Carlow in the 1820s, I found useful Desmond Bowen's *The Protestant Crusade in Ireland, 1800-70* and Kerby Miller's *Emigrants and Exiles*. For background on relevant Irish history, conditions of tenant farmers and reasons for emigration to British North America, see J.A. King, *The Irish Lumberman - Farmer* (1982), especially pp. 21-48, and Margaret E. Fitzgerald and J.A. King, *The Uncounted Irish in Canada and the United States*, especially pp. 1-8 and 33-82.

Canada. Canadian Catholic Church records on the Breens are elusive. The Catholic community of St. Thomas, Ontario, and surrounds (e.g., Southwold, Yarmouth) was served in the late 1820s and early 1830s by several visiting missionary priests of the Diocese of Kingston, who made their entries for baptisms and marriages on their "home" registers, some of which have not been located. Entries by Fr. James W. Campion and Fr. J. Cullin from 1828-31 for ceremonies at Yarmouth and Southwold have been found on an early register of St. Augustine's Parish in Dundas, Ontario. They include the marriage of Charlotte Breen and Patrick Burns (1829), the bride's parents cited as "Edward Breen and Mary Wilson"; the baptism of their son Thomas (1831); the baptisms of two children of Samuel Breen, Edward (baptised 1828, birth year given on the same record as 1826) and William (1830). The names of Patrick Breen, Peggy Breen, James Breen and others appear as witnesses or sponsors. An early Wardens' Account Book for the Catholic Church in St. Thomas records the baptism of Charlotte Burns, daughter of Patrick and Charlotte (Breen) in 1939. Headstone inscriptions in Holy Angels Cemetery in St. Thomas note the death of William Breen (brother of Patrick) in 1872, and that of his wife, Mary Roche, in 1890. The register for the church in St. Thomas records the baptisms and marriages in the 1850s and 1860s of several of the children of Patrick Breen, son of William and Mary.

The best description of the early missionary activity around St. Thomas, and information on existing record collections, is in a 1974 paper by Daniel Brock, delivered to the London & Middlesex Historical Society (copy obtained from Diocese of London Archives). Records of the marriage of Patrick Breen and Margaret Bulger (c1830) and the baptisms of their sons John and Edward have not yet been located, despite considerable searching.

Illinois. No records have been located for the brief period the Breen family spent in Springfield, Illinois (*circa* 1834-35).

Iowa and Missouri. Five Breen children were born near Keokuk, Iowa, between 1837 and 1845. Among the Breen Papers at Bancroft is a yellowed newsclip from a Minnesota paper about French-born Fr. Lucien Galtier. In the margin is a handwritten note, apparently made by a descendant, that Fr. Galtier gave Patrick Breen a prayer book before the family left for California. Baptismal records for the five Breen children born near Keokuk have not been located, despite considerable searching and the help of Msgr. Edgar Kurt of the Archdiocese of Dubuque and Sr. Madeleine Marie Schmidt, C.H.M., archivist and historian of the Diocese of Davenport. The account of Fr. Galtier's experiences in Keokuk can be found in Fr. M. M. Hoffmann, *Church Founders of the Northwest* (Milwaukee, Bruce Publishing Co., c1937). After leaving Keokuk in 1845, Fr. Galtier served at Prairie du Chien, Wisconsin, until his death in 1866.

A brief account of the Catholic Church in Keokuk, before the arrival of Fr. Galtier, can be found in *The History of Lee County, Iowa* [no author or editor cited], Chicago, Western Historical Co., 1879, pp. 637-37: "The first church building erected in Keokuk was a frame building, which stood on the southeast corner of First and Blondeau streets, and was called St. John's Roman Catholic Church. This was built in 1838, and services were held therein and mass celebrated by the Rev. Father J.G. Allemann, A.M. Pelamourgues, and other Missionary Priests, until 1848, when Rev. John M. Villars was appointed Parish Priest by the Rev. Mathias Loras, first Bishop of Dubuque." In 1840, according to the same source, p. 605, Fr. Allemann resided at Ft. Madison, and was the only priest within one hundred miles.

Notes to Chapter 2: California Bound

I have drawn heavily on John Breen's manuscript, "Pioneer Memoirs," and other items among the Breen Papers in the Bancroft archives; also on Julia L. Altrocchi, *The Old California Trail;* George R. Stewart, *The California Trail;* and T.H. Jefferson, *Map of the Emigrant Road from*

Independence, Mo., to San Francisco, California. The prices that emigrants could expect to pay for wagons and livestock are given by Jefferson, who crossed with the Hastings (Harlan-Young) group in 1846.

Notes to Chapter 3: Joining the Donners

For the members of the Donner company, I have drawn on a composite of primary and secondary sources, especially McGlashan, Bancroft, and Stewart, with some contributions of my own, such as the Trudeau surname for John Baptiste, assigning "Mrs. Wolfinger" her first name, Doriss or Doris, and giving more accurate ages for Trudeau, Mrs. Wolfinger, and Patrick Breen. "Mr. Wolfinger" may be the Jacob Wolfinger, age 10, who arrived with his parents, John J. and Elizabeth Wolfinger, at the Port of Baltimore on September 30, 1830 (*Passenger Arrivals at the Port of Baltimore, 1820-1834* from *Customs Passenger Lists*, Baltimore, Genealogical Publishing Co., 1982, transcribed by Elizabeth P. Bentley). They may be among the Wolfingers who settled in Fairfield, Lucas and neighboring counties in Ohio, in the 1830s and 40s.

Augustus Spitzer of the Donner Party may be the person of that name, no age given, an Ohio settler of record, 1839-46, cited in Filby and Lower, *1986 Supplement to Passenger & Immigration Lists Index*, the reference being *An Index to Indiana Naturalization Records Found in Various Order Books in Ninety-two Local Courts Prior to 1907*, Indianapolis, Indiana Historical Society, Family History Section, 1981.

Nothing is known about "Mr. Hardcoop," except for the questionable information found in J. Quinn Thornton's account, repeated by Stewart and others. It was Thornton who wrote that "Mr. Hardcoop....was from Antwerp, Belgium....a cutler by trade, and had a son and daughter in his native city....he owned a farm near Cincinnati, Ohio, and intended, after visiting California, to go back to Ohio, sell his farm, and return to Antwerp, for the purpose of spending with his children the evening of his days." I have been unable to confirm any of this. Michel Parys, Belgian Vice-Consul in Los Angeles, wrote me that "the name 'Hardcoop' does not bear any resemblance to any Belgian name I know," nor does any similar name appear in the current Antwerp phone directory. A "Daniel Hartcop," age 50 to 59, appears as head of a household on the 1840 U.S. Census, Greene Co., Ohio, but he seems to be the "Daniel Hartkofs" who also appears on the 1850 Ohio Census, Dayton Ward 2, age 70, native of Germany.

Notes to Chapter 4: The Long Dry Drive

The research of Charles Kelly (*Salt Desert Trails*, 1930) indicated that the dry drive was seventy-five miles. I have used this figure in preference to Stewart's eighty-three miles (*The California Trail*). The most authoritative description of the exact trail taken by the Donner wagons across the Salt

Desert to Pilot Peak is in Stookey, *Fatal Decision: The Tragic Story of the Donner Party* (1950).

Notes to Chapter 5: A Digression on Indians, Survival, and Charity

For information on the Indians of the Humboldt and Truckee, I am indebted to *The World of the American Indians*, edited by Jules B. Billard, National Geographic Society, 1974; Barbara Leitch, *A Concise Dictionary of the Indian Tribes of North America*, Algonac, Michigan, 1979; Ferol Egan, *Sand in a Whirlwind: The Piute Indian War of 1860*, New York 1972; Gae Whitney Canfield, *Sarah Winnemucca of the Northern Paiutes*, Norman, Oklahoma, 1983. I have also relied on information acquired many years ago when conducting field research with my colleague Alfred Pietroforte for his book *Songs of the Yokuts and Piutes* (Healdsburg, California, 1965).

The wealth of the Donner brothers is discussed in Chapter XX of Mc-Glashan's *History of the Donner Party* (1880):

> Hiram Miller, of the relief parties, is authority for the statement that [George] Donner owned a quarter section of land within the present city limits of Chicago. This land was sold for ten thousand dollars, shortly before Mr. Donner started for California. Mr. Allen Francis, who has been mentioned as the very best authority concerning the family, camped with them on the evening of their first night's journey out of Springfield, Illinois, saw Mr. Donner's money, and thinks there was ten thousand dollars. Mrs. F.E.Bond of Elk Grove, Sacramento County, California, does not remember the exact amount, but knows that Mr. Donner started with a great deal of gold, because she helped make the belts in which it was to be carried in crossing the plains. The relief parties always understood there was at Donner's camp a large sum of money, estimated at from six to fourteen thousand dollars belonging to this family. Yet Capt. Fallon's party claimed to have found very little. It was clear to their minds that some one had robbed the Donner tents.

If the Donners were robbed, prime candidates for the theft would be members of the relief parties. Research into land acquisitions in California by certain members of the relief, and sums paid, might lead to interesting speculations for one with the inclination to pursue such an arduous line of research. Only relatively small sums of money have been accounted for. Captain Fallon's party reported the several hundred dollars they retrieved from the cache Keseberg directed them to, as well as the few hundred dollars they found on his person. Cady and Stone of the second relief seem to have been given at least $500 by Tamsen Donner for carrying out three children from the Alder Creek camp, a task that they aborted when they left the children at the lake camp. Hiram Miller (second relief) may have been given some money by Elizabeth Donner. The following note, in James F. Reed's handwriting, was transcribed and printed by Carroll D. Hall in *Donner Miscellany*:

Money of J. Donners	
given to H Miller	
8 soverins 4.85	*38.80*
29 five Dolls.	*145.00*
7 ten Dolls.	*70.00*
1 two & half Doll	*2.50*
Gold	*256.30*
Silver	*45.00*
	301.30

James F. Reed and Hiram Miller seem to have been solicitous of the interests of the Donner orphans. Reed took Mary Donner, and later Frances, into his home in San Jose. Miller acted as guardian for Frances, Georgia, and Eliza Donner, but did not raise them. They were taken in by a Swiss couple named Brunner. McGlashan mentioned (in Chapter XXIV) that the citizens of San Francisco raised money for purchasing town lots for George and Mary Donner, son and daughter of Jacob Donner, shortly after they were rescued. Two lots were granted them (one hundred varas each) on the petition of James F. Reed at a price of $32 per lot, which was paid out of the fund. The lots were occupied by squatters and years of litigation were in the offing as the land became very valuable. Mary Donner lost her lot because of a technicality (the alcalde's name had been omitted on her grant). George managed to maintain his grant, but litigation continued until after his death.

Notes to Chapter 6: To the Humboldt and Truckee

I have deliberately been guarded about assigning exact dates for the trail points from Fort Bridger to Truckee Meadows. The itineraries in Thornton, McGlashan, Stewart, and Virginia Reed, are impossible to reconcile, and have been further confused by the latter-day appearance of the strange diary composed by Miller, Reed, and at least one unidentifiable person. Professor Stewart addresses the problem in his foreword to the second edition of *Ordeal* in 1960, changing his own previous itinerary for this section of the trail to conform to the new diary. I see no more reason to accept the itinerary in this diary than I do the dates given by Thornton, on which Stewart largely relied for the first edition of *Ordeal*.

For the trail from the Weber River across the Wasatch, the Salt Lake Valley, and the Great Salt Desert, I have relied less on Stewart and more on the later research of Altrocchi and Stookey.

As to the exact spot where Reed slew Snyder, Stewart goes to some length in his foreword to the second edition of *Ordeal* to disprove Mc-Glashan's claim that the event happened at Gravelly Ford near Beowawe, about twenty miles west of today's Carlin, Nevada. Stewart held that Mc-Glashan misread a passage in a narrative prepared by William C. Graves in 1877, and that the killing took place at least two days' journey beyond Gravelly Ford. The evidence seems to be on Stewart's side.

Notes to Chapter 7: Entrapment in the Snows

My figures on the number of emigrants at the two camps – a total of eighty-one people, fifty-six at the sites near the lake, twenty-five in the Alder Creek Valley – are very close to those of Stewart. The exact figure depends on how Denton and Burger, both of whom began the entrapment at Alder Creek but later moved to the lake, are counted. Burger seems to have camped with Spitzer at the lake, but the evidence is not clear as to whether they shared Keseberg's cabin or a makeshift shelter of their own.

Notes to Chapter 8: Breen's Diary

Patrick Breen turned over his diary to Sheriff George McKinstry on his arrival at Sutter's Fort, for his use in preparing a report on the events for American authorities. It is evident that Breen was not aware of the great historical value of the diary, nor was anybody else in the Breen family during his lifetime. The diary came into the possession of Hubert H. Bancroft as a gift from McKinstry in 1871 when Bancroft was collecting documents for his history of California. It ultimately became part of the great Bancroft Library collection at the University of California in Berkeley.

The first transcription of the diary was done by McKinstry himself, for the May 22, 1847 *California Star* (copy in Bancroft fF 592 D6B52). Breen was not mentioned as the author, and the transcription was extremely poor, heavily edited for grammar, spelling and punctuation, some names blanked out, many omissions. McGlashan used this inadequate version.

The first accurate transcription was done by Teggart in 1910. His text is essentially that reprinted in the second edition (1960) of Stewart's *Ordeal*, with only very minor changes, as far as I can determine, mainly in formatting. The sources of my own text are Teggart and a facsimile and transcription of the entire diary published by Stewart in 1946.

Notes to Chapter 9: Attempts to Escape

Eddy cannot be blamed entirely for mythologizing the experience of the Snowshoe Party. Regarding Thornton's account of the killing of the deer, even Stewart granted in his notes, in an unusual admission, that he "suspected a certain elaboration on [Thornton's] part." Interestingly, Peter H. Burnett, later to become Governor of California, when he was prospecting in the mines in 1849 sometimes stayed at "Nye's House" above Marysville where he became, he said, "intimately acquainted" with four Snowshoe Party survivors: William Foster and his wife, Sarah Murphy; Harriet Murphy Pike Nye, and William Eddy. Later he reported in considerable detail what they told him. He is silent about the cannibalism. He barely mentions the shooting of the deer, with none of the fictional flourishes of Thornton and Stewart that include William Eddy and Mary Graves off by themselves praying, then the shooting and the drinking of the blood, then the pair slumbering together alone and peacefully until the next morning. (See "Burnett's Recollections of the Past," vol. 1, pp. 375-96, 1878. Bancroft MS P-A 12.)

As for events at the cabins in the mountains, especially at the lake sites, the Breen Diary is a main source of events related in this chapter and others. Nothing in the testimony of other witnesses contradicts Breen's reporting, as Professor Stewart admits. Occasional additional bits of information come from the manuscript material at Bancroft, especially the McGlashan Papers.

Notes to Chapter 10: The Relief Parties

McGlashan does not mention Lieutenant Kern at all in connection with the relief efforts, and Stewart tends to slight Kern's efforts. For an account of the relief efforts, especially the first relief, I am especially indebted to *The Fort Sutter Papers, Reference Volume: A Literal Transcript of the Manuscripts and Commentaries*. Twenty-six copies were published by Edward Eberstadt in 1922, one of which is Bancroft call no. fF864.K36x. The documents include Kern's papers, showing names of those employed by him, the day they commenced service, number of days served, pay per diem, and total amount. Daniel Rhodes, for example, was employed for thirty-nine days from January 31 to March 15 at $3 per diem, total $117; Adolph Bruheim for forty-eight days, January 31 to March 19, at $1.50, total $72, for "butchering and assisting in carrying provisions from Johnsons to Bear V"; John Stark for serving thirty-nine days at $3, total $117, plus $50 "for bringing out John Graves." Coffeemire earned $104 for "60 days Services at $3.00," from "Last day of Jany to 9th of April" (which should add up to about sixty-nine days).

The role played by William Thompson has generally been slighted in the literature from Thornton to Stewart, which mentions him only in connection with the third relief. The *Fort Sutter Papers* indicate he served from February 10 to April 9, fifty-nine days at $3, total $177, plus $50 for "bringing out F. Donough [Frances Donner]." Edward Pyle [Pile, Pyles] Jr. is not mentioned at all in the literature, yet Kern's payroll credited "Edward Pyles, Jr." for nineteen days service, February 20 to March 10, including "for packing Child 2 days," in the "Cal. Mts." at $3 per day, total $57. On another statement, however, he is credited at the rate of only $1.50 per day, as is his father, Edward, also unheralded in the Donner literature. They apparently hauled provisions to Mule Springs and Bear Valley.

Stewart credits Eddy with writing a letter of appeal to Alcalde Sinclair at Sutter's Fort the day after he arrived almost dead at Johnson's, and giving it to an Indian messenger to deliver. Stewart's source, predictably, was Eddy himself, via Thornton. I cannot find any such letter among the Sutter's Fort papers, nor apparently could Eberstadt. It appears to be just another invention of Eddy that beguiled Thornton and George R. Stewart. McGlashan, who spoke to survivors, gave a vivid description of how John Rhoads carried the news to the fort, with no mention of Eddy's alleged letter. I think that McGlashan is the more reliable source.

I have drawn also on an undated letter (the contents indicate it was written during the last week of January, 1847) from Kern to Hull, in the Huntington Library collection. The letter describes the arrival of the seven survivors of the Snowshoe Party at Johnson's and the plight of those still in the mountains, and Kern asks Hull for authority and government funds to finance relief efforts, even though Kern, with the help of Sinclair and Sutter, had actually begun the relief. The Ritchie-Tucker Diary is extremely critical of Kern's performance, claiming that he arrived four days after Sinclair, encamped with eight Indians on the other side of the Bear River, and never crossed over to Johnson's until the rescue party had departed for the mountains. Further, according to the diary, when the rescue party was returning, Kern was slow to bring up horses from his camp (somewhere between Mule Springs and Johnson's) to Mule Springs, was niggardly with food and other provisions (giving first priority to himself and his Indians), despite instructions from Woodworth to provide the survivors and rescuers amply with their needs, including liquor (which Kern denied them but not himself and the Indians). McGlashan was given the handwritten Ritchie-Tucker Diary by Martha Reed Lewis. After referring to it as "brief, concise, and pointed," he proceeded to quote only those entries dated from February 5 to February 19 (although giving the impression he was quoting the entire diary), ignoring later entries as well as two long pages of addenda having to do with preparations at Johnson's and the later treatment by Kern of the survivors and rescuers. (For original document, see MRL folder 86.) It is difficult to excuse McGlashan for his cover-up of Kern while he unfairly faults Woodworth for allegedly "lying idle in the camp at Bear Valley" and taking no active part in the relief efforts. George R. Stewart's trashing of Woodworth was based on an inadequate reading of the evidence and of the chronologies that Stewart himself presented, somewhat confusedly, in *Ordeal*. This was perhaps because of Stewart's compelling need to provide colorful villains, as well as super-heroes, for his fictional approach to the writing of history.

The literature usually lists Patrick Breen, his wife, and five of his children, as having been brought out by the second relief, under Reed. Actually, they went with the second relief only a few miles beyond the pass to Summit Valley. They were brought to the Sacramento Valley by John Stark of the third relief, a giant of a man recruited by Woodworth.

George Tucker's testimony about the children eating pieces of his father's buckskins is contained in a forty-page statement he prepared for McGlashan in 1879 (Bancroft MS C-D 570). His father's account of the burial of the Keseberg child is in the same file.

In answer to a questionnaire sent to him by McGlashan, William McCutchen of the second relief supported the testimony of Mrs. Breen that her son John fell from a log almost into the firepit. McCutchen adds: "He did not have to be brought back to consciousness, he was the fulest [*sic*] – and most healthy person in the party." McCutchen then testified that, when Reed was afflicted with blindness and had become unconscious, he and Hiram Miller took over. "Miller [was] a man of herculean strength," wrote McCutchen (June 1, 1879 letter to McGlashan, Bancroft MS C-D 570). McCutchen's opinion that John Breen was in good health is doubtful, yet John, even in his mother's testimony, was strong enough to maneuver a tree limb to use for climbing down to the bottom of the pit, and then to dig steps in the snow. Reed's own testimony as to what went on at Starved Camp during the storm is unreliable, since Reed was blind or unconscious most of the time.

Some of the events at Starved Camp that I have included in my narrative may be purely the invention of Eddy/Thornton (as suggested in this chapter and in Chapter 15, "Whom to Believe?"). I have relied much more heavily on Mrs. Breen's own account, given to Mrs. Farnham three years after the events, than on Thornton/Eddy, from whom Stewart derives the "facts" for much of his narrative.

The McGlashan materials did not become available to Stewart until a few years before the second edition of *Ordeal*. Even then the mass of hundreds of letters and other documents was unindexed. Stewart found the materials "disappointing," as he wrote in the foreword to the new edition, "the great majority of [the letters having] nothing about the Donner story at all." He concluded that "on the whole, the McGlashan papers require no changes to be made in the structure of the story."

I worked with the advantage of a superb indexing of the papers done by the Bancroft staff. A great many of the letters were concerned directly with the events of the ordeal as the witnesses remembered them. Further, many items were ignored by McGlashan, no doubt in the interest of not embarrassing survivors. Quite a few items, one would think, might have led Stewart to question some of the "facts" in his own narrative, especially concerning the Breens.

My description of the movement back and forth from the lake camp to the creek camp by rescuers Cady, Stone, and Clark I put together as well as I could from a variety of sources, especially letters to McGlashan in Bancroft file C-D 570.

Woodworth's report appeared in the *California Star*, April 3, 1847.

Notes to Chapter 11: Captain W.O. Fallon and the Fourth Relief; and Chapter 12: Keseberg Speaks for Himself

The agreement of April 10, 1846 between Alcalde Sinclair, representing the Donner children, and Fallon, Rhoads, and Sels of the fourth relief is printed in *Donner Miscellany*, edited by Carroll D. Hall. On May 5, Sinclair entered into a similar agreement with John Rhoads, P.A. House, P.C. Stice [?] and Thomas Rhoads (also printed in *Donner Miscellany*), but it is not known if those four men actually made the trip to the camps to recover what the fourth relief had left behind of the Donner valuables.

Regarding the extracts of the journal allegedly kept by "Captain Fellun," I leave it to the reader to decide on its credibility, after comparing it with Keseberg's statement, printed in the succeeding chapter.

Regarding the slim record of Keseberg's suit for defamation against Ned Coffeymire, it is tempting to speculate that the suit at least partially involved the claim of some that he was involved in the disappearance of Mr. Wolfinger. Why else would Mrs. Wolfinger be called by Keseberg as a witness? As for Captain Fallon's description of finding Keseberg in his cabin with "two kettles of coagulated human blood, all supposed to be over one gallon," McGlashan calls attention to his conversations with Keseberg during which Keseberg mentioned the length of time that Mrs. Donner had been dead, the readiness with which blood coagulates, and the fact that no witness testified to such a circumstance at the defamation hearing.

The full written statement Keseberg prepared for McGlashan – and which he showed to Eliza Donner Houghton – has never been published and probably no longer exists. McGlashan printed only long excerpts from it, interrupted by his own commentary, on pp. 206-15, 218-19, 221-222 of his *History of the Donner Party*, and I have reprinted all of this verbatim except Keseberg's account of his latter days on pp. 221-22 (which I have summarized). The full statement may have been among the documents McGlashan burned, according to his daughter, for fear of compromising some of the survivors who had cooperated with him.

There are clearly some errors and inconsistencies in Keseberg's statement, which can easily be attributed to the three decades that had transpired from actual events to recollections of them.

For the information on the career of Captain William O. Fallon I am indebted mainly to the meticulous research of Dale L. Morgan and Eleanor

T. Harris, which they included in their notes, pp. 296-300, to *The Rocky Mountain Journals of William Marshall Anderson*, edited by them in 1967.

Notes to Chapter 13: Survivors and Casualties
With some minor exceptions, reliable lists of casualties, survivors, and rescuers appear in McGlashan and Stewart. McGlashan's list of thirteen members of the rescue party who left Johnson's Ranch on February 5 failed to include Joe Verrot. Stewart is more accurate, although minimizing or ignoring the participation of the back-up men at the camps that were set up at Mule Springs and Bear Valley. On the lives of the characters after the rescue, McGlashan has much information, and Stewart has many updates. Bancroft's "Pioneer Register" in his *History of California* is an invaluable tool, although not without errors and significant omissions of pioneers. Many little details in my narrative were found in the McGlashan, Reed, Breen and other files at Bancroft having to do with Donner Party members.

Notes to Chapter 14: John Baptiste Trudeau: An Unsung Hero
Rather compelling circumstantial evidence suggests that the pioneer St. Louis schoolmaster, trader, and explorer, Jean Baptiste Trudeau (aka Truteau, 1748-1827), was the grandfather of John Baptiste Trudeau of the Donner Party. According to a county history (J. Thomas Scharf, *History of St. Louis City and County*, 2 vols., Philadelphia, 1883, p. 823 and footnotes), Trudeau and his wife, Madeleine LeRoy, had two sons, Louis (1794) and John Baptiste II (1800). Louis married Archange du Mouchet in 1814. Louis was still alive with family in 1850, according to the St. Louis census for that year. As for his brother, John Baptiste Trudeau II, the county history gives only his birth year. Was he the father of the John Baptiste Trudeau of this study, the birth place of whose father is given as Missouri on the 1900 United States Census? (There were only two Trudeau families in Missouri at the turn of the 18th century, one headed by the schoolmaster, the other by his second cousin, Xenon Trudeau, who served as governor of the territory under Spanish rule.) If so, the "little frontier mongrel" whose mixed blood lines seemed to offend George R. Stewart, descended from a distinguished pioneer schoolmaster and explorer whose early forebear was Etienne Trudeau, who served in the militia in Montreal in 1663. See Cyprian Tanguay, *Dictionnaire Genealogiques des Familles Canadiennes*, vol. 7, 1890 (UCB Library Newsroom film 20885, 4 reels). See also *Dictionary of American Biography*, vol. xix; *Trudeau Family Tree 1565-1988*, privately printed in 1988 by Robert W. Trudeau, Sr., 718 E. Hoyt Avenue, St. Paul, Minnesota 55106; and "Census of 1791, St. Louis and Its District," Juan Trudeau household, in Louis Houck, *Spanish Regime in Missouri*, vol. 2, Chicago, 1909. For the death certificates, obituaries, and other documents related to Trudeau of the Donner Party and members of his family at

Tomales Bay, California, I am indebted to Mr. and Mrs. Hugh L. Wallace of the Marin County Genealogical Society.

Notes to Chapter 15: Whom to Believe?
Sources are cited in the text itself. Full facts of publication or location of manuscript items can be found in the bibliography section.

Notes to Chapter 16: The Breens in California
The deed conveying 401 acres of land of José and Modesta Castro to Patrick Breen on February 7, 1849, was recorded in the office of the Secretary of State for California on July 5, 1849 by W.E.P. Hartnell, Government Translator. The copy of the document in Spanish that I have in my possession has a note in the corner, "352 Southern Dist. U.S. vs. Breen." This litigation seems to explain why the property was not finally confirmed to Patrick Breen by the Commissioner of the General Land Office until January 22, 1877, nine years after his death.

Patrick Breen's last will and testament, with an appraisal of real estate and personal property, was located just recently in an unmarked and unindexed file cabinet of early probate papers in the basement of the San Benito county clerk's office in Hollister. I have not located the record of the final distribution of the estate by the administrators.

Margaret Breen made her will in 1874, shortly before her death. Her estate was not finally settled until April 15, 1887, when administrators James F. Breen and Edward Breen filed a Decree of Distribution with the Superior Court of San Benito County at Hollister. The file (No. 130) includes a copy of her will and an appraisal of real estate and personal property. The real estate was appraised at $64,881, the personal property at $17,500, including $10,500 in deposits at Hibernia Bank of San Francisco and $5,000 at the Bank of Donohoe, Kelly and Co. of San Francisco. It also included $1,500 rent owed for January 1, 1874 to January 1, 1875 by her son Edward for the "Rancho San Lorenzo" (Topo Ranch, near King City) and 442 acres in the San Juan Valley, under a verbal lease. Margaret's shares of both properties were bequeathed to Edward. Her will provided amply for all but one of her living children and a number of grandchildren. The curious exception was her son Simon, who was left only a token $10, although his wife, Maria, and two daughters received bequests of cash and/or real estate.

My perusal of scores of entries in the grantor and grantee indexes of deeds in Monterey and San Benito counties suggests that the heirs of Patrick and Margaret Breen had to do a lot of complicated negotiating and trading over the course of almost twenty years to settle the estates, which included real estate in three counties.

BIBLIOGRAPHY

Manuscript Sources in Public Collections

Bancroft Library, Berkeley, California. C.F. McGlashan, Correspondence and Papers. An immense file of over four hundred letters to McGlashan from survivors and rescuers, with key, plus newspaper clippings and many other items. BancMs file C-B 570. But this file is only the tip of the iceberg of documents at Bancroft. See also Reed Papers, Breen Papers, etc. The original of Breen's Diary is at Bancroft.

California State Library, Sacramento. See "List of Manuscripts in the California State Library," in *News Notes of California Libraries* (quarterly), vol. 74, no. 1. A valuable file is the "Genealogical Records of California Pioneers."

Gleeson Library, University of San Francisco, San Francisco. Some of the Breen family papers in custody at Gleeson in 1954 (see John S. Enright's list, *CHSQ*, vol. 33, 1954) have since been removed by family members and placed in Bancroft Library. Gleeson still has considerable material, including a number of family photos, John Breen's diaries and account books kept at San Juan Bautista (1850s-1870s), Patrick Dolan's Bible, a large and very worn Fremont map of the California trail by cartographer Charles Preuss (perhaps the one used by Patrick Breen).

Huntington Library, San Marino, California. Sherman O. Houghton Collection, which contains 93 letters from C.F. McGlashan to Eliza P. Donner Houghton. Huntington also has the original Fort Sutter Papers.

Sutter's Fort Historical Museum, Sacramento, California. In the 1940s, papers from the Martha Reed Lewis estate were placed by her heirs in the custody of Sutter's Fort Historical Museum. The curator in 1991 was Michael F. Tucker of the Sacramento District Historic Sites Unit of the California Department of Parks and Recreation. He has prepared a "Finding Guide" for over six hundred manuscript items from the estate, including the Hiram O. Miller and James F. Reed diaries (folders 51 and 85). There is no such guide as yet for a considerable number of photos.

Yuba County Library, Marysville, California. Charles Covillaud and Mary Murphy Papers.

Manuscript Sources in Private Collections

Hudner, Philip, of Kentfield, California A great-grandson of Patrick Breen Jr., Hudner has been a lifetime collector of Breen documents. A number of the most valuable items in his collection, including letters and notes from priests in County Carlow and from relatives and friends of the Breens in Canada, Missouri, and elsewhere, have been placed in the temporary custody of Bancroft Library, with the likelihood of permanent custody in 1995.

Manka, Vivian Breen, of Fort Madison, Iowa. A descendant of Samuel Breen and Margaret Murphy, Mrs. Manka has acquired an enormous amount of genealogical records on her line of the Breen family, Missouri and California periods.

Raven, Dr. Peter, of St. Louis, Director of the Missouri Botanical Garden and great-grandson of Patrick Breen Jr. Dr. Raven has acquired a large collection of genealogical and other materials, especially on the Patrick Breen Jr./Amelia Anderson line.

Ireland

Baptismal Register for the Roman Catholic Parish of Borris, County Carlow, Ireland. Searched from 1792 to 1810.

"Borris, Co. Carlow," copy of six pages from a book, author and title unidentified, in collection of Dr. Peter Raven of St. Louis.

Bowen, Desmond. *The Protestant Crusade in Ireland, 1800-70.* Montreal, 1978.

County Carlow Tombstone Inscriptions: Ballicopagan Cemetery, New Cemetery Borris, Clonagoose Cemetery, Kiltennel Cemetery. Published by St. Mullins Muintir na Tire, County Carlow, 1985. Headstone inscriptions for Patrick Breen's father and grandparents, Kiltennel Cemetery.

Griffiths Valuations, c1850, Ballinvally [*sic*] & Kiltennel (considered one townland) and Barnahasken townlands, Barony of Idrone East, County Carlow. LDS film 101,755, and in bound volumes. Enumerations indicate that John Curry, in 1850, was leaseholder for the greater part of what was formerly Breen land.

King, Joseph A. "The Breens of the Donner Party." *Carloviana: Journal of the Old Carlow Society,* no. 39, 1991-92, Carlow, Ireland. Mainly excerpts from an early draft of this book.

Letter from P. Carey, Parish Priest of Borris, to Margaret Breen in San Juan Bautista, December 30, 1869, acknowledging donation to church construction fund. Bancroft Library, Breen Papers, on loan from Philip Hudner.

Letter of introduction from John Walsh, Parish Priest of Borris, County Carlow, April 5, 1828 [1826?], testifying to Margaret Bulger's good character. Bancroft Library, Breen Papers, on loan from Philip Hudner.

Letter of John Canning of Cranberry, Pennsylvania, to Patrick Breen of San Luis Obispo, California, October 15, 1860. Original in collection of Philip Hudner, on loan to Bancroft Library.

Letter of John Canning of Sugar Grove, Ohio, to Patrick Breen of San Juan Bautista, California, January 5, 1858. Original in collection of Philip Hudner, on loan to Bancroft Library.

Lewis, Samuel. *A Topographical Dictionary of Ireland*, 2 vols. London, 1837, and Baltimore, Genealogical Publishing Company, 1984. Entries for Borris and Killedmund.

Miller, Kerby. *Emigrants and Exiles*. New York, 1985.

Raven, Dr. Peter. "Visit to County Carlow, Ireland." Five-page MS, March 25, 1987, copy in author's file.

Tithe Applotment Books, year 1826, townlands of Ballonvally [*sic*]and Barnahasken (Breens), Parish of Kiltennel, Barony of Idrone East, County Carlow, Ireland. LDS film 256,653. Also year 1834, townland of Rathgeran (Bulgers), Parish of St. Mullins, Barony of St. Mullins Lower. LDS film 256,684, end of reel, out of order.

Canada

Baptismal and Marriage Registers. St. Catherine's Catholic Church, Dundas, Ontario, entries for 1828-31, recorded by missionary priests who visited Southwold and Yarmouth; Holy Angels Parish, St. Thomas, Ontario; "Church Wardens of St. Thomas Church Account and Memorandum Book," 1834-39 (Diocese of London Archives); later registers for same church, entries for years 1852-60.

Brock, Daniel J. "The Beginnings of the Roman Catholic Church in the District of London." A talk given before the London and Middlesex Historical Society, January 15, 1974, typewritten MS, 14 pp. Diocese of London Archives.

Dignan, Bishop Ralph H. "History of the Diocese of London, Ontario." Unpublished MS in Diocese of London Archives, with ltr. of November 18, 1972 from Father Joseph P. Finn to Monsignor F.J. Laverty, P.H., evaluating the MS.

Flynn, Lt. Col. L.J. *The Story of the Roman Catholic Church in Kingston, 1826-1976*. Published by the Archdiocese of Kingston, Ontario, 1976. See pp. 17-18 and Appendix 2, p. 370, St. George (Yarmouth), and St. Thomas, and London parishes.

Letter of September 7, 1830, Yarmouth, signed by ten Catholics including Patrick Breen, to Bishop Alexander Macdonnell of the Diocese of Kingston, petitioning him for a resident priest. Archdiocese of Toronto Archives, cited by Enright in *California Historical Society Quarterly* article, vol. 33, 1954, and quoted by him in *Academy Scrapbook* article, February 1954.

Letter of William Breen and his son Patrick of Southwold, Ontario, to Patrick Breen in San Juan Bautista, California, March 3, 1853. Collection of Philip Hudner, original in temporary custody of Bancroft Library.

Letter of William Breen and his son Patrick of Southwold, Ontario, November 2, 1852, to Patrick Breen of San Juan Bautista. Collection of Philip Hudner, original in temporary custody of Bancroft Library. California.

Map of Southwold Township, Elgin County, Ontario, showing lots for assessment purposes. LDS call no. 971.334 R42sw. Patrick Breen (son of William), lot C CR p. 26, and lot 7 S(LP) p. 24; and William Breen, lot 9 N(LR) p. 21.

Ontario Genealogical Society, ltr. of July 17, 1987 to Dr. Peter Raven, with results of a search for Breens. Includes headstone inscriptions, Holy Angels Cemetery, St. Thomas, Ontario, for William Breen (1798-1872) and wife Mary Roche (1798-1890) and others; 1848 and 1852 assessments for Southwold Township – William and Patrick Breen; 1873 Collectors Roll, Southwold – James and Patrick Breen and P. Burns; 1861 and 1871 Census of Southwold – Patrick Breen family, James Breen.

West, Monsignor (no first name given). *History of St. Thomas Parish (1803-1921).* Compiled by Monsignor West, 1921 (place of publication not cited), Diocese of London Archives.

Illinois
Power, John Carroll. *History of the Early Settlers of Sangamon County, Illinois.* Springfield, 1876, pp. 258-60. Sketch of James Frazier Reed.

Record of the Service of Illinois Soldiers in the Black Hawk War. Springfield, 1882, pp. 100, 174-76.

Missouri and Iowa
Bond (deed) signed December 13, 1841, Richard F. Barrett to Patrick Breen, 320 acres of Section 10, near Keokuk, Iowa.

Letter of Mary Breen Daly (daughter of Samuel) of Clark County, Missouri, to her aunt-in-law, Margaret Breen of San Juan Bautista, California, March 12, 1852. Original in collection of Philip Hudner, on loan to Bancroft Library.

Map showing Section 10, Township 65, North of Range 5, south half of which section Patrick Breen purchased from Richard F. Barrett in 1841. Provided by Vivien Breen Manka of Ft. Madison, Iowa.

Naturalization Certificate. Patrick Breen of Ireland, District Court, West Point, Lee County, Iowa, signed November 1, 1844. BancMs C-B 503:1.

Territorial Census of Iowa, 1840. Patrick Breen, Lee County, 381.

Territorial Census of Missouri, 1840. Samuel Breen, Jackson Township, Clark County. Also families of John, Nancy, and Edward Daly, and Nancy Cowgil (mentioned in Mary Breen Daly ltr.).

United States Census of 1850, Clark County, Missouri, District 19. Household 571/597, Samuel Breen family; neighbors include households of John, Edward and Patrick Daly; Nancy Cowgil; Edward Breen.

United States Census of 1860, Jackson Township, Clark County, Missouri. Households of John Daly (1623/1601), Thomas Breen (1681/___), John

Daly (1732/1709), Thomas Breen (1733/1711), Edward Breen (1772/1749).

United States Census of 1900 , Dickerson Township, Montecello, Lewis County, Missouri. Edward Breen (son of Samuel) household.

Donner Party: Breen's Diary

Breen, Patrick. The original Diary is in Bancroft Library. See also *The Diary of Patrick Breen*, introduction and notes by George R. Stewart, San Francisco, Book Club of California, 1946, facsimile and transcription of the Diary; and *Diary of Patrick Breen: One of the Donner Party*, edited by Frederick J. Teggart, *Publications of the Academy of Pacific Coast History*, vol. 1, no. 6, July 1910.

Donner Party: Accounts of Contemporaries

Annals of San Francisco. Frank Soule, John H. Gihon, and James Nisbet, editors. Appleton, New York, 1855; Authors and Newspapers Association, New York and London, 1906. Portrait and biographical sketch of Selim E. Woodworth, the information probably furnished by himself.

Breen, James F. Letter to C.F. McGlashan, June 8, 1889, expressing fear that McGlashan might include defamatory material on Mrs. Breen in forthcoming edition of McGlashan's *History*. BancMs C-B 362.

_____. Letters to C.F. McGlashan. Eight letters in 1879. BancMS C-B 570, box 1, folder 5.

Breen, John. "Pioneer Memories." an 81-page MS prepared for C.F. McGlashan, dated November, 19, 1877. Bound, BancMS C-D 51.

_____. Letters to C.F. McGlashan. Three letters, 1879. BancMs C-B 70, folder 11.

Breen, Margaret. Account of her experiences with Donner Party, including Starved Camp, as told to Mrs. Eliza W. Farnham about 1849 and published as an appendix (pp. 380-457) to Farnham, *California, In-Doors and Out*. New York, 1856. Farnham also quotes John Breen at some length.

Bryant, Edwin. *What I Saw in California*. University of Nebraska Press, Lincoln and London, 1985 (1848).

Burnett, Peter Hardeman (1807-95). "Burnett's Recollections of the Past," San Francisco, 1878. A two-volume bound manuscript, BancMs P-A 12-13. In vol. 1, pp. 377-94, Burnett, who became governor of California, recalled the conversations he had with four survivors: William Eddy, William Foster and his wife Sarah Murphy Foster, and Harriet Murphy Pike Nye. This may be identical to a published work by Burnett, a citation to which has just come to my attention: *Recollections and Opinions of an Old Pioneer*. New York, 1880, pp. 275-82.

Donner Family History Records. Compiled by Barbara Warner of Huntington Westerners, San Marino, California. Copies provided the author, courtesy of Mrs. Warner.

Donner, Tamsen. Letter of May 11, 1846, written on the trail to her sister in Independence, Missouri. Huntington Library manuscript.

Early Day Romances: Sutter's Fort 1847-48." The Nuggets Edition Club of C.F. McClatchy Senior High School, Sacramento, California, 1943. Photocopy of marriage record of George Zins and Doriss Wolfinger, and biographical sketches of both parties.

Eberstadt, Edward, publisher. *The Fort Sutter Papers, Reference Volume: A Literal Transcript of the Manuscripts and Commentaries.* Bancroft fF864.K36x, one of twenty copies, edited with long commentaries by Eberstadt and published by him in 1922.

Fallon, "Captain" William O. "Extracts from a Journal Written by a Member of the Party Latest from the California Mountains," by "Capt. Fellun." *The California Star*, San Francisco, June 5, 1847.

Farnham – see Breen, Margaret.

Graves, William C. Letters to C.F. McGlashan. Five letters in 1879; also a 20-page undated MS (c1879) from Graves addressed to C.F. McGlashan. BancMs C-B 570 folder 98, carton 1. A garbled and embittered account, many errors in fact. Graves' most valuable contribution was a map showing relative locations of the three camps at the lake, in McGlashan file. Graves, who lived in Calistoga, published his version of events in a series of newspaper articles, "Graves' Crossing the Plains in '46," in the *Healdsburg Russian River Flag*, April 26 to May 17, 1877, and December 30, 1875.

Hall, Carroll D., editor. *Donner Miscellany: 41 Diaries and Documents.* Contains transcriptions of the Hiram O. Miller and James F. Reed diaries.

Houghton, Eliza P. Donner. *The Expedition of the Donner Party and Its Tragic Fate.* Chicago, 1911.

Jones, Elbert P. "A most shocking scene...." *The California Star*, San Francisco, April 10, 1847. Wildly lurid and inaccurate account of the ordeal, but accepted by Bryant.

Kern, Edward. Undated letter (but late January, 1847) to Governor Hull about arrival of Snowshoe Party survivors, conditions in the mountain camps, etc. Huntington Library manuscript HM-21355.

Keseberg, Lewis. Statement of his experiences with the Donner Party and his life thereafter prepared for C.F. McGlashan in 1879, printed in McGlashan's *History of the Donner Party* pp. 206-15 and 218-24 (1880 edition) and in this book (Chapter 12).

Lienhard, Heinrich. *A Pioneer at Sutter's Fort, 1846 – The Adventures of Heinrich Lienhard*, translated and edited by Marguerite E. Wilbur from the original manuscript in German. Los Angeles, 1941.

Lyman, George D. "Victor Fourgeaud, M.D.: Second Physician and Surgeon in San Francisco, Writer of California's First Promotion Literature." *California Historical Society Quarterly*, vol. XI, no. 2, June 1932. Describes Fourgeaud's experiences on Sutter's launch captained by Lewis Keseberg.

McCutchen, William. Statements about Donner Party in *San Jose Pioneer*, May 5, 1887 and in *Pacific Rural Press*, April 1, 1871. Manuscript versions are among the Sutter's Fort papers, see Reed entry below.

_____. Letter of January 27, 1847 to James F. Reed from Younts Ranch in Napa Valley. MRL folder 84. He spells his name "McCutchan."

McDougal, Frances H. "The Donner Tragedy." *Pacific Rural Press,* January 21, April 29, 1871.

McGlashan, C.F. Correspondence and Papers. BancMs C-B 570, two boxes and a carton, including over 450 letters from survivors, 1878 *et seq.* Among the letter writers are Leanna Donner App, Frances Donner Wilder, Georgia Donner Babcock, Eliza Donner Houghton, James F. Breen, John Breen, Simon Breen, Nicholas Clark, Mary Graves, Nancy Graves Williamson, William C. Graves, William McCutchen, Martha Reed Lewis, Virginia Reed Murphy, William G. Murphy, Naomi Pike Schenck, George Tucker, Reasin P. Tucker.

McKinstry, George. "Documents for the History of California, 1846-9." BancMs C-B 84. Data on population of Sutter's Fort, November 1846; also bound volume, "McKinstry Papers," includes copy of summons to Mrs. Wolfinger, witness for plaintiff, Keysburg vs. Coffeymere [sic], May 5, 1847, BancMs C-E 70.

Miller, Hiram O. A diary composed partly by Miller, in several scripts including that of James F. Reed and one or more unidentifiable hands, 1846-47. MRL folder 51. See also folder 382, handwriting analysis.

Moultry, Riley Septimus. Interview in *Santa Cruz Sentinel,* August 31, 1888.

_____. Petition for compensation for services in relief party, including affidavits by James F. Reed, William McCutchen, Edward Pyle. 1872, Huntington Library MS, San Marino, California.

Murphy, Mary. "Mary Murphy's Story," a letter quoted in its entirety by Jack and Richard Steed in *The Donner Party Rescue Site: Johnson's Ranch on Bear River*. Sacramento, 1988, pp. 15-18; same book, pp. 18-20, Mary Murphy's letter to "Dear Uncles, Aunts and Cousins," May 25, 1847. The Steeds found these two letters in two separate Charles Covillaud files in the Yuba County Library, Marysville, California.

"New Helvetia Diary of Events from 1845-8 by Swasey, Bidwell, Looker, Sutter." Copied from the original by Bancroft in 1881. BancMs C-E 134. This was published as *New Helvetia Diary: A Record of Events Kept by*

John A. Sutter and His Clerks at New Helvetia, California, from September 9, 1845 to May 25, 1848, by the Grabhorn Press, San Francisco, 1939, in arrangement with the Society of California Pioneers.

Reed, James Frazier. "The Snow-Bound, Starved Emigrants of 1846." *Pacific Rural Press,* March 25, 1871 and April 1, 1871, which were Reed's responses to articles by Frances H. McDougal in January 21 and April 29 issues. (H.H. Bancroft, in vol. 5, p. 6 of *History of California,* gives February 1, 1871 as the date of a McDougal article in the *Hollister Central Californian,* with Reed's and McCutchen's replies appearing in the *San Jose Pioneer,* April 18, May 5, 1877 [*sic*]; also *Santa Cruz Sentinel,* April 28 and May 18, 1877.) A copy of Reed's manuscript is among papers in BancMs C-B 570, Box III, Carton 1, folders 74-82. The original manuscript in rough draft on forty-nine pages of legal size paper, written mostly in one clear and firm hand with occasional insertions by a second writer in a shaky hand, probably Reed's own, is in MRL folders 459 through 468, containing various manuscript versions of the replies of both Reed and McCutchen, including account of relief efforts.

_____. Letter from Reed to James W. Keyes of Springfield, May 20, 1846, published in part in *Illinois State Register,* Springfield, July 5, 1849. Mentions finding one-half ounce of gold while cache-ing a wagon on the Great Salt Desert. BancMs 70/193c. Another letter, same file, to Keyes, July 5, 1849, regarding his approval of marriage of Eliza Williams; same file, mentions being accepted into wagon train of Colonel Russell in letter to Keyes, May 10, 1846, written on the trail.

_____. A diary and notes of rescue efforts by James F. Reed. MRL folder 85.

_____. Deposition of James F. Reed, December 3, 1872, testifying on behalf of Riley Moutrey (Moultry), who had made claim for compensation for services on relief efforts; also briefly describes his own experiences on the trail, including an untruth about why he left the Donner Party in Nevada. MRL folder 307.

_____. Letter that Reed wrote from Fort Bridger, July 31, 1846, printed in *Sangamon Journal,* November 5, 1846. Describes Fort Bridger favorably; discusses Hastings Cut-Off enthusiastically and naively; warns about trading with independent trappers ("as great a set of sharks as ever disgraced humanity, with few exceptions"). Quoted by Dale L. Morgan in June 17, 1949 ltr. to Carroll D. Hall. MRL folder 388.

_____. Narrative based on a "journal" Reed sent back home, passed on by his friend, J.H. Merryman, to the press and published in the *Illinois Journal,* December 9, 1847, partly quoted in letter, Morgan to Hall, *ibid.*

Reed, Martha "Patty" (Mrs. Frank Lewis). Letters to C.F. McGlashan, including a bound volume of fifteen letters, 1879. BancMs C-B 70, folders 29-32.

Reed, Virginia (Mrs. John Murphy). *Across the Plains in the Donner Party: A Personal Narrative of the Overland Trip to California, 1846-47.* Outbooks, Golden, Colorado, 1980 (1891). Also many letters to C.F. McGlashan, including bound volume, BancMs C-B 570 folder 48; and "Letter of Virginia Reed," May 16, 1847, to a cousin in Springfield, Missouri, edited and reprinted by George R. Stewart in second edition (1960) of *Ordeal by Hunger.* One version was printed in the *Illinois Journal* (Springfield), December 16, 1847 ("Deeply Interesting Letter").

Rhoads, Daniel. "Relief of the Donner Party, 1846." Statement of Daniel Rhoads of Kingston, Fresno County, California, 1873, 15 pp. plus 4 pp. of biographical notes. BancMs C-D 144.

———. Letter of Daniel Rhoads to Jesse Esrey, 1849, quoted by Steed and Steed, pp. 24-30.

Ritchie, M.D., and R.P. Tucker. Manuscript diary and notes on first rescue mission, by Ritchie (February 5-14, 1847), and by Tucker (February 15 to arrival at Johnson's Ranch). This has been called a "diary" but it appears to be a report in a single handwriting that was jointly composed by Ritchie and Tucker. Attached to the "diary" are two pages of afterthoughts highly critical of the activities of Kern. See MRL folders 81 and 86.

Sacramento Bee. "Donner Party Obituary File" in this newspaper's library.

Sinclair, John. Original copy of agreement dated April 10, 1847, signed by Sinclair as Justice of the Peace for the Sacramento District, Territory of California, with three members of the fourth relief – William Fallon, John Rhoads, and Joseph Sel. MRL folder 106.

Thornton, J. Quinn. *Camp of Death: The Donner Party Mountain Camp, 1846-47.* Outbooks, Golden, Colorado, 1986 (1849). An account relying heavily on interviews with William Eddy.

Trudeau, John Baptiste. Statement given to a reporter of a St. Louis newspaper and reprinted in the *San Francisco Morning Call*, Sunday October 11, 1891, p. 16. "One of the Donners: A Chat with a Survivor of the Ill-Fated Donner Party." Name cited as "Juan Baptiste Truvido" and "Juan Baptiste Truxido" in this article; also U.S. Census for 1900, Tomales Township, Marin County, California, household of John Trubador, LDS film 1,240,093; death record of "John Baptist Truevido," Recorder's Office, Marin County, California, Death Index, vol. 3, p. 385.

Tucker, Reasin P. Letter to C.F. McGlashan, May 26, 1879. BancMs C-B 70 folder 49; also 40-page account of Donner Party by his son George in same file. See also Ritchie entry, above.

Wise, Henry Augustine, Lieutenant, U.S.N. *Los Gringos; or an Inside View of Mexico and California*, New York, 1849, and Paris, 1850. A grossly distorted view of the Donner Party based on an alleged conversation with John Baptiste.

Woodworth, Selim E. Report regarding first three relief expeditions from "S.E. Woodworth, P's M'd U.S.N., Com'dg Expedition to the California Mountains," April 1, 1847, printed in the *California Star*, April 3, 1847.

Donner Party: Books and Articles (Secondary Sources)

Bancroft, Hubert H. *History of California*. San Francisco, 1890. See vol. 5, pp. 527-44, Donner Party.

Breen, Harry J. Letter to Dr. Walter M. Stookey, from Hollister, California, February 12, 1947. Printed in Stookey, *Fatal Decision*, pp. 189-94.

Clark, Nicholas. "Nicholas Clark: One of the Rescuers of the Donner Party." *Truckee Republican*, October 24, 1885.

DeVoto, Bernard. *The Year of Decision, 1846*. Boston, 1943.

Farnham, Eliza W. "Narrative of the Emigration of the Donner Party to California in 1846," in *California, In-Doors and Out*. New York, 1856, pp. 380-457.

Foley, Doris. "Mary Graves, A Heroine of the Donner Party. *Nevada County Historical Society* (Nevada City, California), vol. 8, no. 3, July 1954.

Grayson, Donald K. "Donner Party Deaths: A Demographic Assessment." *Journal of Anthropological Research*, vol. 46, no. 3, fall 1990, pp. 223-41. See also Pat Shipman, "Life and Death on the Wagon Trail," *New Sentinel*, July 17, 1991, based on Grayson.

Hine, Robert V. *In the Shadow of Fremont: Edward Kern and the Art of American Exploration, 1848-1860*. Norman, Oklahoma, 1962, pp. 41-43.

Lyman, George D. "Victor J. Fourgeaud, M.D." *California Historical Society Quarterly*, vol. XI, no. 2, June, 1932. Account of Keseberg as navigator for Sutter's launch.

McGlashan, C.F. *History of the Donner Party: A Tragedy of the Sierra*. Stanford, California, 1947 (1880).

McGlashan, M. Nona. *Give Me a Mountain Meadow*. Fresno, 1981; and *From the Desk of Truckee's C.F. McGlashan*. Fresno, 1986.

McHugh, Thomas P. *Hazeldell Charivari, Christmas at Zayante, 1856, being the story of the wedding of Patty Reed to Frank Lewis and a recount of the Donner Party Tragedy, 1846*. Pamphlet, Santa Cruz, 1959, from materials first assembled for the *Frontier Gazette*, Christmas 1948 issue. Society of California Pioneers Library, San Francisco.

"Pioneer Cemeteries Near Sacramento," prepared by Ilene Hunter, mainly "from notes left by Julie K. Brennan." *Tour Guide Book*, Oregon-California Trails Association, 9th Annual Convention, August 14-18, 1991, Sacramento. Long list of burial places of Donner Party survivors.

Stewart, George R., Jr. *Ordeal by Hunger: The Story of the Donner Party*. New York, Henry Holt and Company, 1936.

Stewart, George R. (no "Jr."). *Ordeal by Hunger: The Story of the Donner Party*. University of Nebraska Press, Lincoln and London, 1986 (1936, revised 1960). This edition includes a long foreword, and transcripts (preceded by commentary) of the "Diary of Patrick Breen," the "Diary of James F. Reed," and the "Letter of Virginia Reed," but is without the photographs that were included in the 1936 edition. A number of small changes have been made in the "Notes and References" section. In the 1960 Notes, there is less citing of the unreliable *California Star* as the actual source.

_____. Letter of August 24, 1949, to Carroll D. Hall, enclosing five pages of notes on Hall's *Donner Miscellany* and the Miller and Reed diaries as transcribed by Hall. MRL folder 390.

Shumate, Albert. "A Note on the Donner Party Tragedy," *Pacific Historian*, vol. 23, no. 1, Spring 1979. Short piece indicating that Solomon Sublette, as well as Clyman, warned the 1846 emigrants not to take the Hastings Cut-Off.

Stokes, Frank Jr. "The Last Man Out: a brief for Lewis Keseberg, and a defense of his conduct as a member of the tragic Donner Party." *Touring Topics*, vol. XXI, February 1929.

Steed, Jack and Richard. *The Donner Party Rescue Site: Johnson's Ranch on the Bear River*. Sacramento, 1988.

Stookey, Walter M. *Fatal Decision: The Tragic Story of the Donner Party*. Deseret Book Company, Salt Lake City, 1950.

Walsh, Henry L., S.J. *Hallowed Were the Gold Dust Trails*. University of Santa Clara Press, 1946. Bishop Eugene O'Connell's letter in 1861 to colleagues in Dublin, Ireland, seeking advice on the complicated marital status, in the eyes of the Catholic Church, of Mary Murphy Covillaud. Also genealogical information (in "Notes to Text") on the Murphy and Covillaud families, and William Johnson.

Wells, Evelyn. A long series on the Donner Party that appeared in the *San Francisco Call and Post*, beginning June 11, 1919; includes photo of document carried by James F. Reed – muster roll of his company in Black Hawk War, Reed and Abraham Lincoln listed consecutively, also Stephen Douglas. BancMs C-B 570, Carton 1.

The Donner Party: Maps, Trail, Camps

Altrocchi, Julia Cooley. *The Old California Trail*. The Caxton Printers, Caldwell, Idaho, 1945.

Dary, David. *Entrepreneurs of the Old West*. University of Nebraska Press, Lincoln and London, 1986; Bison Book Printing, 1987.

Franzwa, Gregory M. *Maps of the Oregon Trail*. The Patrice Press, St. Louis, 1990.

Hafen, Leroy R. and W.J. Ghent. *Broken Hand: The Life Story of Thomas Fitzpatrick, Chief of the Mountain Men.* Denver, 1931. Map, "Forts and Trails of the Old West."

Haines, Aubrey. *Historic Sites Along the Oregon Trail.* The Patrice Press, St. Louis, 1981.

Hardesty, Donald L. "The Archaeology of the Donner Party Tragedy." *Nevada Historical Society Quarterly.* Winter 1987, vol. 30, no. 4, pp. 246-68.

Hawkins, Bruce, and David B. Madsen. *Excavation of the Donner-Reed Wagons: Historic Archaeology Along the Hastings Cut-Off.* University of Utah Press, Salt Lake City, 1990.

Jefferson, T.H. *Map of the Emigrant Road from Independence, Mo., to San Francisco, California* (1849). Republished with introduction by George R. Stewart, San Francisco, California Historical Society, 1945. Contains practical advice for emigrants on the trail. Jefferson probably crossed with Hastings on the cut-off in 1846. Original map is in Map Room Collection, University of California at Berkeley Library, call no. F2 C7 Ro 1949d B.

Kelly, Charles. *Salt Desert Trails.* Salt Lake City, 1930, p. 84.

McGlashan, C.F. *The Location of the Site of the Breen Cabin.* Oakland, California, 1920.

Steed, Jack. *The Donner Rescue Party Site: Johnson's Ranch on Bear River.* Graphic Publishers, Santa Ana, California, 1991.

Stewart, George R. *Donner Pass and Those Who Crossed It.* Menlo Park, California, 1964. Includes copy of map drawn by William C. Graves showing locations of the cabins at the lake.

———. *The California Trail.* University of Nebraska Press, Lincoln and London, 1983 (1962).

Tour Guide Book. Oregon-California Trails Association, 9th Annual Convention, August 14-18, 1991, Sacramento. Especially good maps.

Unruh, John D., Jr. *The Plains Across: The Overland Emigrants and the Trans-Mississippi West,* 1840-60. Urbana, Illinois, 1982.

Weddell, P.M. "Location of Donner Camp and Marking Trail." *The Pony Express,* May 1949.

The Donner Party: Fiction

Reviewed in Chapter 15:

Birney, Hoffman. *Grim Journey.* New York, 1934.

Croy, Homer. *Wheels West.* New York, 1955.

Fisher, Vardis. *The Mothers: An American Saga of Courage* (1943).

Keithley, George. *The Donner Party.* New York, 1972.

Maino, Jeannette Gould. *Left Hand Turn: A Story of the Donner Party Women*. Privately printed, Modesto, California, 1987. This book, with extensive notes, qualifies as history as well as fiction.

Pigney, Joseph. *For Fear We Shall Perish*. New York, 1961.

Rhodes, Richard. *The Ungodly: A Novel of the Donner Party*. New York, 1973.

Stewart, George R. *Ordeal by Hunger: The Story of the Donner Party*. University of Nebraska Press, Lincoln and London, 1986. First published 1936, revised 1960. Classified as historical fiction, for reasons explained in Chapter 15.

Other fiction, not reviewed in Chapter 15:

Altrocchi, Julia Cooley. *Snow-Covered Wagons, A Pioneer Epic: The Donner Party Expedition, 1846-47*. New York, 1936. In verse.

Anderson, Edna M. *Tamsen*. Fort Washington, Maryland, 1973. A children's book.

Bonner, Geraldine. *The Emigrant Trail*. New York, 1910.

Galloway, David. *Tamsen*. San Diego, 1982.

Harte, Bret. *Gabriel Conroy*. Boston, 1871.

Headon, William. *Beyond the Pass*. New York, 1955.

Laurgaard, Rachel. *Patty Reed's Doll: The Story of the Donner Party*. McCurdy Historical Doll Museum, 246 North 100 East, Provo, Utah 84601, 1981. A touching account intended for children.

Lofts, Nora. *Winter Harvest*. New York, 1955.

McDonald, Kay L. *The Vision is Fulfilled*. New York, 1983.

Sutton, Margaret. *Palace Wagon Family*. New York, 1957. For children.

Whitman, Ruth. *A Woman's Journey*. Cambridge, Massachusetts, 1985.

Wilbur, Margaret E. *John Sutter: Rascal and Adventurer*. New York, 1949.

Wagner, Harr N. *Pacific History Stories*. San Francisco, 1918. For children.

Mabie, Mary Louise. *The Long Knives Walked*. Indianapolis, 1932.

The Breens in California

Anzar vs Fallon, litigation concerning the orchard at Mission Santa Cruz, 1848-54, BancMs C-B 421, box 4, folders 442-48, and also file 76/65c depositions. Patrick Breen's deposition in favor of Fr. Anzar.

Assessment Rolls, 1850 and 1854, livestock owned by Patrick Breen. The data, which is cited in Chapter 16, is recorded on one typewritten page, unsigned and undated, in files of San Juan Bautista State Park (Vicky Cottage).

Breen, Barbara, of Hollister, California. Letters and interviews, 1991, regarding her grandfather, Edward Breen.

Breen, Harry J. "A Short Sketch of the Lives of Patrick and Margaret Breen
and Their Family: Members of the Ill-Fated Donner Party of 1846."
Pony Express Courier, March 1937. See Appendix D.

Breen, John and Patrick Jr. Statement of livestock and land holdings in San
Benito Counties in June 1889, on "California As It Is" questionnaire.
BancMs C-B 503.

Breen, Margaret. Last will and testament, appraisal of real estate and
personal property, and decree of distribution of final estate (filed April
15, 1887). File 130, Superior Court records, Hollister, San Benito County.

Breen, Patrick. Burial entry 179, p. 36, Book I, *Death Record*, Old Mission
San Juan Bautista. English translation from Spanish (quoted in Chapter
16), BancMs C-B 503.

_____. Last Will and Testament and other probate papers of Patrick
Breen including appraisal of property. San Benito County Clerk's office,
Hollister, in an unindexed and unmarked file cabinet.

Breen, Patrick Jr. Map of land in San Benito County held in 1982 by nineteen heirs of Patrick Jr. Collection of Peter Raven of St. Louis.

Browne, John Ross. *Crusoe's Island: A Ramble in the Footsteps of Alexander
Selkirk with Sketches of Adventures in California and Washoe*. New York,
1872. Account of visit to the Breens' residence and inn at San Juan
Bautista in 1849.

California State Census of 1852. Monterey County, p. 245, household of
Patrick Breen (including his brother, Samuel).

Castro, Jose and Modesta. Deed of land to Patrick Breen, document dated
February 7, 1849. In Spanish, copy in author's files, courtesy of Joe Cullumber of San Juan Bautista.

Cowan, Robert G. *Ranchos of California: A List of Spanish Concessions,
1775-1822 and Mexican Grants, 1822-1846*. Academy Library Guild,
Fresno, California, 1956. Entry No. 478, p. 81, abstract of patent to
Patrick Breen for 401 acres in San Juan Bautista purchased from Jose
Castro. In Philip Hudner's collection is an 1877 "Map of the Ranch Land
Finally Confirmed to Patrick Breen....Containing 401 Acres."

Cullumber, Joe, of San Juan Bautista. Letters and interviews, 1991,
regarding Cullumber's ancestor, Simon Breen, and others.

Diocese of Monterey, California. Record of burials, marriages, confirma-
tions. LDS film 913,311.

Enright, John Shea, S.J. "Catholic Pioneer in the Donner Party." *Academy
Scrapbook* (Diocese of Fresno, California), no. 7, February 1954.

_____. "The Breens of San Juan Bautista: with a Calendar of Family Pa-
pers." *California Historical Society Quarterly*, vol. 33, 1954, pp. 349-59.

Guinn, J[ames] M[iller]. *Historical and Biographical Record of Monterey and
San Benito Counties and History of the State of California*, vol. II. Los

Angeles, 1910 (first published in 1868, New Haven, Connecticut). Biographical sketch of Edward J. Breen, p. 780.

History of San Benito County, California, Elliott & Moore, Publishers. San Francisco, 1881. Photographs of James Breen; sketches of residences of John Breen and Patrick Breen Jr.; account of the Breen family and the Donner Party (long extract from Farnham) by Hon. James F. Breen, pp. 105-08; biographical sketches of Patrick Sr., John, and James Breen, pp. 105, 108-09; general account of the Donner Party, pp. 53-55.

Hollister Free Lance. "Edward J. Breen/San Benito County Loses a Prominent Citizen," obituary, September 5, 1890.

Hoover, Mildred Brooke, and others. *Historic Spots in California,* 3rd edition, revised by William N. Abeloe. Stanford, California, 1966.

Letter of August 4, 1991, Joanne Ciccone of California Department of Parks and Recreation to J.A. King, enclosing copy of the sherriff's bill of sale of brick house in Monterey to Patrick Breen, August 11, 1851, copy obtained by Ms. Ciccone from Colton Hall Museum in Monterey.

McBride, Michael. "A Piano with Roots." *Sacramento Union*, Sunday, April 15, 1979. Article about grand piano purchased by Simon Breen in late 1860s, now in museum at San Juan Bautista.

McKevitt, Gerald, S.J. *The University of Santa Clara: A History, 1851-1977.* Stanford, California, 1979. Appendix, p. 334, Hon. James Breen, president of Alumni Council (1882-85); photo of class of 1898, including Eugene Breen, p. 83.

Mylar, Isaac L. *Early Days of the Mission San Juan Bautista.* Published by *Evening Pajoronian*, Watsonville, California, 1928, and Valley Publishers in cooperation with San Juan Bautista Historical Society, 1970.

"New Helvetia Diary of Events from 1845-8 by Swasey, Bidwell, Looker, Sutter." Copied by Bancroft from the original in 1881. BancMs C-E 134, bound. Arrivals and departures of Patrick Breen at Sutter's Fort in summer of 1847. Several references to Breen.

Ordway, Ed. Letter June 23, 1991 from Angel's Camp to J. A. King about Ordway's ancestor, Simon Breen.

Pierce, Marjorie. "Castro-Breen Adobe Reflects Page from Early California." *San Jose Mercury News*, Sunday, November 7, 1971, p. 48.

_____. *East of the Gabilans.* Western Tenager Press, Santa Cruz, 1977, pp. 37-48, all about Breens of San Juan Bautista and Topo Ranch.

Prendergast, Thomas F. *Forgotten Pioneers: Irish Leaders in Early California.* San Francisco, 1942, pp. 134-46.

Quigley, Hugh. *The Irish Race in California and on the Pacific Coast.* San Francisco, 1878.

San Juan Bautista District Cemetery. Headstone inscriptions for Patrick and Margaret Breen and their children. Also headstone inscriptions for some members of Samuel Breen family.

San Juan Mission News, San Juan Bautista, California, June 7, 1968, pp. 5-6. "Breen Plaque Dedicated by Historical Society."

The Pinnacle (San Benito County weekly), January 21, 1988 article, "Gold Rush Led to a Bustling San Juan."

Trescony, Julius. *An Heir to a Land Grant*. Oral History Project, Regents of the University of California at Davis, 1978. Information on Edwin Breen's connection with "California Rodeo."

United States Census of 1850. Monterey County, San Juan Township, pp. 119/237 (dually numbered page sequences). Household 128/209, Patrick Breen.

United States Census of 1860. Monterey County, San Juan Township. Household 529/481, Samuel Breen family; John Breen 552/502; Edward Breen 551/500; Patrick Breen, postmaster 552/503.

United States Census of 1900. El Dorado County, Placerville Township. Household of Dennis Daly (grandson of Samuel), enumeration district 28, p. 23; household of brother William H. Daly nearby.

Vera, Dorothy. "Breens were First Americans in San Juan." *Salinas Californian*, May 16, 1970.

Wells, Evelyn. "Mrs. M'Mahon Still Fears '46 Memory." Interview with Isabella Breen McMahon, undated and unidentified newspaper clipping in author's files.

INDEX